A DETAILED GUIDE TO
SELF-PUBLISHING
with
AMAZON
AND OTHER ONLINE BOOKSELLERS

VOL **2**

Chris McMullen

COPYRIGHT

A Detailed Guide to Self-Publishing with Amazon and Other Online Booksellers, Vol. 2
Proofreading, Author Pages, Marketing, and More

Chris McMullen
Cover design by Melissa Stevens: theillustratedauthor.net

Third edition published in May, 2014 (for new cover and minor updates)
Second edition published in January, 2014 (to add **index** and minor updates)
First edition published in April, 2013
First printing in April, 2013

Books > Education & Reference > Publishing & Books > Authorship
Books > Business & Investing > Marketing & Sales > Marketing

ISBN-10: 1484037243
EAN-13: 978-1484037249

Disclaimer: Every effort was made to describe the information in this book very accurately as of the publication date. Companies make periodic changes to their websites, practices, and policies, and so this information is subject to change. The author makes no guarantees regarding the information in this book. You should check directly with each company for the most up-to-date information regarding their practices, policies, pricing, etc.

CONTENTS

Volume 1 Contents

INTRODUCTION

The fact that you're reading the introduction to the second volume of this book shows that you're not only interested in putting an excellent book together, but are also motivated to perfect and promote your book. This makes a huge difference, and therefore we will reconsider a few suggestions from the first volume. For example, in Volume 1, I recommended making a free cover for two reasons (which I didn't reveal at the time; rather, I only emphasized saving money and how long it may take to recover the investment). First, you will see firsthand how well you can design your own cover, which will serve as the basis for comparison. If you shop for cover help, you will be able to measure how much the artist is improving over your own ability. Secondly, whether or not you should invest in a fantastic cover depends on several factors, such as how much time and effort you will put into revisions and marketing. You're showing some interest in this because you have this book open presently, so we'll reconsider this point in Volume 2.

Self-publishing success involves several factors. Just having a great book concept is the tip of the iceberg. There are tens of thousands of incredible books and hundreds of thousands that had the potential to be incredible books (but the execution wasn't perfect). The first step is to have an attractive cover. Nobody will discover how good your book is until they first discover your book. The second step is to have an interesting blurb, which shows how much harder it can be to write just a few words than very many. Next, customers look inside your book. It takes professional editing and formatting to get customers who discover your work to read it. Once they begin to read, the book must be well-written and engaging. Finally, a great story (for fiction) or excellent content (for nonfiction) will help to establish the book as a good book. If also the book evokes powerful emotions and has memorable characters (for fiction) or is extremely useful or entertaining (for nonfiction), it may be a great book.

Marketing is only useful if the packaging (cover, blurb, and formatting) is professional. There isn't much point in drawing interest into a product that many people won't buy. If the cover, blurb, or sample doesn't look professional, the customer will wonder if the content is similarly lacking in effort. There are hundreds of thousands of books that are professional all the way through. So why read a book that appears less than professional?

A great cover and blurb will only be effective if the book is first perfected. Reviews and the very important prospect of word-of-mouth sales depend on this. Edit and revise your book to perfection. If you're willing to do this, then a fantastic cover and an effective marketing plan can significantly impact the potential success of your book. In this book, you will learn how to perfect your book from cover to cover and how to market your book successfully.

Chapter 5

Editing Your Proof

Chapter Overview

5.1 Proofing Your Paperback
5.2 Proofing Your eBook

This chapter answers questions about the following topics, and more:

- ☑ How the cover, title, and other elements of your book can help market it.
- ☑ Getting feedback before your publish and how this can help create "buzz."
- ☑ How to make even-page headers show the name of each chapter.
- ☑ Using Roman numerals for front matter and Arabic numerals for the main text.
- ☑ Perfecting your cover design and the importance of having an excellent cover.
- ☑ What to look for when you receive your paperback proof.
- ☑ Why you should receive at least one proof as a hard copy.
- ☑ When it's okay to proof your paperback book electronically.
- ☑ Possible variations and differences between your proof and customers' paperbacks.
- ☑ What to do if the proof is significantly different from your interior or cover file.
- ☑ Submitting revisions to your interior or cover files.
- ☑ Other things you need to proof besides your book, like your description and biography.
- ☑ Improving the description for your book.
- ☑ Using Word's Styles and perfecting the formatting of your eBook.
- ☑ What to look for when you proof your eBook.
- ☑ Warnings that some eBook publishing services may make you wait one or more days before submitting changes once you publish your eBook.
- ☑ Submitting revisions to your eBook interior file or thumbnail image.

5.1 Proofing Your Paperback

5.1.1 Before Submitting Files for Review

Many indie authors submit their files for review prematurely, and also approve their proofs too early. You want your book to appear as professional as possible, which will help it to stand out in a good way, and you want to give your book the best possible chance of success. Take your time, consider everything carefully, invest a little more time and effort where it may help, and strive to avoid amateur mistakes (like rushing the book to market too soon).

This mistake is very natural. It takes a great deal of time, effort, writing, revising, and commitment just to write the book in the first place. The process consumes some authors to the extent that they are often up in the middle of the night working. After months of writing, you feel a strong desire for the project to be complete and to get some recognition and appreciation for your hard work.

That's when you discover how much more effort is needed for editing, formatting, cover design, preparing a blurb, and marketing. Writing the book is actually the easy part, especially since you enjoy writing. Most authors don't enjoy editing, formatting, and marketing, but they are just as important for the potential success of your book. It's easy to shirk on these aspects and rush the book to market for that feeling of satisfaction and the prospects for reaping some rewards from the time that you've invested (and any money that you may have put into it, too). However, you'll be far more satisfied and have much better prospects for some measure of success if you strive to perfect the full package.

I'd rather read a book that tells a great story, but has a poor cover, some editing and formatting mistakes, and wasn't marketed well than to read a book that tells a mediocre story, but has a fantastic cover, professional editing and formatting, and was marketed effectively. But that's not a choice that customers face. Most people won't find a book that's not visibly marketed, several won't read a book if the reviews complain of editing or formatting problems, and many won't notice a book among other thumbnails if the cover doesn't appeal to them. As a result, a mediocre writer with highly effective marketing skills will often be much more successful than a great writer who struggles with marketing. I'm not saying that it's necessarily fair, but it is what it is. Strive to perfect the full package and your book will have the best chance for success.

In a few paragraphs, we will consider a few important details that you can still change before you approve your proof. I believe that you'll be happy that you didn't skip ahead to the next section. Have a little patience, as there are a few other important points that I feel compelled to make first. For example, if you think it may be too late to make changes, you might be wrong. Also, I would like to stress the importance of trying to perfect your work now.

If you used a free CreateSpace ISBN, you can still delete your title and start over if you haven't already approved your proof. If you invested in an ISBN or other services and would still like to make changes, contact CreateSpace to discuss your options. Depending on the situation, you may still have the opportunity to start fresh without a sunk cost. Once you choose your ISBN information, you can't change your title, author, and other information that relates to your ISBN, but you can delete your book all together and add a new title if you haven't already approved your proof. If you have approved your proof and haven't enabled any sales channels, then you can also just start a new title. Even if you have enabled sales channels, you can disable sales channels (but in this case, your original title will probably still show on Amazon for potential used sales, even though it won't be available for sale new). Where there is a will to start fresh, there probably is a way. The main issue is that if you've already invested in money in the title, you want to contact CreateSpace and ask if there is any way to transfer that investment into a new title (or if they can revise your current title).

Most self-published authors have very little money to invest toward cover design, professional editing, marketing, etc. But authors do have time; they may not always exercise the patience to take as much time as they could, yet this is much easier than finding money to invest. Time is money. So if you lack money, invest time. There are many resources available to help you design a better cover. You can proofread and revise repeatedly and find other pairs of eyes to help. You can collaborate with other authors and help one another edit. There are many free marketing tools available. Lack of money is not a valid excuse for not perfecting your cover, writing, promotion, etc. Invest the time to do it right.

Don't get caught in the common lazy trap. If you just want to get your work out there to find out if it's good before you invest time in it, don't publish your work. Instead, join a writing group (online or in person) for such feedback. Once you publish your work, you're beginning to develop your image and reputation. Do this with your best work from the onset. Don't think, "If my book sells and people like it, then I'll invest in a cover," or, "If anyone complains about the editing, then I'll fix it." These things can actually affect, quite significantly, if your book sells and how much, and whether or not people will like it. Also, if anyone leaves a one-star review complaining about editing, it's permanent. Make every effort to put your best work out there in the beginning. There are thousands of indie authors wishing they had.

So which features of your book should you consider possibly changing before submitting your files for review? Let's reconsider your cover, title, blurb, price, and your image as an author. It's also very important to develop a marketing plan before you publish. The vast majority of indie authors first publish, then later on consider marketing as an afterthought. A marketing plan – which can be relatively simple – can give your book a significant edge.

Test your book out before you publish. You can show your book to family, friends, and acquaintances, but it's far more important to gauge how complete strangers will react. Don't ignore family and friends – try both. Make a revised version of your front cover where you change the text to something like, "This is not the real title of this book," and print it out (in color). Show this to dozens of strangers and ask them two questions: (1) What do you think this book is about? (2) What do you think about the cover? If 70% of your sample thinks that your book is a romance, when it's really a thriller, you have a problem. Even if your book is a romance, but they think it's erotica, you still have a problem. It's much better to receive invaluable feedback like this before you publish than afterward.

With your second question, you may receive helpful suggestions, like whether or not the font is legible, if the cover seems too busy, and whether or not the colors work well together. You might come to learn that while only a few people are talented artists, almost everybody is an art critic. Be prepared to show a "thick skin." You want to solicit honest advice. Don't defend your work and you'll receive more honest opinions. Don't try to satisfy every comment that you hear. You have to try to filter out the good from the bad, and you also have your own tastes and style to consider. If you did the art yourself and tend to get defensive easily when others criticize your work, find a friend to do this for you (in your complete absence). Start building a positive image as an author. If you get in an argument with a stranger about your cover and they post this story on the internet, your book might be sunk before the ship ever sails. Be professional at all times to build the best possible author image.

You can get such feedback just about anywhere. Keep the cover with you for one day and show it to everyone you interact with. If you absolutely can't make yourself feel comfortable doing this for one day (or persuade a friend to do it on your behalf), then use the internet. Even if you do feel comfortable asking in person, you can also supplement this with the internet. Post online and get feedback, but not just from people who know and like you (as would be the case with social media – their feedback may be helpful, too, but you really need to gauge the opinions of strangers).

Next, print out a page that has just the title as it appears on your front cover (remove the picture, author, and everything else – however, if your font color is light, change the background to a dark color instead of white). Show this to a different group of strangers (i.e. people who haven't seen your cover). Ask them what they think your book is about. You want your cover, title, and blurb to present a unifying picture and to reinforce one another. Ideally, anyone who looks at your cover, reads your title, or reads your blurb (any one of the three all by itself) should be able to identify your book's genre and have some idea of what to expect.

Therefore, you should separately print out your blurb (your book's description) and show it to several people who haven't seen your cover or read your title. By doing this three times (once for the cover, title, and blurb), you actually get more exposure for your book prior to its release. Don't think of it as more work. Think of it as a combination of valuable input and free marketing. Remember, you're also trying to establish your image as a professional author.

When you solicit opinions on your cover and title, here's something else you would like to gauge. First, watch closely to see how they react. If the cover has a striking image, you should see some pop in their reactions; if your cover is just so-so (or worse), you may be able to judge this from their reactions. Next, you want to judge whether your cover or title are memorable. At some point during your interaction, put these papers away, then just as they're about to walk away, ask them to please describe the cover or repeat the title (whichever it was). Did you have a striking image that they will retain well or a short, catchy title that is easy to remember? You want them to remember your title easily and for a long period of time because this significantly improves your chances of getting word-of-mouth sales, which are the most valuable sales you can get (the book also has to be good – both content and aesthetics – to get these). If the picture is memorable, it will help them recognize your cover. Some customers don't make immediate purchase decisions, but those who don't often wind up buying products that they remember. How many times do you choose one brand over another in the store simple because you've heard of it? Recognition – both by sight and by name – is important.

Now you may see the value of having a short title. If you browse the bestseller lists, you may learn that most of these books have just three words or less in their titles! We'll return to this issue in Sec. 5.1.5.

Remember, these polls give you exposure. This way, you're beginning a small marketing campaign before your book is even published. If your cover looks nice or your title sounds interesting, a few people whom you interact with may ask when your book will be available. Be prepared for this marketing opportunity. You want people to look for your book later (even if they don't ask you directly, you can still make this effort). When will it be available? How will they find it? Think about the answers to these questions. Even better, prepare a press release package (see Sec. 8.1.14). We'll return to the necessity of developing a marketing plan in the next section, along with other valuable pre-release marketing suggestions, like preorders.

Strive to perfect your cover, title, and blurb before you seek opinions. You're more likely to generate interest in your work this way, and you'll also receive more effective feedback. We will discuss how to this in Sec.'s 5.1.3-5. If you revise your cover, title, and/or blurb significantly after receiving feedback, consider showing them again after the revisions. You'll receive new feedback and, if the feedback is better, develop a helpful measure of confidence. (Confidence is an important skill in marketing success, but so is humility. You need both. Beware of overconfidence and bragging, and also avoid the other extreme of lacking confidence.) You will also increase your pre-sale exposure. (This exposure is a minor thing in itself. If you interact with a hundred people who show interest, it might be just a few – but you never know; people do like to read books by authors they have met, and they might appreciate that you sought their advice – who actually buy your book, and it might not be for quite some time. Do it for the feedback, not for the promotion. At the same time, all of the little things that you can do in the way of marketing do add up.)

I recommend reading this chapter *before* submitting your files for review. In addition to considering possible changes before it may be too late to make them, you might also avoid some common mistakes (such as those described in Sec. 5.1.6). It's much better to prevent mistakes than to correct them later.

Copyright registration is another thing that you might want to do before you publish. Your work is already under copyright protection once you have typed or written it. I recommend that you keep your files (especially, a sequence of versions showing the development of your book over the course of time), just in case. If you are the copyright owner of the work (i.e. you wrote it yourself and were not a work for hire, and have not granted the copyright to anyone else, such as a publisher), then you provide your copyright notice in the copyright page of your book. Copyright registration is optional protection that you can obtain by filling out a form and submitting a copy of your manuscript to www.copyright.gov with a fee ($35 online and $65 via mail, presently).

Amazon has contacted a few authors to request verification of copyright ownership. Presently, it has only happened to a small percentage of authors, but it has happened. For example, if Amazon realizes that two different authors have published essentially the same material or if someone complains to Amazon that copyright may have been violated, Amazon will ask the author(s) to verify copyright ownership. In such instances, the simplest, most effective way to respond is to submit proof of copyright registration. If you don't have copyright registration, your work is still copyrighted, and there are still ways to demonstrate copyright ownership – it's just not quite as easy. I'm not an attorney. If you would like legal advice, contact an attorney. You can also find some helpful resources and learn more about copyright law at www.copyright.gov.

5.1.2 The Importance of Having a Plan

Most authors click Approve Proof to publish their first book without any sort of plan for how they will help stimulate sales. As we will learn in this section, you can start out with a simple, yet effective, marketing plan, which can make a significant impact on the success of your book. The problem is that most writers excel at writing or storytelling, but don't have any marketing skills – or associate marketing with social media, advertising, and salesmanship (but it's not!). We'll explore free and low-cost marketing ideas in detail in Chapter 8. For now, we'll focus on simple, yet effective ways to help stimulate sales when you release your book.

As of February 2013, there are 20,000,000 paperback books, nearly 8,000,000 hardcover books, and almost 2,000,000 Kindle eBooks for sale on Amazon. Just in the last 30 days, 80,000 paperbacks, 30,000 hardcovers, and 60,000 Kindle eBooks have been published. More than 5,000 books are released every day just on Amazon.[1] What do these numbers mean to you? How will anyone ever discover your book? Customers must discover your book before there is any chance that they will read or buy it.

---

[1] These numbers were found by browsing Books and Kindle eBooks, respectively. Some of these books are different editions of the same book or re-releases of previous books, and so the actual number of *new* books may be somewhat smaller than these figures suggest.

Publishing is a highly competitive business. There are millions of books on the market, including a hundred thousand new releases. Out of these millions of books, only the top 5,000 sell several copies per day on average; the top 50,000 sell a couple of copies per day on average; and millions of books just sell a few copies per month or less.

You're not just competing with other self-published authors. Many of the top selling books are published by the big traditional publishers or were written by established popular authors. It may be instructive to browse the bestsellers in your genre. You may see that you don't have to be a big name or have a big publisher to achieve success, and you can learn a few of the secrets to success by studying (and even reading) books that are proven to sell well. The bestsellers tend to have excellent covers, short and clear descriptions, and a visually attractive sample in the Look Inside. Their product pages tend to look professional. Look for other features, like editorial reviews, quotes from readers, an author picture and link to an author page, and which categories the book is listed in. This should help give you some ideas.

A marketing plan can help jumpstart sales, which may help make your book discoverable by other potential customers and which helps improve your prospects for reviews (since customers need to read your book before they can review it). If instead you just throw your book out there and very few people discover your book, your book will have a history of poor sales rank, which itself can affect sales. You don't need to invest in the marketing. There are simple, free ideas available. I will reveal what these are in a few paragraphs. Patience, please.

Let me first discuss something else that's equally important – something that you must do in order to prevent the marketing plan from backfiring. First, you must perfect your book from cover to cover and your product page. It won't do any good to drive sales to your book if any feature of your book or product page seems unprofessional – that will put many prospective customers off, and may result in negative customer reviews.

Your cover will show up next to other covers in search results. Customers are more likely to notice a cover that attracts interest. If your cover and title attract interest (and signify the correct genre), customers will check out the product page and read the description. If the product page appears professional and the description engages their interest, customers will Look Inside. If the sample looks professional, customers will read the first chapter. If the first chapter holds their interest and customers don't encounter mistakes or anything that spoils their mood, customers will buy your book. If the book is professionally edited and formatted, the story is good, and the characters are memorable, customers will leave good reviews; but if there are mistakes or issues that you could have corrected, these are likely to show up in bad reviews. So many factors affect the prospects for sales and reviews.

Some authors think along these lines: "You shouldn't judge a book by its cover," "Great storytelling is more important than technically correct writing," and, "If the story is great, customers will spread the word." You're absolutely right, philosophically, but that's not the way book buying works in practice. The reality is that the cover strongly impacts buying decisions, the quality of the writing does affect reviews, and you need people to read your book (and not be distracted by editing or formatting issues) before they can spread the word. The other side is this: Why should customers spend money on a book that wasn't perfected?

Here's the thing. There are tens of thousands of books that have fantastic covers, enticing descriptions, professional product pages, a professional Look Inside, are professionally edited and formatted, tell great stories, and feature memorable characters. If your book only has a few things on this list, why should customers buy your book when there are tens of thousands of books available that have everything on this list? Remember, you don't necessarily need money to perfect these things – you can invest some time instead. We'll discuss how to perfect your cover, interior, and blurb in Sec.'s 5.1.3-5.

You need to have your book and product page perfected when you release your book if you want your marketing plan to be effective. If instead you release your book and save these things for later, your book is more likely to start out with a mediocre sales rank and – if there are writing or story issues in the content – receive some negative reviews. It's much more difficult to overcome a history of a mediocre sales rank and negative reviews than it is to do everything right in the first place. So don't procrastinate. You can favorably impact the potential success of your own book by doing everything right in the first place.

What simple, free ideas are available for a marketing plan that can help stimulate initial sales (and through those sales, hopefully, some reviews, too)? Note that a complete list can be found in Sec. 8.1.2. First off, you can begin to develop a following before your first book is ever released. Start with people you know – friends, family, acquaintances, and coworkers who may appreciate your work. Most of the books that people read were written by authors they know very little about. When the rare opportunity presents itself, people like to be able to say, "I know that author," and especially, "I knew her before she became famous."

Start with friends, family, acquaintances, and coworkers. Keep them informed about the progress of your book – but don't overdo it. Show them how much time and effort you're putting into it; emphasize the various challenges that you've come across and how you've handled them. If you've asked them for any input – whether it's on part of the content or just the cover – they may feel a little more attached to and interested in your work.

Next, tap into your social networks (again, don't overdo it or you get tuned out). You may have many more acquaintances there. Have you posted your cover, title, and description there and asked for feedback? You want to increase the "buzz" about your upcoming book. It's unrealistic to expect everyone you know to buy your book or to buy it on the day it comes out. However, the more people who know about your book, the better. Someone who isn't interested in your book, but knows about it, might tell a friend who does read your genre.

Strive to increase the anticipation for your new release. "Did you hear that Jane wrote a mystery and it's coming out next month?" Such word-of-mouth advertising can be very helpful, but you can improve on this. You want them to know a little more. What striking characteristic does your book have? Compare the previous quote to the following quotes. These can be more effective. "Jane's cover is incredible. You have to see it." "One of Jane's characters is just as memorable as Gollum from *The Hobbit*." "Jane spent years just doing the research for her book." "I heard that Jane's book could be the next *Harry Potter*." "I read an excerpt from Jane's book, and the writing conveys some powerful emotions."

You want to identify ways that your book stands out and promote this. Share this. Don't try to tell people to advertise for you – or worse, tell them what to say. Rather, share a part of your book that's likely to generate "buzz" about your book. If your cover is awesome, the more you show it and request feedback, the more buzz you might get about your cover. If you've put a great deal of time into writing and revisions, working with an editor, doing research, and so on, mention this in conversations, occasionally post this on your social networks, etc. Don't heavily plug your upcoming book or the information may be tuned out; less than 10% of your posts might mention your book or your work on it, for example.

Friends, family, acquaintances, and coworkers are just the beginning. If you took my suggestion from the previous section to solicit feedback from strangers, this helps to build your following. Next, look for local press coverage. Local newspapers often like to feature local authors, for example. We'll discuss this and other marketing ideas (such as writing articles, which can be highly effective) further in Chapter 8. I hope that you see the importance of learning more about marketing and developing your marketing strategy <u>before</u> you release your book. It would be a great idea to skip ahead and read Sec. 8.1.2 now.

The following that you build and the "buzz" that develops in anticipation of your book's release can help to stimulate early sales.[2] Strive to visualize this – in a positive way, with the confidence that you can pull it off. Read Chapter 8 before you publish. There you can learn about other important pre-release marketing strategies, like how to get your book listed as Coming Soon on Amazon with the option of preorders (sales that you can get before your book is ever released) – that's what the big publishers do – but note that preorders themselves are described in Sec. 7.1.8. You also want to learn how to develop a long-term marketing plan; what we've discussed so far is just to get you started.

Your author image is very important. Every person you interact with, anything you post online, any email or text message that you send, and every other form of communication that you have with anyone helps to portray your image as an author. You want these posts, comments, blogs, conversations, and such to show you in a positive light as a professional author, knowledgeable about writing in his/her genre, of good character, etc. Strive to build a positive image and establish a "brand" as an author. Above all, accept criticism (and offer thanks for it – except in written reviews on your book's product page), don't act rashly or emotionally, and don't respond to any criticism defensively, snobbishly, or accusingly. A single outburst of unprofessional conduct can bring an avalanche against your book far greater than any marketing that you can do. We will discuss this further in Chapters 7-8.

---

[2] Beware that anyone who may have a financial interest in your book, such as immediate family, is not permitted to review your book on Amazon.com. If they do, their reviews are very likely to be removed at some point. We'll discuss marketing and the prospects for receiving reviews further in Chapters 7-8.

If you will be releasing both paperback and eBook editions, you will want to time their availability. In order for them to become available simultaneously, you should have them all ready and set to go (meaning that you've already inspected your printed proof and previewed your eBook on all devices, and are happy with both), so that all that remains to be done is to click the buttons to publish. It will take about 12 hours for your eBook to go live and although your paperback might show up in one to three days (but not always), it will take longer for your product page to grow (see Chapter 7). You can also establish your paperback early with preorders, or launch a hardcover edition first (learn more in Sec. 7.1.8 and Chapter 8).

You may want your eBook edition to be released prior to your paperback edition, or vice-versa. This way, provided that you successfully market the release of your book, you may be able to stimulate early sales twice – once with each release – since some people prefer eBooks, while others prefer paperback (or hardcover). Many traditional publishers apply the multi-release strategy with different editions. They often release the more expensive hard-cover first; but in your case, you might actually draw a greater royalty on a cheaper edition.

Will you be publishing one book, several books, or a series? The answer to this question affects your marketing strategy. If you have a series, or if you will have a few related books, you want to maximize your exposure for the first book. In this case, your goal isn't to make the greatest profit from the first book, but to maximize the number of sales. The idea is that the more people who read your first book, the more people will get drawn into the series. The catch is that your first book better be very good in order to make customers come for more. Many authors actually give their first book away for free or offer giveaway promotions with their first books with long-term success in mind (we'll return to this point in Chapter 8).

5.1.3 Perfecting Your Paperback Cover

Your cover is a very important marketing tool. A great cover helps to get your book discovered in search results. The cover should attract attention and signify the genre. Customers browsing through search results on Amazon are usually looking for a specific type of book, and they tend to click on appealing covers that look like the types of books that they normally read. Therefore, it's very important to study the covers in your genre to see what customers are accustomed to seeing.

A great cover can make a huge difference for a book that has a good description, professional product page, great story, memorable characters, and a professional Look Inside. A mediocre cover on a great book can significantly deter sales. A great cover on a mediocre book can inspire original sales, but then the reviews may eventually reflect that the book is mediocre. You won't be guaranteed success by having a great cover, but not having a great cover may greatly limit your book's potential. Give your book the best chance of success with the best cover you can make given your resources (which may be greater than you think).

Almost all top-selling authors believe that a highly successful book needs to have a fantastic cover. The content is more important to the reader, but the cover significantly helps in determining to what extent your book will be noticed in search results. The content is irrelevant when customers don't notice and explore the book. Just imagine your book lying atop a customer's desk or table when company comes over. If the guests notice your book and think, "Wow, that looks interesting," your book suddenly becomes a conversation piece. It's not just Amazon search results that may be affected by your cover: Your cover may be seen on buses, subways, airport terminals, and anywhere else that a customer might read your book in public. Word-of-mouth sales can make for highly effective, yet free marketing.

The cover has more importance than just attracting attention, signifying the genre, and emphasizing a few words that suggest what the book is about. It also represents an image of your professionalism and attention to detail. In practice, people *do* judge a book by its cover. When the cover is poor or mediocre, a potential buyer naturally wonders if the content is similarly lacking in effort. If the content isn't lacking, make a cover that isn't lacking either.

Does *every* book need a super cover? The cover is very important for most books, but there may be a few exceptions where a good cover may suffice. A cover is extremely important for most genres in fiction and for many nonfiction books that are more likely to sell by being wanted than by being needed. Nonfiction books that inform readers how to do something, provide technical help, include valuable knowledge, and so on may be able to get away with just a good cover. In this case, a simple cover can be quite effective, so long as it is visually appealing, the right words are emphasized and clear in the thumbnail, and the cover doesn't violate any of the rules for making a good cover (to be described soon). But here's the thing: If there are two similar nonfiction books providing helpful information – all other things being roughly equal, as far as the customer can tell – the one with the better cover will win.

I've heard some amazing success stories from authors who significantly improved their original covers – in many cases, going from one sale per day or less to several copies per day. Their blurbs, stories, editing, formatting, and characters were good, too; the new and improved covers helped call attention to their books. If the book is good, it's worth the cover.

What makes a cover good or great? It's not just about the art. There are some lousy covers that are highly detailed artistically or have well-crafted images, and there are some exceptional covers that are virtually lacking in art. However, for fiction, you definitely need some sort of imagery to signify the genre and show what the book is about. It doesn't have to be art (except perhaps for a few genres, like fantasy, where art is common); it could be a quality photo.

Covers involve many factors. If any aspect is poor, it can single-handedly ruin the effect. There is text for the title and author (at least), there may be art or photos, there can be decoration, and covers have a background. The quality of the images must be high – not just in terms of DPI, but also by being "clean," not having red-eye, looking sharp, etc. The text must be clear. Colors must coordinate well. Even the layout is important.

Shortly, we will consider a variety of ingredients that go into designing a cover and how to perfect them. In Volume 1, I described how to make a cover, while I have saved the secrets for perfecting the cover until Volume 2. Why? Partly, I didn't want to limit your creativity; if you've already attempted a cover, then you have a draft to serve as a useful starting point. Secondly, since you're reading the half of the book that concerns perfecting your proof and marketing, it suggests that you have the motivation to produce a good enough book for which an excellent cover may make the difference.

For this very reason, we should also reassess whether or not it may be worthwhile to invest in a nice cover. In Volume 1, I suggested saving money. If you will be following the advice of Volume 2 on how to perfect the content and if you're also motivated to market your book (e.g. by trying to create "buzz" for its release), then investing in a nice cover is more likely to reap dividends for you. You may have witnessed your own cover design potential firsthand if you've already attempted a draft of your cover. If so, this may help you decide how much a professional cover may improve over your own ability. Many successful authors have invested in cover design. For people with highly effective marketing skills, it's a no-brainer – they already have a plan for how to recover the investment through sales. Ask yourself how confident you are in your own book. Do you believe that it's good enough to succeed? Bear in mind that if you do hire a professional designer, your book may be featured on their website, which offers you a little exposure in return. If you're wondering about costs, hold onto your question for a moment.

There is an exception. There are a few indie authors who expect to sell most of their books in person. This is common for salesmen or speakers who travel around the country to give presentations. They sell most of their books in person when the presentation is over. If that's you, and you don't expect your book to be discovered through search results, then just having a satisfactory cover may be in order. Otherwise, strive for a great cover.

Now let's get into the cover secrets! The first step is to avoid common mistakes, which can turn a potentially great cover into a lousy cover:

☺ **Text that is hard to read** because of a poor or fancy font. Clear and legible is much better than fancy. Some fonts often create a negative reaction. Research your font selections online to find out for which context they're more often used and how appealing they seem to be (Wikipedia lists research statistics on this for many fonts).

𝔒𝔩𝔡 𝔈𝔫𝔤𝔩𝔦𝔰𝔥 text is not that easy to read.

Comic Sans has a tendency to produce a negative reaction from readers.

☺ Problems with image quality. Pictures that appear **blurry, jagged, or pixelated** – in print or online – create a poor impression (we'll discuss how to correct these issues in Sec. 5.1.6). Inspect the quality of the images in the printed proof carefully.

☺ Poor photographs. Photos should be **well-lit**, properly **touched up** (like removing red-eye), precisely **cropped** (if needed), and professional in appearance.

☺ Using low-resolution images. Google images and other stock images often have 96 DPI. (These images may also be easily recognized from having been used on many occasions.) Ideally, all images should be **300 DPI** in the native program and if you insert them into Word you must take steps to avoid automatic compression (see Sec. 5.1.6).

☺ Text or pictures are not clean. It's very common for letters or pictures to have little **stray marks** around them. Either find a graphics program that can help you clean these up or don't use those pictures. Stray marks or dots around letters or pictures offer a poor first impression of your book.

 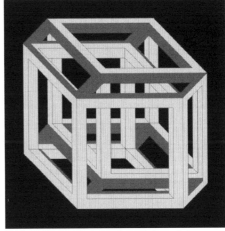

☺ Wrong choice of words emphasized in the title. If some words of the title are larger (or otherwise emphasized) over others, choose just the most relevant words. It's a common mistake to make the long words smaller and the short words larger just because the larger words wouldn't fit otherwise. Keep the author(s), other contributors, and subtitles smaller than the title. Names shouldn't be prominent unless they are famous.

☺ Poor contrast, **colors clash**, or poor color coordination. Research (online) which colors work well together – two colors that create good contrast often work well next to one another – and which colors tend to clash with one another. There should be good contrast between the text and background so that the text is easy to read. Red text on an orange background, for example, will be very difficult to make out. It's so important to seek feedback (as described in Sec. 5.1.1) on your cover because what seems fine to you might turn out to be fairly unpopular.

☺ The cover is **too busy**. The purpose of the cover is two-fold: First, grab attention (in a positive way), then lure readers from the intended audience. For the second part, the cover must make it clear which genre it falls in (by having a cover that fits into the styles common in its genre) and indicate what the book is about (from a primary image and a few emphasized words that stand out on the cover). Extra images and details make it this more difficult to determine. Many artists want to show off their talent by including artistic detail and indies feel a natural inclination to fill up every blank space on the cover, but it's a mistake. Some very popular traditionally published children's books with artists who have a knack for artistic detail have simple covers with one main image. The reason for this is that they want the main image and a few empha-sized words to stand out and they want the main image to be memorable. (I have made this mistake myself, as you can see in the pictures below.)

☺ Text arranged in a way that is **difficult to read**. Words that appear vertically, diago-nally, or have the letters staggered take longer to read. Occasionally, it may be pos-sible to achieve a good effect by using a special effect for one or two words, but it's a risk. The title should be clear and easy for the reader to figure out. Definitely, don't write an entire title with a font that's not quick and easy to read, and don't apply any fancy fonts or text effects to nonstandard words (like names or foreign words). Layout all words horizontally because they're much easier to read this way.

☺ Hand drawings that aren't expertly done. There are many magnificent covers in this age of graphic arts. Unless you're selling a coloring book, crayons are a really bad idea; so are colored pencils. Drawings or paintings must be professionally done. If a potential customer can find any fault in it, this will be used as an excuse not to buy the book. It's a challenge for hand-drawn cover art to compete with covers that take advantage of the possibilities of graphic arts. Even photos must appear **professional and clean** in order to compete.

☺ Something on the cover looks **unnatural or out of place**. Check all of the objects in the background to make sure that none of them are in an awkward position compared to the foreground images. If there are any semi-transparent images in the foreground, check if any background objects are inside them. I saw a book once with a semi-transparent man in the foreground and ski slopes in the background, and when I looked closely, there was a skier inside of his head! Such a mistake is a sales killer.

☺ Picture looks **distorted**. This common mistake occurs when the author uses a picture for the front cover that doesn't have the same aspect ratio as the cover size. Changing the aspect ratio to match the shape of the cover will distort the images. This especially makes people appear very unnatural.

☺ Text embedded in a jpeg picture appears **blurry or pixelated**. Use a textbox instead. Go to the Insert tab and choose WordArt or a textbox. While this is selected, go to the Format tab and set both Shape Fill and Shape Outline to no color (these are different from Text Fill and Text Outline, which you may wish to adjust). Text prints much better when it's not part of a jpeg picture.

TEXT TEXT

☺ Including the word "**by**" before or above the author name. Some people view this as amateurish. The author clearly wrote the book – there isn't really any reason to include this word. Don't give anyone an excuse not to take your work seriously.

by
Chris McMullen

There is more to making a great cover than simply avoiding mistakes. Following are some of the 'secrets' to designing a successful cover. I selected some examples from covers that you can find on Amazon. It will be highly instructive to take the time to check out these covers.

☺ **Striking cover designs** grab attention; the cover just pops out at you. It's not necessarily a picture that has to be striking; some other effects can also elicit a *Wow!* Stark contrast – bright against dark – can catch attention, even without images (but for most fiction, you really need a relevant image). An interesting picture can also stand out, but you want to make sure than anything that stands out does so in a good way (and signifies the genre and relates to the content).

- *Shatter Me* by Tahereh Mafi literally is an eye-opener.
- *CIN: "Lynn, Lynn, the city of sin. You never come out the way you went in"* by Christina Leigh Pritchard stands out among other thumbnails.
- *Grace Lost* by M. Lauryl Lewis features a striking zombie picture.
- *Random Rationality* by Fourat Janabi is unique and simple, yet detailed.
- *The Guardian of Threshold* by A. A. Volts is bright, yet soft.

☺ It's not just the quality of art or a photograph. It doesn't take a Picasso to sell books. Strive to make the cover appealing. Good use of color, nice **contrast**, **bright** imagery, pleasing to look at, a main image that catches attention – such things help to build cover appeal. Nothing out of place or **distracting**, not **too busy**, easy to understand images and text, one main image (and no more than three images) – these things help to avoid an unappealing cover. **Shadows must be consistent with the light source.**

- *Merry Christmas* by Susan Rohrer effectively uses a touch of color.
- *Instant Feng Shui* by Trish McCabe, Caleen Mulock, and Ken McCabe features just a simple picture, yet looks warm and appealing.

☺ Having a **memorable cover** helps with marketing. When people recognize your cover upon seeing it again, it helps establish the book's brand (people generally purchase products they have heard of before – i.e. they recognize it). You want buyers to think, "I remember seeing this before." One main image is easier to remember than multiple images. A **short title** is easier to remember than a long title. You're more likely to get invaluable word-of-mouth sales if you have a short, memorable title (no hard words to spell, relates to the content). Research actually shows that people best recall covers that send a **unifying message** (single font used, title and images signify the genre and relate to the book). Having something zany on your cover – like a rhinoceros doing cartwheels – may catch attention, but doesn't provide the same recognition that we strive for as a cover that sends a unifying message relevant to the content and genre.

- *Illusions* by Chantilly Chanel Austin is memorable for its unique concept.
- *Reapers Inc.* by Dave Hunter has a simple, yet highly effective style.
- *Money Saving Emergency Plan* by Dave Ramson is a little zany, yet this works because the signal clearly relates to the content and genre.

☺ **Simplicity** is key. Don't get carried away with artistic detail. Artists and indie cover designers naturally feel inclined to try to fill every void. Supplemental images cause the primary image and title to be less memorable. An artistic border design may be okay, but shouldn't detract from the main image and text. Adding a little detail that makes the book appear more professional is good provided that it doesn't interfere with sending a clear message and recognition (many traditionally published books have a starburst, for example, that does this – sample traditionally published books in your genre to see what features they add to help distinguish their covers without detracting from the simplicity of design).

- *My Vampire Prom Date* and other stories by Shawn Pfister is striking, yet simple and not too detailed.
- *Through These Eyes* by Tom Bradford and Michael Risley creates an eye-catching effect with a simple design.

☺ Limit the number of images on the front cover to **three or less**. One is often best – it stands out better and it's easier to recall that way. If there are multiple images, they must all be **related**. What do a witch, a lion, and a knight all have in common? Nothing, so they shouldn't be on the same cover! They might all be in the story, but you're trying to sell books to people who haven't read the story yet. Don't include multiple images that aren't inherently related. While one image is usually best, there are occasions where two images can work together well – such as separation between protagonist and antagonist, or a romance (although a couple can also appear together with the effect of one image). Images may also appear in the foreground with another image in the background. If so, ensure that the background is not too busy.

- *Abandoned Treasure* by Ken Acha features a single, yet striking, image.

☺ Create good **contrast** – especially between text and the background. For example, white and black provide excellent contrast, yellow contrasts well with blue or purple, and red stands out well on black. Yet there are different hues and tones, so what's true in general doesn't always hold. Try playing with the colors (there are many color programs on the web that you can experiment with – i.e. programs that designers use to place colors beside one another and see how they look together) to see what produces nice contrast to your eye, and also seek external opinions because not all perceptions are identical and you want the cover to appeal to a majority of buyers.

- *The Black Dragon* by W. D. Newman features a dragon silhouette.
- *Fated* by Kazine Phoenix has contrasting butterfly wings.
- *Fine to Fab* by Lisa Lieberman-Wang has white text contrasting with purple.
- *Miso for Life* by Mai Xuan Bui, Wendy Toliver, Jenny Baranick, and Quyen Ngo has a busy foreground that contrasts well with the empty background.

Primary	Colors it often stands out with
red	yellow, black, white, gray
green	blue, black, gray, purple, pink, yellow
blue	yellow, white, pink, green
yellow	blue, black, red, orange, gray, brown, purple, pink
orange	black, white, yellow, brown, purple
brown	white, yellow, orange, pink
purple	yellow, white, black, pink, green, orange
pink	black, blue, brown, purple, green, yellow, white
black	white, yellow, pink, red, orange, green, purple, gray
white	black, brown, purple, blue, red, orange, gray, pink
gray	white, yellow, green, red, black

☺ At least part of the cover should be **nice and bright**. Even if most of the cover is dark, there at least needs to be some part that is quite bright to create contrast. In general, bright covers tend to attract more attention than dark covers; they also tend to put the buyer in a better mood. Dark covers may be more common specifically in horror, but even then the text or part of the imagery must still be bright to offset this and create the needed contrast. When you look at the top sellers in your genre, see how many of them look bright (also check if they agree with the advice in this book).

- *The Psychology of the Soul* by Angel Cusick is glowing.
- *The Haunted* by J. A. Templeton looks bright among other thumbnails.
- *I Don't Think So!* by Debbie Happy Cohen broke some of these rules (that's okay given its title), but uses color effectively in a different way.

☺ Try to restrict your cover design to **three colors**. This goes hand in hand with simplicity, recognition, easy to understand, unity of presentation, and having colors that work well together. Three is the magic number that traditional publishers use. Most of the imagery should feature just three main colors. Photographs and artwork sometimes have many colors. In this case, which colors stand out? The entire cover – text, artwork, photos, designs, etc. – should revolve around just three main colors. There should be one dominant color, so instead of having three equal colors, an old rule of thumb is to use 60% for the primary color, 30% for the secondary color (the primary and secondary should stand out well from one another), and 10% for the accent color (which should complement the primary or secondary). If you need more than three colors, try using different tints and shades of the three main colors.

- *Kindle Marketing Ninja Guide* by R. L. Adams is black, purple, and white.
- *Cinder* by Marissa Meyer makes use of black, white, and red.
- *The Girl Who Fell Beneath Fairyland and Led the Revels There* by Catherynne M. Valente and Ana Juan features purple, orange, and red.
- *Thoroughly Modern Monsters* by Jennifer Rainey uses green, white, and black.

☺ Another way that three is a magic number for cover design has to do with the **rule of thirds**. This rule suggests that the primary image might be better placed one-third the width and height from the edge than it would if it were centered. The problem of centering the main image is that it divides the cover into equal halves. Rather than cause the viewer to see the cover as equal halves, the rule of thirds helps the main image stand out. One main image is more memorable than two equal halves, so this helps with recall and associating the main image with what the book is about. There are a few exceptions, such as a mirror image contrasting design (e.g. portraying the protagonist and antagonist) or a cover that is symbolic of a battle (which may be appropriate for a war book).

- *Your World is Exploding* by Christopher Dessi applies both the rule of thirds and the three-color rule effectively.
- *Debugging with Fiddler* by Eric Lawrence has the center of the fiddle's body positioned approximately one-third from the right and bottom edges.
- *Happiness in Your Life – Book One* by Doe Zantamata features a butterfly that is one-third down from the top.

☺ Use colors that work well together. First, choose two colors that **stand out well** from one another for the primary and secondary. The third color – the accent – should **complement** one of the first two colors. If you have a main image, the colors need to **coordinate** with this. Since text needs to be clear, black text often appears against a light background and white text is usually used on a dark background. However, red text can stand out well on black, and red also catches attention. Yellow text can also stand out well on black, purple, and navy blue, although white tends to be more clear.

It's a challenge to coordinate all of the colors of the cover – text, images, and background. That's why it's so important to check out the colors that work well together in the top sellers and also to seek external opinions on your cover design.

- *The Last Man* by Vince Flynn blends white, red, and black effectively, and the title text – in orange – complements the red.
- *Book Writing Made Simple* by Kalinda Rose Stevenson has an appealing blue that contrasts well with yellow pencils and white letters.
- *Ever After* by Kim Harrison blends red, black, and yellow with a fiery effect.

☺ Use colors that send **relevant messages** for your genre and content. Different colors convey different emotions – e.g. red may evoke a sense of passion, while yellow may evoke cheerfulness. Observe that a single color is often associated with multiple emotions – e.g. green may be associated with money (especially dark green), but it also represents safety. Soft pastels are used for a feminine book, strong bold colors indicate a masculine book, and bright vibrant covers are geared toward children. Certain colors are common within a genre – e.g. romance covers often feature red for passion, while financial books tend to have dark green for money or blue for trust.

- *Touched* by Corinne Jackson features a red rose, which symbolizes the romance and power featured in the novel.
- *Freakonomics* by Steven D. Levitt utilizes green to signify money and safety.
- *Etiquette & Espionage* by Gail Carriger attracts females with a pink background.
- *The Power of Habit* by Charles Duhigg seems to promise happiness with its bright yellow background.
- *The Money Class* by Suze Orman combines white for safety, black for power, and gold for wealth – symbolizing a powerful, safe means to establish wealth.

Color	Emotions that it may evoke
red	passion, strength, power, danger
green	safety, healing, money
blue	stability, trust, health
yellow	happiness, intellect
orange	joy, enthusiasm, encouragement
brown	confidence, casualness
gold	wealth, prestige, wisdom
purple	power, luxury, ambition
pink	feminism, romance
black	power, elegance, mystery, death
white	purity, perfection, safety
gray	tradition, dullness

☺ Some colors also have **specific effects** in cover design. Red text and images tend to stand out and catch attention; it is sometimes used as an accent to help stimulate a sense of urgency (it's common on "click here" buttons on the internet). Green provides a sense of relaxation. Yellow and orange can be used effectively to call attention as highlighters. However, yellow needs to appear with dark colors to create contrast, and shouldn't be used when trying to convey masculinity, prestige, or stability. High quality is symbolized by gold. White suggests simplicity, while blue represents knowledge and expertise. Blue also helps to convey trust. Navy blue is cheaper, whereas purple is luxurious and gold is prestigious. Black adds a sense of depth. A black background helps light colors stand out, yet text is harder to read on a black background. Black and white together look formal.

- *Think and Grow Rich* by Napoleon Hill symbolizes knowledge and expertise with blue, high quality with gold, and has an orange accent in the background.

☺ **Consistency and unity** are very important factors for getting a potential buyer who notices your cover to click on your book. The images need to be unified – i.e. they must clearly go together. For example, a spaceship goes with a picture of the stars; but a cheerleader does not go with a robot (even if the story has both a robot and a cheerleader – remember, the buyer doesn't know the story yet). Use just a couple of different fonts on the cover to have consistent text. All of the fonts should be easy to read, but most of the text should be in the clearest font. The font styles should go together, too. The images, color scheme, and font styles of the cover must all send the same unified message, and this message must be consistent with the title, description, and content of the book. This is critical because inconsistent, non-unified messages among these elements deter book sales. If the title sounds like a romance, while the images look more like erotica, for example, this mismatch will create buyer confusion, and confused buyers tend to prefer a book that sends a clear message. It's a very common mistake for one of the elements – title, images, colors, font, blurb, and content – not to fit in. Check all of this carefully and seek external feedback to check that your message is 100% unified. Your cover helps to market your book.

- *Dangling Without a Rope* by Barbara Belmont sends a unified message.
- *Bible Cryptograms* by Marie Matthews focuses on the theme of the book.

☺ Design a cover that clearly **signifies your book's precise genre**. Readers are accustomed to reading books in that genre. When they see a cover that looks like the kind of cover they are used to seeing, it mentally registers that this book might be something they would read, and they click on it. If your book doesn't signify the genre, your intended audience won't be clicking on your book in search results. Check out the top sellers in your genre – and separate traditional publishers from others; both may be useful, but it may be helpful to know the difference – to see what imagery, color schemes, and font styles are characteristic of the genre. Also explore similar genres (e.g. in romance, compare adult, young adult, and erotica) to see how those books are distinguished from your genre. Don't make the mistake of using a cover that belongs in a slightly different genre. If the wrong audience clicks on your book, they won't buy it.

- *Die for Me* by Amy Plum screams teen romance.
- *Wait for You* by J. Lynn is a contemporary romance; it is distinguishable from both teen romance and erotica.

☺ The cover needs to relate to your book's content. Can people guess what your book is about just by looking at the cover? Obtain external (i.e. not from friends and family) input on your cover as described in Sec. 5.1.1 to learn what people think your book is about just by looking at the cover. This will help you see if your cover relates to the content. If you want to have just a few words in your title, which is common among the top sellers (especially, in fiction), you can add a little further clarification with a subtitle or an informative line on your front cover. However, a subtitle will appear together with your title – separated by a colon – in search results on Amazon, which may give the appearance of a longer title in the search results. If you don't want a subtitle, you can still add an informative line on the front cover (much like a subtitle). However, keep in mind that people will only read this line if they see the cover in person or take the time to enlarge the front cover view on Amazon; you can't expect this line to make up for anything that the title, images, or color scheme may be lacking.

- *Space! A Kids Book about Space* by Brian G. Johnson appears child-oriented.
- *Who Dat Cookin'* by Todd-Michael St. Pierre, Jeff Walsh, and Lori Walsh sends a clear message this this is a Louisiana cookbook.

☺ The entire cover needs to look professional, including the back cover and spine. The spine text (if your book has at least 102 pages) should be well-positioned and easy to read from a distance. Write the spine text in CAPS to make more effective use of a very narrow spine. While the front cover needs to be appealing both as a thumbnail and in person, your back cover should primarily be designed around its look in print. Back cover text needs to be clear and arranged in a very appealing way. After you order your first printed proof, show it to people for opinions – be sure to ask about the back cover, too – as described in Sec. 5.1.1. Visit different locations and don't stand in one place like a solicitor. You don't have to make special trips – just carry your cover, title, blurb, or proof with you and seek advice from people you naturally interact with (you don't need to approach complete strangers – it can be people you were going to briefly speak to anyway; but if you do intend to approach strangers, bring a friend for company and safety). Sometimes, you might even be able to approach people who may have an interest in your book. For example, if you're writing a book that relates to golf, bring this material with you every time you visit a golf course.

- *Men Are from Mars, Women Are from Venus* by John Gray, the hardcover edition, has the same style throughout the front, spine, and back.

☺ Minor professional touches can make a big difference. Develop a little logo that you can put on your books – both on the cover and on the copyright page. This will help you establish a visual brand – readers will come to associate this logo with your work. Traditional publishers often use little design marks, add fine print, include a starburst, and apply subtle touches that help give the cover an overall professional feel. Study the front, back, and spine of several professionally designed covers in your genre to learn these secrets.

- *Boundaries* by Henry Cloud and John Townsend includes the website, logo, and category on the back cover in addition to quotes (see the customer image).

Of course, there are exceptions to every rule. Just remember, there are millions of covers that break one or more of these rules that aren't selling well, but only a few covers breaking the rules that do sell very well. At the very least, don't break any of these rules unless you can think of a compelling reason to do so.

Should you pay for professional cover help? That depends on your situation. If you plan to sell most of the books in person (e.g. following a presentation), then a basic cover may suffice. For technical nonfiction or how-to books, a simple cover can be effective and the information that people need will help drive sales. Fiction, especially, along with nonfiction that people may want, but don't necessarily need (a chemistry workbook or a book that describes how to paint a house fall under need, whereas a guide to wine tasting or a biography of Napoleon fall under want) are more likely to sell when seen in online searches if they have great covers. Even word-of-mouth sales strongly depend on the quality of the cover.

Unless your book happens to fall under an exception (like selling mostly in person or a nonfiction book that people need – and even then, if there is much competition, a great cover can give you an edge), you need a wonderful cover in order to be highly successful. The next thing to consider is how well you can do by yourself (which you can gauge best if you first attempt this), and how much better a professional cover may be. Try the free and low-cost options first (to be discussed toward the end of this section) and try to get honest input from strangers. If it turns out that you have a gift for the graphic arts, you might wind up with a great self-made cover. At the very least, you will see how little or how much a professional cover might be able to improve upon what you can do by yourself.

Next, you must consider how good the book is and how much marketing you are willing to do. If there may be any issues with the storyline, editing, formatting, blurb, characteri-zation, etc. – or if the book concept just might not be of much general interest – then a great cover may not pay off. It would be a waste to have an incredible cover attract a great deal of attention, only for most of the potential buyers to wind up not purchasing the book because (a) the blurb didn't catch their interest, (b) they found typos, grammatical errors, or format-ting mistakes in the Look Inside, (c) there were several bad reviews that mention editing or storyline problems, or (d) the free sample wasn't what they were expecting from the cover.

Do some research to see how well similar books are selling. This will help you judge the potential of your concept. You don't want to invest heavily in a concept that has little interest.

How strongly do you believe in your book? How much time and effort are you willing to invest in your book? Are you seeking help with editing? If you feel strongly that your story is great, that your editing and formatting will be excellent, and that there will be popular interest in your book, then you should be willing to invest in your belief. This investment will give your book the best chance of success.

Also, consider how much time and effort you are willing to invest toward marketing (even if it's just free and low-cost marketing), and how effective your marketing campaign may be. We will discuss several free and low-cost marketing strategies in Chapter 8; the question right now is how motivated and diligent you may be in pursuing this. Any author who has any natural aptitude for marketing – e.g. if you are in the advertising business, that must be the case – should easily be able to make an investment in an amazing cover pay off. If you have a unique situation that may be of interest to the press – like writing a book that draws on your experience as a triplet or overcoming dyslexia to produce a well-written book – this is a marketing edge that you may be able to apply to help recover the cost of professional cover help. However, even if you don't have any marketing advantages, provided that you're willing to learn about how to market your book effectively and are also willing to make a long-term commitment to diligently marketing, an investment in a great cover can pay off in the long run (especially, if the content of your book is as good as the cover, both in terms of ideas and the editing and formatting). If you're highly motivated to try to create "buzz" for your book and to seek external opinions as I've already recommended, then you're already on the right track.

Professional cover design comes in a variety of price ranges. Some graphic artists sell premade covers from $10 to $100. This requires browsing to find one that's a good fit for your book. When using this option, find out whether or not other authors may be able to use the same cover – otherwise, there may be several similarly looking books. Many illustrators work with writers to provide custom cover designs for $100 to $1000. It's not necessary to spend $1000 to get a great cover; many wonderful cover designs are produced at the lower end of this price range.

CreateSpace also offers professional cover services from $400 to $1200, but note that you don't get much interaction with the artist or custom illustrations except at the high end of this price range. Their Custom Illustrations package provides up to five illustrations that can be used in the interior or cover for $225, but you must use the illustration to make your own cover; this option includes some samples and allows you to choose an artist. CreateSpace also provides cover help through crowdSPRING (http://www.crowdspring.com/createspace/book/) starting at $300. The cheapest CreateSpace option is _free_, since you can use the Cover Creator tool or upload your own PDF.

There are a few advantages of searching for your own custom cover designer online: there are less expensive options ($10 to $100 for premade covers and custom covers starting at around $100), you can learn more about the artist's ability and experience before signing up, and you may be able to interact with the artist extensively throughout the project (inquire about this before you commit). I had always designed my own covers until I wrote a 100-page fictional work called *Romancing the Novel* – an extended analogy about a man who has a very passionate relationship with a book. This cover stumped me, so I searched online for help. I discovered a talented artist, Melissa Stevens, at http://www.theillustratedauthor.net, and was very pleased both with the result and the process. I spent $300 on my cover. There are many great artists out there, and you can find very good custom designs starting at around $100.

When shopping for an illustrator, first check out the artist's portfolio. Look for samples that suit your genre and content, where the artwork pops out at you and looks professional. See if the sample covers follow the rules that I have listed previously. Browse for the books on Amazon to make sure that they are real books and see if the illustrator is listed on the cover or copyright page. See if anyone you know has ever hired a professional illustrator that he/she can recommend.

Next, contact the artist and try to interact with him/her for a while through the exchange of some emails. Such interaction will help you judge the artist's character, interest in your project, knowledge, etc. Here is a sample of what to inquire about:

- ✓ What is the artist's background, experience, etc.?
- ✓ What technique(s) does the artist use?
- ✓ Does the artist create the images or use stock images?
- ✓ How does the artist know that the images are not under copyright?
- ✓ How will you know that copyrighted images from others have not been used?
- ✓ To what extent will you be involved in the process?
- ✓ Can the artist describe briefly his/her vision for your cover?
- ✓ Can you see a brief mock-up before you sign the contract?
- ✓ Who owns the cover (probably the artist) and under what circumstances will you be able to use it (probably just for the cover of one book for as long as it's available)?
- ✓ Will the cover be displayed on the artist's website (if so, it increases your book's visibility, but bear in mind that most people who will see it are themselves writing books, and so it might not affect sales)?
- ✓ Can you display the cover on your own website, too?
- ✓ If you have legal questions about the contract, you should consult an attorney.

Whether you invest $10 or $1200 on cover design, it's worth calculating what it will take just to recover the investment. Divide your (potential) investment by the book's royalty (see Sec.'s 4.1.5 and 4.2.5) to determine how many books must be sold just to break even. For example, if you invest $300 on cover design and your royalty will be $3.27, you will have to sell 92 copies just to break even. A top-selling book can recover this quickly, whereas it can take several months to recover this investment if the book only sells a few copies per week.

Finally, we'll explore free and low-cost solutions. Designing your own cover is free, but can be a challenge to do professionally. Chapter 3 provides a tutorial on how to draw with Microsoft Word, but some objects are much easier to draw well than others. A digital camera with sufficient resolution can be used to take a high-quality photo. You want to make sure that your images have 300 DPI. Divide the pixel count of the width and height by the actual width and height that the image will have on the printed page (click on the image after you insert it in Word and go to the Format tab to see its dimensions) to determine the DPI. Also see the notes in Sec. 5.1.6 about how to prevent Word from compressing the images.

Although drawing skills aren't involved in photography, there are some photography skills needed to produce good results – e.g. the person or object should be well-lit, the objects must be in focus, the background needs to be suitable, etc. If you photograph a person, get written permission to use the photo (unless, perhaps, they are minor people in the background in a public place). Some objects, like the Eiffel Tower at night, are trademarked. I'm not an attorney. If you have legal questions, contact an attorney.

There are many free and low-cost stock photos and artwork collections online or on CD's. As described in Sec. 3.1.11, be sure that the owner of the image clearly allows commercial use of the image (some collections do not allow commercial use even for paid images). Check that the images will be 300 DPI. Many free images that allow commercial use are just 96 DPI, which may look blurry or pixelated in print. Many of the images available on the internet are copyrighted, do not allow free commercial use, and are only 96 DPI. If the image is over 80 years old, it is now in the public domain. If it is less than 80 years old, you need express written permission to use the image. The best thing is if the image or collection clearly states that commercial use is allowed. Otherwise, you must contact the copyright holder, who will probably charge a fee for use of the image. If somebody gives you a picture, make sure that they hold the copyright and get their express written permission to use it for your cover.

There are still many free and low-cost image collections that do have 300 DPI and allow for commercial use. Take the time to explore these options and you might be able to make a fantastic cover economically. Find authors whose covers you like and ask where they got their images, or inquire about stock images on a community forum for writers or self-publishers (such as CreateSpace).

You can also get free help. There are many experienced small publishers on the CreateSpace community forum, for example, who often provide helpful answers to questions asked by aspiring authors. If you have any friends or acquaintances with experience using Photoshop or other graphic arts programs, they may be willing to help you get started. If you have Photoshop or other photo-editing software, you should spend a few days playing with it. Once you learn the basics, you might find that you can make a nice cover yourself this way.

This section of the book has been quite long, but it is fitting because cover design is that important. Just a few details remain, and we will finally move on. It would be wise to read the other sections of this chapter before you finalize your cover. For example, you should allow for printing variations and tolerances and other issues described in Sec. 5.1.7, and learn how to prevent Word from compressing your images in Sec. 5.1.6.

Remember, your cover is also a reflection of you and your image as an author. However you make a cover, you should be happy with it. I enjoy making my own cover. Not every one of my self-made covers is perfect, but I enjoyed the satisfaction of creating them myself. (I hired a designer for this book.) I even have the experience of making a few of the mistakes that I have outlined in this book (such as making a few covers that are too busy). May you benefit from my experience and research on cover design by avoiding those mistakes. ☺

5.1.4 Perfecting the Interior for Your Paperback

Many little details, like avoiding widows, orphans, and rivers, or adding design marks to the copyright page, can help make the formatting look much more professional and less amateurish. Compare with a variety of traditionally published books – including some in your genre – to help discover what details can help your book stand out in a good way.

One thing you'll notice is that the title page, copyright page, contents, dedications, acknowledgements, and preface usually don't have any page numbers, the introduction and foreword generally have lowercase Roman numeral page numbers (iv, v, vi, etc.), and starting with Chapter 1 the page numbers are Arabic (7, 8, 9, etc.). When page numbering does begin, it's not with page 1, but the actual position in the book. For example, if the introduction begins on the fifth page in the book, page numbering will start on page v, and if the first chapter begins on the seventh page in the book, its page number will be 7.

There is a trick to using a different style of page numbers for different sections of the book in Microsoft Word. The first step is to use section breaks instead of regular page breaks. Remove page breaks and instead go to the Page Layout tab, click on Breaks, and select Next Page (both going to Insert and clicking Page Break and going to Page Layout and choosing Breaks and then Page prohibit professional page numbering and headers) anywhere that you wish to tell Word that you want to start using a new style of page headers or numbers. Using Next Page (instead of an ordinary page break) tells Word when a new section is beginning. If you want to have different page numbering styles (including none at all for the first few pages), you must first tell Word (by using Next Page) when the new sections begin.

If you haven't already done so, insert page numbers as described in Sec. 2.1.9. Note that you can add symbols before and after the page number – e.g. your page numbers can look like -31- instead of just 31. Highlight the page number to change the font size or style. To remove page numbers, click the bottom portion of the Page Number button.

Place your cursor in the page number area to pull up the Design tab for headers and footers. Check the box for different odd and even pages. If you would like the first page of the section to have different formatting, check that box, too.

I like to start at the beginning of the book and work forward. I adjust the page numbering and headers section by section through the book, each time checking the previous sections to make sure that any changes made to the new sections don't mess up the prior sections (it will probably happen a few times, so you want to inspect it frequently). It's also wise to back up your file at this point two different ways – like email and jump drive – and to make a new version number for your file (like Book2.docx instead of Book1.docx). If you experience file corruption issues while working on headers and footers, you'll be glad you have a back-up.

The 'magic' button is called Link to Previous. The Same as Previous flag disappears when the Link to Previous button is clicked. This allows you to change the footer style from none to Roman numerals or from Roman numerals to Arabic numbers, or to change the starting page number of that section. Double-check that all of the odd-numbered pages are actually on odd pages in your document.

Headers can be changed between sections the same way. Many traditionally published books have the title on odd-numbered pages and chapter names on even-numbered pages (in cases where the chapters have names). To change the header name between sections, use Next Page under breaks in Page Layout to define new sections in Word, place the cursor in the header area, and use Link to Previous to remove the Same as Previous flag.

Word sometimes gets a little fussy when several page numbering and header changes are made. Occasionally, you just have to remove the page break, reinsert the Next Page section break, and try it again. You may even have to delete the current break between chapters, reinsert it and the Next Page section break, and change the header again. If you have a PDF converter that allows you to combine PDF files together, a simple fix when Word gets fussy is simply to split the file into two or more separate files – then after converting to PDF, you can join the files back together.

Note that Word's two-page view does <u>not</u> correctly show what the book will look like: This view shows the odd pages on the left and the even pages on the right, whereas when you open the actual book, the odd pages will appear on the right with the even pages on the left. You can temporarily adjust this by inserting a blank page at the beginning, but that might mess up your page numbering and headers. You will be able to see the two-page spreads correctly in CreateSpace's Interior Reviewer when you upload your book (if you choose the Guided Setup option) and Digital Proofer after file review (and you can still make revisions after using these tools).

All of the odd-numbered pages must be on the right in the open book, which means that the odd-numbered pages must appear on the left in Word's two-page view. Word's two-page view is simply backwards: Just understand and realize this, but don't try to 'fix' it. The first chapter should begin on an odd-numbered page. There are books where every chapter begins on an odd-numbered page, even if it means inserting a blank page to do this; but there are more books where the chapter (except for Chapter 1) begins wherever it happens to be – odd or even. Check what is most common in your book's genre and go with that.

Times New Roman and Calibri are default fonts on different editions of Microsoft Word, such that many self-published books use these font styles. Some people feel that these fonts give an amateurish look. However, there are many fonts similar to these, and it's hard to pick a font out from another that is very similar. I used Calibri for this book because I felt that it looks clean and clear for this how-to guide. Garamond, Palatino Linotype, and Georgia are popular for fiction in size 12 fonts among many indie authors looking for something different than Word's defaults. Minion and Dante are popular fonts for traditionally published fiction, but these aren't preinstalled on Word. It is worth researching fonts online to see what may be common in your genre. Wikipedia even provides statistics for how readers react to a variety of fonts – Comic Sans, for example, often creates a more negative impact.

Many well-educated people believe that there should be two spaces after a period and before the first letter of the following sentence. I believed this myself until I read an interesting article called "Space Invaders" by Farhad Manjoo in *Slate Magazine*. This is what our teachers were taught, and so this is what they passed onto us. However, if you examine traditionally published books carefully, you will see that they only use one space after the period. This can make a marked difference on full justification, for example. So if you want a professional appearance, use a single space after a period; this will become even more important in eBooks, as we will learn in Sec. 5.2.1. I actually used 2 spaces in Volume 1, but 1 space in Volume 2. This way, you can compare the two volumes and see the difference. **Tip**: If you have a habit of two-spacing, use the Replace tool on the Home tab to see if you had any double spaces.

Word's default indent is 0.5", which is larger than what most traditionally published books use – 0.2" to 0.3" is common. I used 0.3" for this book, which has wide pages. Compare Volume 2 to Volume 1, which had a wider indent. Which fits your eye better? Measure the indentations for a variety of books in your genre to see what is common. Traditional publishers actually measure their indents in terms of an 'em,' where 1 em is the width of the uppercase M. In this way, the size of the indent depends on the font style and size.

The indentation of this book is set to just over 2 ems. In full justification, the spacing of the first line tends to look better if the indent is smaller. Thus, an indent of 1 to 1.5 ems is common with smaller pages or wider margins. However, the indent needs to be clear, and an indent of 1 em isn't as easy to recognize on a large printed page.

Traditional publishers almost always use full justification[3] – not left alignment. Self-published authors sometimes align the body text left because this is the default alignment in Word; other times, they do it because they don't like the gaps that they see in fully justified

---

[3] Like many words in English, 'justified' has multiple meanings. Sometimes, 'justified' is used to imply that both sides are even, in which case 'fully justified' would seem redundant. However, 'justified' has a broader usage to mean that the text is even or properly positioned, in which case left-aligned text or right-aligned text are partially justified. Hence, some people refer to 'left-justified' and 'right-justified.' Since these terms are not uncommon, the use of 'fully justified' here may help to avoid possible confusion.

text. However, if you think about it, there are really large gaps at the end of the line when text is aligned left – this is called "ragged right" because the ends of the lines look ragged. Use full justification for a professional appearance.

There is a way to reduce the size of the gaps in fully justified text: hyphenation. You can manually hyphenate words by looking up the natural breaks in a dictionary. Don't bother with this until your manuscript is complete; otherwise, any revisions may cause hyphenated words to move and no longer appear at the end of a line. An alternative to hyphenation is kerning.

Word actually has a built-in Hyphenation tool in the Page Layout tab. Turn it on by setting Hyphenation to Automatic. If you use this tool, go into Hyphenation Options and increase the Hyphenation Zone to about 0.4" to avoid excessive hyphenation. You can also limit the number of consecutive hyphens. Check the final manuscript carefully because it may hyphenate words that you don't want hyphenated (e.g. a long heading that spans two lines might look funny if hyphenated). To manually correct an automatic hyphen, place the cursor before the first letter of the word, then hold down Shift and press Enter (then also delete the space that precedes this word at the end of the previous line). Again, don't bother with any manual hyphenation until your book is perfected. **Tip**: Go to the File tab, scroll down below Help to find Options, click Options, find Advanced, click on Layout Options at the very bottom (you can click this, even though it doesn't look like something to click on), and check the box that says to hyphenate the way that WordPerfect does.

There are two types of dashes, which are longer than hyphens and are used differently. The short en dash (–) and the long em dash (—) are used as separators; they are different from hyphens (-). A hyphen (-) appears in some compound words and is also used to join two words together to make compound adjectives, as in, "This is a well-known way to make a compound adjective." A dash is used to create separation between parenthetic elements. Either use the shorter en dash (–) with spaces around it or the longer em dash (—) without spaces, but not both – it's generally better to be consistent—don't be inconsistent like this sentence. Note the space around the en dash (–), but not the em dash (—), in the previous sentence. Word's AutoFormat feature can turn two consecutive hyphens into an en dash, but you can make the en and em dashes more properly by holding down Alt and typing 0150 and 0151, respectively. The Alt method is better if you may be making an eBook edition, too. Not everyone agrees on which dash is better to use; see what traditional publishers use in your genre. The em (—) dash is also used following the end of a quotation in lieu of quotation marks to indicate the author (but this time, with space), as in the example below.

Better to write for yourself and have no public, than to write for the public and have no self. — Cyril Connolly in *The New Statesman*

Traditional publishers use approximately single line spacing. Setting the line spacing to double or even just 1.5 is not only unconventional, it makes the text much more difficult to read (however, those settings are good for proofreading as they allow room for editing marks). The best line spacing might not be *exactly* single spacing, though. Traditional publishers refer to 'leading,' which is the distance between the baselines of two consecutive lines of text. For example, for 12-pt font, the leading may be set to 14 pts, which is 17% leading (comparing the 2-pt difference to the 12-pt font size). Setting the leading to around 20% to 25% is typical. To do this, go to the Paragraph dialog box (click the funny icon in the bottom-right corner of the Paragraph group in the Home tab), choose Exactly under the Line Spacing option, and set the size of the leading in pts (e.g. 14 pts). Check to see how closely this compares to single spacing in Word. Print out a page and compare it to traditionally published books in your genre that have a similar font height (measure the font height of similar letters to check this), and adjust your leading if you would like to reproduce those models.

You can make your book look much more professional by eliminating widows, orphans, and rivers from your book. Don't bother adjusting these until your book is virtually complete, otherwise you may need to adjust them again after making revisions. A widow is a single line of a paragraph that winds up being on a different page from the rest; an orphan is a single word or a few short words on the last line of a paragraph; and a river is formed when the gaps between words happen to line up to create a long gap running down a paragraph. A widow (left), orphan (center), and river (right) are shown in the figure below. (In the middle diagram, you can also see gaps in the bottom line that could be corrected through hyphenation.)

Traditionally published books usually do not have widows or rivers, but orphans are not uncommon. Widows, rivers, and orphans can be removed by editing the text, in principle, but in practice, writers first perfect the text and then design the formatting around the text – authors generally don't design the text around the formatting. Other ways to remove these features include adjusting individual lines (by adjusting hyphenation or forcing a short word onto the next line – by placing the cursor before the word and pressing Shift + Enter), kerning (highlight the text that you want to kern – i.e. adjust the space between characters – then right-click, choose Font, and select the Advanced tab), or making slight adjustments to the spacing before or after paragraphs (in the Paragraph dialog box) or to the line spacing. You'll need to remove these features from the eBook edition (if you make one).

Word does have automatic Widow/Orphan Control (open the Paragraph dialog box and select the Line and Page Breaks tab). However, using this automatic control will result in gaps at the bottom of the pages. Therefore, it's best to remove widows and orphans manually. The CreateSpace templates often have one or more of the boxes checked in the Line and Page Breaks tab in the Paragraph dialog box: Uncheck these boxes for optimal results.

Professional publishers also take the time to vertically justify the text – i.e. to make all of the pages of full text line up at the top and bottom. Viewing multiple pages at once, you can go page by page through the book and adjust vertical spacing, as needed, to achieve this. If you have mostly text, like a novel, you should also have the same number of lines on almost every page. You can adjust the spacing before or after paragraphs (in the Paragraph dialog box) for stand-alone lines – like headings, figures, and equations, adjust the kerning, or make slight adjustments to line spacing, for example, to vertically justify text. The two volumes of this book are littered with pictures and bullets, so you might not have noticed it (unless you have an eye for such formatting details – which will help you greatly with the layout of your own book). Compare them: Volume 2 shows a subtle improvement. In comparison, a novel or other book that consists mostly of text will stand out visually if it is not vertically justified.

A few pages should be centered vertically, while most of the pages should be aligned at the top and vertically justified to also line up at the bottom. However, the initial and final pages of a chapter may not line up at the top and bottom. The title page, copyright page, and a few other pages (consult traditionally published books in your genre to see which) are often centered vertically. You can center these pages vertically by going to the Page Setup dialog box, choosing the Layout tab, setting Apply To on This Section, and changing Vertical Alignment to Center. Make sure that you used Page Layout > Breaks > Next Page to create the page breaks (if not, remove the page break and use Next Page instead), otherwise you might find a blank page inserted or other pages affected vertically when you make this change.

The first page of a chapter usually doesn't start at the top of the page, but is generally dropped down a few lines (alternatively, increase the space before the chapter heading in the Paragraph dialog box). Chapter headings are often boldfaced and centered, but not under-lined. Look at some traditionally published books in your genre for ideas regarding what the beginning of each chapter can look like. You should also use a drop cap (see Sec. 2.1.11) unless you have any chapters where the first paragraph doesn't have enough lines to exceed the height of the drop cap. (In that case, don't use any drop caps; consistency is important.) The first few words of the chapter often also appear in UPPERCASE (again, use traditionally published books in your genre as models).

Self-published authors often neglect the formatting and details of the first few pages of the book – i.e. the title page, copyright page, contents, etc. These are the first pages that a prospective buyer sees when he/she clicks to Look Inside. Make these as professional as possible to make a striking impression. Inspect these pages closely in a variety of traditionally published books to see what information, details, formatting, and fancy design marks they add to these pages. The printing codes on the copyright page won't be relevant since your book is printed on demand, and you won't have library information (unless you purchased an LCCN – see Sec. 4.1.7). You also won't have a publisher name unless you use an ISBN option with your own imprint (see Sec. 4.1.6); you <u>can't</u> write "published by CreateSpace" (but "with" is okay). However, there are many ways to make these pages look highly professional, so taking the time to research your options and perfect these pages can give you an edge.

Traditional publishers have an appealing logo. If you use your own imprint, you should also develop your own logo (if so, you should explore any legalities involved). The logo may appear on the spine, back cover, title page, and/or copyright page (see where traditional publishers place their logos).

Avoid writing The End when you reach the very end of the content. Just like writing "by" on the cover or title page, some people perceive this as amateurish. Why risk losing any sales?

Remember that there are marketing opportunities in your front and back matter. Keep in mind that if your email address is in the front matter, it may get spammed – and possibly just from the Look Inside. Some authors create a special email address just for their books, but then they must remember to check them periodically. Readers can also connect with authors through Facebook, Twitter, a discussion forum at the author's website, and so on.

You might not want to go overboard on contact information and marketing. Readers who enjoy your book will be interested in learning more about you and seeing what else you've written, but at the same time people tend to have an aversion to advertising and salesmanship. I usually don't include a catalog of my books. I only included it with this book to show what a catalog might look like. In my recent books, however, I have included a couple of pages that have pictures and descriptions for a few related books; you can see a sample of this on the page following the catalog at the back of this book (but those don't relate to this book...).

Many authors include an About the Author section at the back of the book with a photograph, biography, and contact information – such as the link to their blog or author website, email address, and Facebook and Twitter author accounts (you probably want to create a separate account for your author profile, which will be in addition to a personal profile that you may already have). Thinking ahead to marketing, consider adding a book club or fan club. If so, you want to set this up before releasing your book so that you can provide information about it at the end of your book. We'll talk more about this in Sec. 6.2.6.

Another thing you can do is include a sample chapter at the end or your book. If you write a series of books, include the first chapter (but no more than what the Look Inside will show for free) of the next book in the series. Remember that customers like to receive a good value for their money. This means that the front matter, back matter, sample chapter, etc. shouldn't make a large percentage of the overall content (otherwise, customers may complain about this in reviews).

Some of the comments that I made about formatting the cover in the previous section also apply to formatting your interior, especially if you have images, tables, or textboxes. For example, text embedded in jpegs doesn't format well – it's better to leave the text out of images and instead add WordArt or textboxes.

We've mostly examined how to format your interior file professionally in this section. The art of proofreading and editing will be discussed in Sec. 5.1.8. I've made a few of these formatting 'mistakes' myself in previous books (such as avoiding hyphenation); or, rather, my own style has changed with time and experience. Vertical justification, for example, didn't seem as important as maintaining precise consistency in vertical spacing, for example, when I first began writing and publishing, but I've since come to see the light.

Before we move on, I want to say a few words about content. Mainly, since this book also covers the important subject of marketing, I want to point out and emphasize that content and marketing do share a relationship. As the writer and publisher, you have the flexibility to be as creative as you wish with your content (and even with the formatting). However, you should beware that the choices you make regarding your content do impact how successful your marketing efforts may be.

Ask yourself how much artistic freedom you wish to embrace as a writer versus how successful you want sales to be. You can write to explore this freedom or you can write toward successful sales – and very often writing mainly with the freedom and independence in mind doesn't provide optimal sales. So another thing to ask yourself is whether you're willing to compromise on the freedom to some extent.

Let me address the issue of how to write with successful sales in mind, with the understanding that the more you deviate from this path, the more it may affect the sales of your book. If your goal is to have a bestseller, the answer is right there before your eyes: First read bestsellers in your genre to learn what readers in that genre are accustomed to, what attracts those readers, what content has proven success, what rules you absolutely aren't allowed to break (go ahead and break them – but some rules, like not having a happy ending for a romance novel, may greatly deter sales if broken), which writing styles work, etc. Read the top sellers in that genre, including the top self-published sellers – since you also want to see how those other indie authors broke through. Hopefully, you've already read some books in your genre; you want to truly understand what your intended audience loves and expects.

Research takes time, but it can pay off. In addition to reading bestsellers to master the genre, there is also the issue of mastering the craft of writing in the genre. In order to gain a professional edge, many authors join writing groups, book clubs, and critique groups in an effort to improve their grammatical writing and their writing style. You learn some basic rules of writing – like writing actively instead of passively, and which types of writing to avoid – and some more subtle tips that can help your writing stand out. Developing bestselling content takes much time and effort, but in the long run it can make a huge difference.

If you want to exercise your creativity and independence, consider this: If instead you write your first two books traditionally, geared toward excellent sales, once you attain some measure of success and have a following, you can then afford to exercise creative freedom in your third book and it will actually reach a large audience. If instead you exercise your creative freedom in your first book, you might not have much of an audience for it. Look, creativity can mean many different things. By all means, feel creative and artistic as a writer. When I speak of exercising creative freedom in regards to sales, I mean that if you exercise the freedom to break the rules and expectations for your genre, it will probably hurt sales. Readers appreciate certain kinds of creativity, but most readers don't like it when authors break the unspoken rules for what is or isn't accepted in each specific genre.

5.1.5 Perfecting the Blurb and Other Features

The description for your book – called the blurb – is a sales pitch. It shouldn't sound like a sales pitch, but it should be designed to help sell the book. After seeing your cover and title, the blurb is the next thing that customers see – and it's the one major hurdle that you have to jump to make customers Look Inside instead of walking away. Only a percentage of the potential customers who read your blurb will click to Look Inside. You want to maximize this percentage as much as possible by writing a highly effective blurb.

I like to joke that it's very easy to write 50,000 words, but quite a challenge to write 50 words or even just 5. Many self-published authors can relate to this when they try to condense their 50,000 word (maybe more, maybe less) book down to the size of a modest blurb. But therein lies the problem: Your description is not a summary of your book. It's a sales pitch that should sound like it's telling the reader what your book is about, while not sounding like a sales pitch. But don't forget that the blurb is your salesman, and the only salesman standing there at the doorway to your book online!

I didn't mention this in Sec. 4.1.2 when I described how to prepare the description. Then, I wanted you to prepare a first draft of your description, and I also didn't want to hamper your creativity by providing too much direction. But now it's time to talk about how to improve your blurb to be more effective.

Most likely, your present blurb is too long, especially if your book is fiction. Shorter blurbs tend to be more effective. I happen to write technical books – like how-to guides, science books, and math workbooks – so my own descriptions are fairly long. Unless you're writing similar books, your description should be quite short. Some blurb writers will tell you that your blurb should even be short if you write technical books. However, in the case of technical nonfiction and textbooks, expertise is an important factor, and so a longer description that makes that expertise clear can also be effective. For fiction and less technical or entertaining nonfiction, shorter is better.

Why? Because people tend to be impatient. Just visit any metropolitan area and experience the traffic for a few hours and you will see firsthand that most people are impatient. It doesn't just apply to traffic; it applies to book buying, too.

One reason that bestselling books tend to have short titles – three words or less – is because buyers are impatient. The general rule of thumb is that you have 3 seconds for the customer to get interested in your title and thumbnail image – so both have to be very clear and send a unified message to attract the right reader in just 3 seconds. (But all of the details of the cover are important because some customers will stare at the large image of your cover for a while once they open your book's product page.) Then, when the customers click on your book, there is a 5-second rule for the blurb. The beginning of the blurb should attract the reader's interest – and reinforce the message conveyed by the title and cover – within 5 seconds. If they like what they read, you have another 5 seconds to hold their interest.

Some customers see a long blurb and instantly return to the main page; that's the danger of overwhelming the customer who sees more than he/she wants to read to learn about your book. Consider separating your blurb into two or three block paragraphs with spaces in between. (The description that you enter in CreateSpace will be consolidated into a single paragraph on Amazon, unless you use basic HTML as described in Chapter 6. What you need to do to format your cover is go to AuthorCentral; you can revise your description there with some basic formatting tools. We'll learn how to do this in Chapter 6.)

The blurb is a challenge for authors to write because the description has much to accomplish with a minimum of words and judicious word choice. Here is what the blurb needs to accomplish:

- ✓ Grab the reader's attention right off the bat.
- ✓ Relate to the content and reinforce the title and cover; and clearly signify the genre.
- ✓ Build interest in your book and hold the reader's attention throughout.
- ✓ Express ideas very clearly and with a vocabulary appropriate for the audience.
- ✓ Use perfect spelling and grammar, with an appealing writing style.
- ✓ Include the same keywords that you entered through CreateSpace (or, for your eBook, through KDP), but only if the blurb sounds good as you do this. Keywords must be less than 15% of your blurb, at the most (and a list of keywords at the end will look funny). This may affect your book's visibility in search results to some extent (probably not by introducing new keywords, but by reinforcing those you enter when you publish).
- ✓ Provide an idea of what the work is about; but not with a detailed summary.
- ✓ Arouse the reader's curiosity.
- ✓ Let the work speak for itself; bragging deters sales (however, accurately describing the author's related qualifications or what distinguishes this from other books is relevant).
- ✓ Accurately describe the content; making it seem better than it is will backfire.
- ✓ Be concise and written in the third person.
- ✓ Ultimately, persuade the reader to Look Inside. Many blurbs end with a question.

Writing a highly effective blurb is a formidable task, but can really pay off. Many authors revise and revise and revise their blurbs in an effort to perfect them. Some authors do extensive research on effective blurb writing (there are even books that describe this art, but you may be able to find free examples and ideas online). The problem with doing all of that research is that your description will still be unique and geared toward your book. These guides and books will teach you some terminology and discuss a few key concepts, but when it comes down to it, it will still be a challenge to come up with a great blurb geared toward your own book.

You need a starting point: If you have a short summary, begin with this. Look at your summary and decide what main ideas may interest readers. Not the plot itself, but some ideas from the content may be relevant. For fiction, if the first chapter sells the book, start by summarizing *only* that. Do you have any characters that you can make the reader fall in love with in a very short description? You'll need to introduce the protagonist briefly, at a minimum (for fiction). What features would interest readers most? If you've shared drafts of your work with others, their feedback can help you answer some of these questions.

Then you try to write the description. It's a draft – just a place to start. Then read my checklist for what your blurb should accomplish, and rate how your blurb accomplishes each step on a scale of 1 to 5 (1 very little, 5 very well). Getting opinions from others on this would be wise – since a variety of other people will be reading your description when they find your book. (If anyone rewrites your blurb, be sure to get their written permission to use it.) This checklist will then help you see which elements of your blurb need improving.

Revise the description, get more feedback, and so on. Initially, spelling and grammar are the least of your worries. Think structurally, conceptually. How effective are the ideas, which ideas are best and worst, what can you remove to shorten it? But after several revisions, you also want to perfect your spelling and grammar. **A single mistake in the blurb may cost you many sales.** If you make any spelling, grammar, or style mistakes in a short description – which is very prominently placed and vital to the success of your book – it doesn't bode well for the book itself being well-written. Your final blurb should <u>not</u> be a summary of the book.

In Sec. 6.1.4, we'll learn how you can use AuthorCentral to format your blurb with boldface, linebreaks, and so forth. You can do this prior to publishing with HTML, but once your book is available on Amazon, you can also reformat your blurb through AuthorCentral.

Note that there are two common uses of the word 'blurb' in publishing. Sometimes, it refers to the text that appears on the back cover, and other times it refers to the description on the product page; the latter is often different, and may be shorter. The blurb I have been discussing in this section is the description for your book on its product page, although some of the same ideas may apply to the back cover text. Back cover text may also include quotes from customers or reviews (but not Amazon's), or information about the author, for example.

Next, you need to make a strapline for your book. The strapline is a single, short sentence designed to attract interest in your book. Now you must condense your blurb down to a single sentence. Well, the strapline doesn't have to accomplish as many things. It functions a little more like an advertising slogan (but not quite). Here is what an effective strapline should do:

✓ Include a hook that gets people interested in your book.
✓ Signify the genre and relate to the content.
✓ Be short, concise, and easy to remember (maybe even catchy).

The strapline can serve many purposes. You can include it on a stand-alone line at the beginning of your blurb, with a blank line between (remember, blank lines must be added through AuthorCentral after publishing – or using HTML in CreateSpace). Use it at presentations or anytime that you have a chance to speak to a group of people about your book. Even if you also provide a longer description of your book or read a sample chapter, still use your strapline before and/or after. People are much more likely to remember the strapline, and it has your hook – some idea that will help to get people interested in reading your book. They are more likely to buy your book – and even tell others about it – if they can remember something about it, so you want your strapline to be memorable. Your strapline may even come in handy on a website, on your blog, and in your marketing efforts.

As long as we're considering condensed descriptions of your book, let's reconsider your title one more time. Remember, most top sellers have titles with just three words or less because they convey information quickly and are easy to remember. This also comes in handy when marketing – you can write, "Your Name, Author of __, __, and __," concisely if you use short titles. A great title has impact, hidden subtlety, signifies the genre, and relates to the content (such that a potential reader can guess how without already having read your book).

A descriptive title that uses keywords may work in nonfiction – especially, for more technical books. Shorter titles tend to be more effective in fiction and less technical or more entertaining nonfiction; but even for technical nonfiction, longer can be a deterrent.

There is one more place where the 5-second rule comes in play: the Look Inside. Once the customer looks inside, the front matter and first pages need to seal the deal. Format and design these pages as professionally as possible. Perfect the beginning of your book. Again, grammatical, spelling, or formatting mistakes in the Look Inside are sales killers as they don't bode well for the remainder of the book. The more professional the appearance of the Look Inside, the greater the chances that the customer will buy the book. The first chapter needs to grab and hold attention – and send a unified message along with the title, cover, and blurb. If your book has a slow start (you're more likely to close the deal if you come out with your best stuff), consider adding an excerpt of a better part to your front matter. Choose the front matter wisely because you don't want to bore the reader with a great deal of dull front matter before getting into the action. The style and quality of the writing will also impact the reader's decision. You want the words to flow well, for the reader to enjoy the read, and to be fascinated by the content and characters (which need to fit the genre – it needs to match up with the type of audience your cover, title, and blurb attract).

While you must strive to perfect the blurb and Look Inside, you don't want to create a huge disparity between these and the rest of your book. If your title, cover, blurb, and Look

Inside are effective at getting sales, this will backfire if the rest of your book doesn't live up to the expectations that these create – through negative customer reviews. Once you succeed in getting sales, to have continued sales – or to benefit from word-of-mouth sales – the content itself must be very good in terms of ideas, writing style, grammar, spelling, and formatting.

How about your name? Is it easy to spell, and easy to remember? Does it sound good, and fit your genre? If not, that might be one reason to consider using a nickname or pen name. On the other hand, your own name may be easier to market than a pen name. Everyone you meet is a potential reader – and if you tell everyone you meet what your pen name is, it kind of defeats the purpose of having one. If your first name is tough to spell or remember, but your last name isn't, you might use your first initial (or first and middle initials) along with your last name – or use a nickname if you have one (you can always start now).

One more piece of writing to perfect is your biography. As mentioned in Sec. 4.1.2, the About the Author section that you can submit through CreateSpace will be in addition to a biography that you can add through AuthorCentral. As with the description, you can modify and reformat the About the Author section through AuthorCentral once your book is published. If you include an About the Author section when you publish and add a biography at AuthorCentral, both of these will be visible on your book's product page. Therefore, you want these sections to be different if you include both. For starters, the About the Author section might be shorter, with the biography more detailed. If you write multiple books, the About the Author sections might be catered to each book, whereas there is just one biography for your AuthorCentral account.

You want your biography to read well and be interesting, provide curious readers some information about you, and build credibility as the author for the kinds of books that you write. If you have relevant experience, include that. Write your biography in the third person, so that it sounds like someone else wrote it (you can even ask someone else to write it – provided that they write biographies very well – but get their written permission to use it). Biographies are often boring, so if yours reads well (yet appears professional – a little fun and personality can be effective, but don't cross the proverbial line), this bodes well for the book. On the other hand, any mistakes in the writing may deter sales.

Other writing that you may want to perfect before you publish is marketing material. Consider reading Chapter 8 before you publish your book. For optimal results, marketing is something that begins months before your book goes live and continues for years afterward.

Lastly, let's reconsider price one last time. Price was discussed in great detail in Sec.'s 4.1.4-5, so I will restrict myself to two new points that relate to marketing. First, writing is an art, and as with all art, value is based on perception. Perceived value is something that you can create through marketing. Also, customers often perceive a low price as being of little value, and a higher price as having greater value. On the other hand, if you price your book higher, your book better deliver the perception of high value – otherwise, customer reviews may reflect the disparity. Also, if the price is too high, many customers will have to pass on it.

It's a common mistake for self-published authors to undervalue their work. Intuitively, authors feel that if they drop the price, sales will increase. Usually, dropping the price doesn't increase sales unless the book was originally priced higher than similar, popular titles. Even if dropping the price does increase sales, it still might not increase the overall royalties because your per-book royalty is less with a lower list price. What often happens is that customers see a price that's too low compared to similar, popular books and perceive it to be a cheap book in terms of content. If you price your book fairly compared to similar, popular titles and your book is good, the best thing you can do for sales is marketing. Part of marketing is about creating a good, accurate perception of your book and spreading awareness of this. This way, marketing and price can work together to suggest that the book has high value.

The second point I wish to make regarding price is relevant if you have a series or if you will write more books that are similar enough that customers who read one and enjoy it may be interested in the other(s). In this case, the primary goal with the first book isn't to maximize royalties – rather, it's to maximize exposure. The idea is that the more people who read your first book, the more people will purchase your other books. Some authors even go to the extreme of giving the first book of a series away for free (economically feasible for eBooks – see Sec. 8.1.18). Alternatives include discounting the price of the first book, creating interest with giveaways and other promotions, and putting the first book on "sale" periodically. We'll discuss this further in Chapter 8.

Your first book has to be very good for this to work. It doesn't do any good to attract more readers of the first volume unless it hooks them to want to read subsequent volumes. Also, while all positive exposure is generally good, you really want to increase your exposure with the right audience. So you should direct any promoting that you do with the first book specifically toward your target audience.

The point is that if you have a series, you want the first book to give you the greatest number of readers, not necessarily the maximum royalty. Provided that the first book is good enough to hook readers into the series, this may give you greater royalties in the long run.

5.1.6 Common Paperback File Review Issues

In this section, we will focus on some issues that commonly arise when uploading and submitting files for review at CreateSpace. We will discuss how to order a proof, what to look for when checking your proof, and how to submit corrections in subsequent sections.

The first place where you are likely to encounter these problems is when you use the Interior Reviewer tool at CreateSpace. This tool is available if you use Guided Setup. Note that the Interior Reviewer is not always 100% accurate in the issues that it identifies. Also, some of the issues are just recommendations, while other issues must be fixed; but Interior Reviewer doesn't tell you which are which.

For these reasons, some experts like to skip Interior Reviewer. However, Interior Reviewer can be helpful, especially as it visually shows you the out-of-live zone and can show you specifically where the issues are. When you submit your files to CreateSpace, they provide a similar (but often somewhat different) list of issues. CreateSpace may not identify exactly where the problem is, whereas Interior Reviewer will flag the problem visually right in your book. This is the advantage of using Interior Reviewer. This tool saved me a great deal of frustration once: It flagged a stray character in the out-of-live zone. I have no idea how that character got there, and never would have believed it was there without this tool pointing right to it; I may never have found it by just browsing page by page through my file. Therefore, I recommend using Interior Reviewer, provided that you remember that some issues that it identifies may be not be accurate and some issues don't necessarily need to be fixed.

If you have trouble with the functionality of Interior Reviewer, try switching browsers (or even computers) – e.g. from Internet Explorer to FireFox (and possibly adjusting browser settings). It may take several minutes (if you have a really large file – approaching the limits of what can be uploaded, it may take much, much longer) for Interior Reviewer to open your book. Once it does, you see your book in a two-page spread, with the odd-numbered pages on the right and the even-numbered pages on the left, just as if you're reading your book (there is even an artificial lighting effect to help create this illusion).

The out-of-live zone is clearly marked, and you can see how your margins compare to these limits. If anything is flagged as being in the out-of-live zone, you will be able to see exactly which objects are in this area. You can also see how your pages look in print layout, aesthetically. If you're not happy with this, now is a good time to modify it.

Interior Reviewer will give you numbered comments (if there are any) in the top right corner. Click on any of these numbers to find the problems in the file – it will jump to that page so you can see it visually. Two common issues that Interior Reviewer finds are problems with margins (such as text in the out-of-live zone) and images with fewer than 200 DPI.

CreateSpace will reject the file if there is text in the out-of-live zone, so if you get this message, you should find the flag(s) to see what Interior Reviewer found. You can't have text (or glyphs or other text-like symbols) closer than 0.25" from the page edges. If you have images that bleed (i.e. images that extend to the page edges), then text needs to be at least 0.38" from the oversized page edges (if you have bleed, your page size in Word must also be 0.25" taller and 0.13" wider than the trim size). Also, if you have any images that extend into the out-of-live zone, then they must extend all of the way to the oversized page edges (and you must choose the option with bleed in order to do this).

If you have any text (or glyphs or other text-like symbols) in the out-of-live zone, your file will be rejected. One way for this to happen is if your outside margins are less than 0.25" (or less than 0.38" if your file has bleed); using the exact minimum may also trigger an error (so 0.26" or 0.39" may be safer than 0.25" or 0.38"). Another way to have text in the out-of-live zone is to have a textbox with Text Wrap set to In Front Of Text or Behind Text, which is placed too close to the edge of the page. If there is any text embedded in the pictures, ensure that such text isn't in the out-of-live zone.

Any images that extend partway into the out-of-live zone will also cause the file to get rejected. Either push the images all of the way to the oversized page edges (if your book will have bleed) or pull them back inside of the out-of-live zone. If you have images that you want to be full-page, (first the book must have bleeds) right-click on them, go to the Format tab, select Wrap Text, and choose In Front of Text (unless *every* page in the book is full-page, then you should use 0" margins and In Line With Text). Full-page images must match your oversized book size (i.e. greater than the trim size) and completely fill the page; if there are any gaps along the edges, these can cause the file to be rejected. (Ideally, a full-page picture should be correctly sized to match the oversized page – i.e. after accounting for bleed – of the book when the picture is made. Otherwise, if you adjust the aspect ratio of the picture to fill the page, the picture will appear distorted.)

Remember, Interior Reviewer isn't 100% accurate. If you checked all of the flags and believe that Interior Reviewer may be wrong, the best way to find out is to submit your files for review. After file review, CreateSpace will tell you if there is, in fact, any problem in the out-of-live zone that must be corrected.

A related issue that you could have is an insufficient interior margin. The interior margin must be at least 0.38" for a book with 150 pages or less, 0.75" for 151-400 pages, 0.875" for 401-600 pages, and 1" for 601 pages or more. The interior margin equals the value that you set for Gutter plus the value that you set for Left/Right in Word. (What Word calls a gutter, most publishing manuals refer to as a half-gutter. The gutter is extra space near the binding that can't be used.) We discussed margins in Sec. 2.1.6.

Interior Reviewer will also flag images that it believes to have a resolution of fewer than 200 dots per inch (DPI). CreateSpace recommends 300 DPI for optimal printing; images with fewer than 200 DPI may appear blurry or pixelated in print. The DPI issue will not cause your file to be rejected – it's recommended that you correct the problem, but not required.

It's also possible to get an image with more than 200 DPI flagged as having less than 200 DPI. Remember, Interior Reviewer isn't 100% accurate. That said, more often than not, the image actually has less than 200 DPI and the self-publisher doesn't realize (or believe) it. The problem is that Word has a tendency to automatically compress images – even if you check the box that tells Word not to do this! Therefore, many times the images have actually been compressed down to as little as 96 DPI, but the author doesn't realize it.

Here is how to avoid having images less than 200 DPI:

1. First, use pictures that are already 300 DPI to begin with. Depending on how you made the picture, you must check the device (e.g. camera or scanner) or software program to see what the original DPI is. Also, if you resize the picture, this may change. Divide the pixel height by the actual height in word to get the DPI for the height, and similarly calculate the DPI for the width. You can increase the pixel count (in Paint may be

better than nothing, but other options are better than Paint), but adding these invented pixels isn't an ideal substitute from having higher-resolution images.

2. Turn off picture compression. Click File, scroll down below Help to find Options, choose Advanced, scroll down to Image Size and Quality, and check the box that says, "Do not compress images in file."[4] You must do this before inserting pictures. Otherwise, remove the pictures and reinsert them after doing this.[5]

3. Don't use copy/paste to insert images into the file. Instead, go to the Insert tab and click on the Picture button.

4. Avoid resizing your images in Word; pre-size them in the native program before inserting them into Word. Also, it's best to format images in the native program, rather than reformatting them in Word.

5. Don't upload a .doc, .docx, or .rtf file to CreateSpace. Instead, convert your Word document to PDF yourself and submit the PDF file.

6. To convert your file to PDF, don't go to File, Save As, and choose PDF. The best option is to use a different PDF converter and print to PDF (instead of using Save As). Make sure that the PDF converter saves the images at 300 DPI and embeds the fonts (depending on what program you use, you may have to adjust the settings). It would also be desirable to have a PDF converter that can flatten transparency. There are many free Word-to-PDF converters available on the internet (but you must beware of viruses, spyware, and malware – so have a good anti-virus program on your computer, and see if you can get a recommendation from a trustworthy source).

Some images look good even if they have less than 200 DPI, while others look blurry or pixelated. The best test is to order a printed proof and see what it looks like.

Don't upload a .rtf, .doc, or .docx file to CreateSpace, regardless of whether or not your file has images. CreateSpace's conversion to PDF often causes unexpected formatting changes. Therefore, it is much better to convert your Word document to PDF and upload a PDF file. If you don't have any images, you can use Word's convenient Save As PDF feature.

Once you have investigated any issues that Interior Reviewer has flagged and are ready to proceed (remember, Interior Reviewer isn't 100% accurate, so sometimes it helps to submit files for review even if there are outstanding issues in Interior Reviewer), submit your files for review. When CreateSpace replies (often in 12 to 24 hours), they will identify any issues that need to be fixed if your files are rejected, and may notify you of any other issues (such as images with less than 200 DPI). Interior Reviewer isn't always consistent with CreateSpace's file review, and CreateSpace's file review isn't always consistent – a number of people have reported resubmitting the exact same file with different results from the previous file review.

---

[4] As with Volume 1 of this book, the instructions are specifically for Word 2010. In Word 2007, go to Format, then Adjust Group to find this option. In Word 2003, right-click on a picture, then choose Format Picture > Picture.
[5] This was also mentioned in Volume 1 on page 120, at the beginning of Sec. 3.1.12.

We'll now discuss a few common issues that are reported after file review (aside from margins and DPI, which we have already discussed). One such issue may be that you need to embed the fonts in your PDF. For this, you need to use a Word-to-PDF converter that allows you to embed fonts and figure out how to do this. However, there are some fonts that don't allow embedding; in that case, the font designer is not permitting commercial use of the font. You may be able to learn more about this by trying to research the font online or inquiring about this in CreateSpace's community help forum.

Another issue that may arise is if your spine text is too large for the spine width. Your spine text must be narrow enough and precisely positioned such that there is at least 0.0625" between the spine text and each spine edge. If not, CreateSpace will shrink your spine text. They will notify you if they do this. If so, you should at least look at the printed proof and see if the resizing meets your satisfaction. The better option is to resize it yourself and submit a new cover file. If your book has 101 pages or less, spine text isn't allowed. In this case, CreateSpace will remove the spine text from your cover.

Most images are created with transparency. CreateSpace will usually tell you if your submitted interior and/or cover files contain images with transparency. If so, CreateSpace will manually flatten these images. The images may look somewhat different if they are manually flattened. You can avoid this problem by using a PDF converter that allows you to flatten the images before you submit the file to CreateSpace. At the very least, inspect the printed proof carefully to see if the images meet your approval (and if not, you'll have to find a PDF converter that can flatten them for you – or you can turn your images into JPEG images as described in Sec. 2.2.5, but then you must do so in a way that retains quality and DPI).

See Sec. 5.1.11 if you encounter problems that you need help with. If you feel that your file may have been rejected in error, try resubmitting the same files and see if you get the same error messages the second time (once in a while, this actually works). If needed, try posting your issue on the CreateSpace community forum. Very often, someone else will have experienced the same problem and will know how to solve it.

Beware that CreateSpace will not revise or edit your files for you. They won't correct any formatting, editing, or other mistakes that you make; they don't read your book. The files print just the way you submit them. It is the author's responsibility to find and correct any and all mistakes in the files. CreateSpace only looks for specific file review issues – like checking for problems with margins, resolution of images, images with transparency, using the exact same title on the cover and title page, using the same author name on the cover and title page, writing "published by CreateSpace," and other things of this sort (and you can't rely on them to catch all of these things, either). Inspect your files and printed proof very carefully.

Occasionally, CreateSpace does make small changes to the cover file. I already mentioned how they may adjust the spine text. They may also shrink or reposition images on the cover (and may not notify you of this). It's also possible for the thumbnail image to be off. We'll discuss these two issues in Sec. 5.1.8.

5.1.7 How to order a Proof

Once CreateSpace approves your files, you can order a proof. There are two options – viewing a digital proof and ordering a printed proof. View the digital proof first and then, if you're happy with that, order a printed proof next. You should at least order one printed proof, otherwise there may be significant problems that your customers will see before you do. For one, images look differently in print than they do on the screen. Also, almost everybody (including grammar experts) catches mistakes in print that they didn't see on the screen.

It would be wise to check the PDF carefully before you submit it to CreateSpace. It's very common to find mistakes in the PDF, and you can save valuable time by catching them before you upload them to CreateSpace.

There are two ways to view a digital proof – Digital Proofer and a PDF proof (which may differ slightly from the PDF that you upload – e.g. if transparency was flattened, the images may look different). Digital Proofer shows you your book in two-page spreads by default so that it looks like an open book, and also allows you to view your cover spread and a 3D cover.

I recommend first using the Digital Proofer. If you have trouble getting this to open, try switching browsers – e.g. from Internet Explorer to FireFox – or updating your browser, or even adjusting the internet options in your browser.

Once you get Digital Proofer to open your book, first study your cover carefully. The spine edges are clearly marked, which helps you check that the spine text is properly centered. Check the text on the cover, including the spine (it's easy not to notice mistakes here) – any typos on your cover will stand out to potential customers like a sore thumb. Check the positioning of images. See if the bar code appeared exactly where you expected it to be.

Look for the row of icons at the top right in Digital Proofer: The left icon shows you a 3D view of your cover. You can even spin the cover in 3D mode. This is a great way to check for centering on the front cover, spine, and back cover. Click the Stop button when the cover reaches the view you want. Close the 3D view when you're ready to check the interior.

Like Interior Reviewer, you can find a list of file issues on the right side of Digital Proofer; it flags issues like images with less than 200 DPI or images where transparency was flattened. You should inspect these flags. Check the title page carefully – the last thing you want to have is a glaring typo on the first page. Scroll through the book in the two-page spread to check for formatting problems. When you finish, change the view to show many pages at once. Some-times your eye will catch a formatting issue the many-page view. Check that the text lines up at the bottom in both the many-page and two-page views.

In the two-page view, check for improper page breaks, and look for consistent styles and formatting throughout the book. Catching these errors now may minimize the total number of printed proofs that you need to order in the long run.

You may also want to view the PDF proof. Some people find it better to look for formatting mistakes in the Digital Proofer and editing mistakes in the PDF proof. If you find any mistakes in the digital proofs, I recommend correcting them and resubmitting your file – and repeating the process as needed until you don't see mistakes in your digital proofs. Then order a printed proof.

As I already mentioned, you really need to have at least one printed proof to see exactly what your customers will be receiving. Don't let your customers see the printed proof before you do; otherwise, they might point out something in a review that you should have caught and corrected yourself before publishing. You should also carefully check what should be the very final proof of your book in print. Almost everyone catches mistakes in the printed proof that weren't seen digitally – except for those authors who don't check the printed proof (their books tend to have more mistakes that they don't know about).

Sometimes, you check a printed proof and find one little typo to correct. If you're just changing one little thing (or a few little things), you may opt to just view a digital proof and skip the printed proof. BUT BEWARE: One little correction can create a chain reaction, causing many major formatting problems. There are true stories of self-published authors who made one little change and wound up with hundreds of defective books because they didn't realize that one tiny change could mess up the whole book. Even the smallest change can affect things like page breaks – and an improperly positioned page break can be a disaster.

If you're just making one little correction, look at your printed proof (which had the mistake) and the digital proof (which has the correction – meaning after the revised file was reviewed) and compare them carefully. Start at the position where the mistake was made. First read that sentence and make sure that the revised sentence is, in fact, correct. Then check the formatting from that point forward slowly, page by page, until the original printed proof (with the mistake) and the revised digital proof match up. Let me recommend ordering another printed proof anyway. Every once in a while, something that wasn't changed comes out a little different the second time. There is no better option than holding the completely final, perfect printed proof in your hands and seeing for yourself that it is indeed perfect.

5.1.8 What to Look for When Checking Your Proof

Begin by inspecting your cover carefully. Since the cover is the first thing that prospective customers will see, it's worthwhile to invest the time to check it very thoroughly; it's also easy to do, since there is just a front, back, and spine.

Read the title slowly. Then speak the title slowly as you read it (you might hear something that you didn't see). Repeat for the author(s) and other contributors, subtitle, spine text, back cover text, and any other text on your cover. The cover is just about the worst place to have a typo. It's easy to have a typo on the spine, especially since it looks small and sideways on the computer monitor. Hence, you should check the spine text very carefully. Also check the orientation of the spine text in the printed proof: Make sure that it's not backwards compared to traditionally published books. It should be obvious if your spine text is upside down if you insert your book between traditionally published books on a shelf.

Does the font look reasonable? Old versions of Word used to squeeze and stretch text if the textboxes and WordArt were resized, so if you used an older edition of Word to make your cover (or if you used another software program that may do this to text), then you should copy/paste the text into a blank document, make it the same size and style, print it out, and compare the text to your cover.

Find a second pair of eyes to check over your cover. You can't expect anyone else to do as thorough a job as you yourself should do, but other people may find mistakes that you are missing and might offer a valuable suggestion.

Check the centering of text and images (that you intended to be centered) on the front cover, back cover, and spine. Another thing you might examine is even spacing near the edges and between different elements (text and images) on your cover.

Images often appear different in print than they do on the screen. We discussed reasons for this in Sec. 3.1.4. Printed images may appear darker than they look on a monitor, and there may be color shifts. Two slightly different hues of the same color may look identical in print. Study the colors of your text, images, and background and compare them with the original cover as viewed on the monitor. If you're not pleased with what you see in print, you need to make adjustments (and it may take a little trial and error to get it just right). Colors don't always print exactly the same every time – if you order 100 copies of your book, the colors won't look the same on all of them. There can be slight printing variations. If CreateSpace flattened transparency, you may be able to reduce some slight printing shifts by instead uploading a PDF for the cover that already has transparency flattened (you just need to find a PDF converter – possibly free, online – that provides this option).

See if any images or text look blurry, jagged, or pixelated. If so, this is likely caused by having images under 300 DPI. Sec. 5.1.6 discussed how to keep Word from compressing images. If you used a different program to make your cover, find the settings that control the DPI. Also check the DPI of the original image – if that's too low, you found your problem.

Look at large plain colors and see if they printed smoothly. Large plain black areas often have issues, especially if there were textboxes lying in front of them; sometimes, the "black" color inside of the textbox is noticeably lighter than the "black" color in the background. Try flattening the cover in the PDF program (find one with this option) and see if that helps. If not, you can try combining the black background object and textbox together into a single jpeg image, although a jpeg image may not have lines and text that are as smooth as the original. Another option is revising the color scheme for your cover – but before going to that extreme, try posting your issue on the CreateSpace community forum to see if anyone can suggest a better solution.

Are there are any straight lines or straight edges of objects near the cover edges? If so, these can accentuate any slight trimming imperfections. For example, if a book is trimmed at a slight angle, it can make a line that should be parallel to the edge look like it's slanted. Also, if you made a border for your cover, due to slight trimming variations, the border may not look perfectly even on every copy of your book that is printed. Use a piece of paper to cover 1/8" of one edge of the cover at a time and see how that appeals to your eye. If you're content with that degree of printing variation, then it's probably not an issue to worry about.

Similarly, the spine may be off by 1/8" on either edge due to slight printing variations. Therefore, spine text won't always be centered, either side (i.e. front or back) may wrap 1/8" onto the spine, and the spine may wrap 1/8" onto either side. This is most noticeable if there is a sudden change in color between the spine and either side. It's just 1/8", and very often the spine may be dead-on. You have to weigh the pros and the cons.

Look closely for possible resizing and repositioning issues. CreateSpace occasionally re-sizes and repositions elements on the cover; and, if so, they may not inform you about it. If you observe this and prefer to avoid it, try cropping the size of your cover file to just the cover with bleeds. A couple of years ago, we used to be able to submit a cover with extra back-ground (i.e. a larger file than just the cover with bleeds), and as long as it was centered, it would print just fine. Recently, however, I and other authors have noticed occasional resizing and repositioning when the submitted cover is larger than it needs to be. You do have to add 0.25" to both the width and height to allow for bleeds, and you do have to figure in the spine width, but don't make the width and height of the cover file any larger than the minimum requirements and this will help prevent possible resizing and repositioning.

I sometimes notice slight centering issues with the CreateSpace thumbnail image, even when the submitted cover file is exactly the minimum size. However, the Amazon thumbnail is often centered properly even when the CreateSpace thumbnail isn't.

Now it's time to open the book and look inside. You need to do two separate things: read the text itself and check the formatting. Trying to do both at once will probably result in many mistakes not getting caught – e.g. formatting mistakes distract from the text, and when you get focused on the text, formatting issues might not be noticed. Therefore, you should browse through once to check formatting and separately read the text for proofreading.

Here are formatting issues to look for:

- ✓ Is the style and size of headers and footers consistent throughout the book? Proofread the header text carefully. If you used the chapter headings for the even-page headers, double-check that these match the actual chapter names.
- ✓ Check that all of the pages are numbered correctly and that the style is consistent throughout the book (except for switching from Roman numerals to Arabic numbers).
- ✓ Spend a few moments looking at each page for possible problems with the page layout. Look for strange page breaks, linebreaks, changes in justification (like a sudden change from full to left or centered), changes in font style or size, inconsistent line spacing, inconsistent indents, and variations in the space between headings and para-graph text.

- ✓ Inspect the table of contents and index. Check each page reference to make sure that it refers to the right page. Do the chapter names from the table of contents match the actual chapter headings? Read these carefully. Make sure that your chapter headings have consistent style both in the table of contents and throughout the book.
- ✓ Search for references to pages (e.g. "see page 42"), figures (e.g. "see Fig. 3"), tables, equations, chapters, etc. and check to see if the numbers are correct.
- ✓ Check for consistency in bullets – e.g. using the same size indents, being consistent with whether or not the indents hang, etc.
- ✓ Inspect page borders, figures, equations, tables, captions, and textboxes.
- ✓ If you intended to line up the bottom of every page, thumb through the book quickly to check the vertical justification.
- ✓ After enough rounds of editing, when you finally believe that the text is perfected, you will need to attend to any manual formatting issues that you may have saved for last – such as manually dealing with hyphens, widows, orphans, and rivers (as described in Sec. 5.1.4). Note that changing one of these issues may affect others, so you'll have to keep a lookout for this. Look for hyphenation issues, wide gaps between words (that could be the result of automatic hyphenation not realizing that a "word" like Create-Space can be split in two), widows, orphans, and rivers in your "final" proof. You will also need to recheck most of the items from this list.

Keep in mind that any changes that you make to the text may cause changes to the formatting. Even a single small change may create a domino effect – e.g. it can create an unnatural page break which can carry over for many pages. Any time you make revisions to your text, you must carefully proof the book for formatting issues afterward.

Following are things that you should look for as you carefully read the text:

- ✓ Examine the title page carefully. Take a moment to make sure that the title and author(s) are exactly the same on the front cover, spine, title page, copyright, and on your member dashboard at CreateSpace. As a customer, I have occasionally spotted a typo in the title of a book in search results on Amazon. You definitely want to make sure that your title is perfect.
- ✓ Don't ignore the copyright page and other front matter. These are the first pages that a prospective customer will see when using the Look Inside feature at Amazon. Invest some time to see if they are as professional as you can get them.
- ✓ Similarly, you want to nail the first few chapters, which may show in the Look Inside. Any mistakes here can cause potential sales to be lost. Make sure that your eyes are fresh and check the beginning of your book a few times. Are these pages captivating?
- ✓ Also rest your eyes and rejuvenate yourself frequently as you read the remainder of the book. If a reader judges that there are too many typos, this may be reflected in reviews, which can potentially impact sales.

✓ Look for spelling and grammatical mistakes. If you haven't already done so, click on the Spelling & Grammar button in the Review tab in Word and carefully check every instance that Word shows as a possible mistake. However, there are many mistakes that Word doesn't catch – e.g. "their playing by the shore" (instead of "they're"), "be there at ate o'clock" (instead of "eight"), and "the boxes punched him in the face" (instead of "boxer"). Use Word's spelling and grammar checker to catch some mistakes, but don't rely on it. You must proofread your book carefully to find many typos and mistakes that Word won't catch for you.

✓ It's very common to mean one word, but use another similar word – such as a homophone or a word that has similar spelling. Some examples include "its" and "it's," "their," "there," and "they're," and "week" and "weak." Such mistakes are easy to make without knowing it, but can really annoy readers if you don't catch them. Hence, it's very important to proofread thoroughly, carefully, and repeatedly.

✓ Also look for repeated words. For example, "the" is often repeated, especially when one "the" comes at the end of one line and the next "the" begins the next line. You can find these in Word by entering "the the" (without the quotes, of course) in the Find tool on the Home tab.

✓ Check the punctuation. Make sure that questions actually end with question marks, and not periods. Consult a style guide to see if you used colons, semicolons, commas, quotation marks, and parentheses appropriately. Even if you already know the rules, you must still check each colon, semicolon, comma, etc. for possible typing mistakes.

✓ Verify the storyline, plot, character development, chronology, etc. Any mistakes in the plot or storytelling can be huge sales killers. The problem you have is that you already know the story, so it's hard to read and think through the story the same way that a reader will. You really need a second (and third, and so on) pair of eyes to read the story and give you feedback – especially, someone you can count on to tell it like it is.

✓ "Make sure that quotes face the right direction," as in this quote, 'and this one.'

✓ Check that the short hyphen (-) is used to hy-phen-ate words – while the longer en (–) or even longer em (—) dash is used as a separator. Also check for consistency – i.e. use either the en dash or the em dash, but not both, for a separator. However, the longer em dash (—) is correct as an interrupter at the end of a line or to attribute the author of a quotation, even if you are using the en dash (–) as a separator.

✓ Look for changes of tense – e.g. suddenly switching from past tense (e.g. "she sang wonderfully") to present tense (e.g. "she sings wonderfully"). (Of course, there are exceptions, such as: "She sang wonderfully back then and still sings wonderfully today.") Also check for incorrect changes in person – e.g. narrating in the first person singular (I, me, my) and suddenly switching to narrate in the third person (he, him). There are occasions where the person should change; you want to eliminate the cases where it shouldn't change, but does. (However, a how-to guide may be less formal.)

- ✓ In general, active writing is favored over passive writing. That is, good writing tends to "show" more than "tell." For example, compare "it is very cold today" with "although he wore a thick jacket, a scarf, a ski hat, and mittens, he was still shivering." Don't change every instance where you "tell" to "show." Rather, try to gauge whether or not you tell too often and show too little – in which case, you want to try to show more and tell less – and when you do tell, consider whether or not showing would have been more appropriate (there are many minor points that aren't worth detracting from the story to show, so sometimes telling is better).
- ✓ Did you overuse adverbs that end with –ly? Adverbs also tend to be passive rather than active. For example, "she returned to her bedroom sadly" tells that she was sad, whereas "she wiped the tears from her eyes on her way to the bedroom" shows that she was sad. Some technical nonfiction books, however, do use –ly adverbs more.
- ✓ Various forms of the verb "to be" (is, are, was, were, been, etc.) also tend to tell rather than show, and are sometimes even useless words. For instance, "to be" is superfluous in "seems to be obvious." However, this style is sometimes used in technical works.
- ✓ Check for other useless words and redundancies like "wastefully useless."
- ✓ Some words and phrases are essentially filler – that is, the same information can often be conveyed without using them. (It's true! See!) Some common filler words include "although," "that," "whereas," "in fact," "in general," and "as opposed to." It's okay to use these words sometimes, but you should check if you overuse them. It also depends on the context; these words tend to be used more frequently in technical nonfiction and textbooks.
- ✓ Are there any words that you personally tend to overuse? If so, search for them in Word and consider finding alternatives to them. Here, it helps to know your own bad habits, which you could learn by receiving unbiased feedback from others.

Be sure to make revisions to both your paperback and eBook files (except for those changes, such as page header adjustments, that only apply to one or the other). You'd hate to have a mistake in your eBook, for example, that you corrected in your paperback, but forgot to also fix in the eBook.

It's nearly impossible to catch all of our own mistakes. For one, we often "see" what we meant to write instead of what we actually wrote. Many top-notch writers who have thoroughly mastered grammar and the elements of writing and style seek editors and other unbiased readers to check through their work to suggest possible mistakes and provide feedback. Even professional editors themselves hire others to edit their own writing. Having another pair of eyes look over your work is invaluable, and quite necessary.

Hiring a professional editor can make a huge difference. Many professional editors charge $300 and up. There are less expensive editing services, too. The challenge is finding someone who will do an excellent job at an affordable price, and who you can trust to protect the confidence of your work. Find writing that you can verify they have edited (easiest, when they are listed as the editor); if spelling and grammar aren't your strong suits, find someone with fluency in this to judge writing that they have edited. Request a free (or at least, low-cost) sample of a small number of pages – such as your first chapter – and see if they edit that to your satisfaction. That way, you have an expectation of what you may be getting before investing too much time and money. The prospective editor or editing service should present you with a contract. A clause in the contract about you retaining ownership of the work and the editor protecting your confidence should help ease any concerns of this sort that you may have. (I'm not an attorney; you should consult an attorney for all of your legal questions, and to check over the contract.) It's mutually beneficial if the editor will accept 50% of the payment upfront and the remainder upon receipt of the edited manuscript. Also, note that CreateSpace offers copyediting services; you might contact support to inquire about this. (I haven't used it myself, so I can't recommend it one way or the other. However, you might be able to learn about experiences that others have had with this by searching their community help forums – but keep in mind that people are more likely to post if they're unhappy.)

Note that there are different types of editors. Basic editing consists of just checking for mistakes in spelling and grammar. You can also get editing help with writing style, storyline suggestions, formatting, etc. If you seek editing help, you want to know exactly what you're getting (and you should first determine which type of help you want).

See Sec. 5.1.11 if you have questions about editing or formatting. There are also some editors and small publishers on the CreateSpace forums who provide professional services. I haven't used them, and so I can't recommend any of them one way or the other; I just know that there are some regulars there who show expertise in many questions that they answer.

In Volume 1, I recommended publishing your book for free, whereas in Volume 2, I'm suggesting that hiring cover and editing help could make a significant difference. Why? By reading Volume 2, you're showing interest in perfecting your book and learning about market-ing. The author who takes the time to perfect the content of the book, attend to all of the details, and is willing to learn how to effectively market (and also is willing to do the work) is much more likely to reap the benefits of a great cover and good editing. Volume 1 was focused on getting the book written and published. The author who rushes through that, but doesn't take time to perfect the book and market, shouldn't invest in cover design and editing. Also, if you tried all of this yourself first, now you have seen firsthand and can assess more properly to what extent your cover, formatting, and editing might be improved through professional help.

There are a few other things that you need to proof besides the book itself. Login to CreateSpace and proofread your description and biography carefully. Also, carefully double-check the tittle, subtitle, and author(s) and other contributors. A second pair of eyes can also be helpful for proofing your description and About the Author sections. These are among the first things that prospective buyers will see, so they are well worth perfecting.

After you publish your book, you should also check the Amazon page for your book. Make sure that the title on Amazon correctly matches the title as you entered it at CreateSpace, for example. It's worth checking your book's product page periodically – if there happens to be any glitch in the system that could affect sales, you want to know about it so you can report it to Amazon (there is a form for this on the page, or ask CreateSpace to report this for you).

5.1.9 Before You Approve Your Proof

Rush, rush, rush! People are usually in a rush, and naturally impatient. This affects cover design and blurb writing through the 5-second rule. But customers aren't the only ones who tend to show impatience – authors do it, too. Most self-published authors rush their work out to the wolves. Slow down, take it easy, resist the temptation to get your work out there as quickly as possible, and avoid this much-too-common mistake.

Authors spend months – sometimes years – writing. This is the result of a great deal of effort, and reflects much diligence and motivation. The completion of the manuscript is a major accomplishment just in itself.

So now what will the author *do* with this book? Publish it, of course. That's when the writer suddenly realizes that writing the book was the easy part! It may have been a great deal of work, but it's something that the author felt that he/she knew how to do, and writing is a hobby that the author enjoys. After the book is written, the author is faced with a great deal of work that is unfamiliar. Publishing the book involves the fickle art of writing a query letter and book proposal, searching for publishers and literary agents, selling your book to strangers who are often more interested in your resume and marketing skills than the writing itself, and dealing with an overwhelming rejection ratio. The alternative, self-publishing, involves a variety of unfamiliar skills – formatting, editing, publishing, cover design, marketing, and even public relations – including skills which the writer may not enjoy or excel at (such as the illustrations involved in making a cover or the social prowess and public relations skills entailed in marketing).

After all of the work done to write the book and the additional work needed to publish the book, the writer naturally feels a very strong compulsion to be finished with it once and for all, to get the book to the market and be done with it, and hopefully get some pats on the back through feedback for the amazing feat of finishing the book. Realize this: Your task is not complete when you publish the book by clicking the Approve Proof button. Successful authors invest much time in marketing, and the most successful authors begin their marketing campaign before the book is launched. The book even has marketing in itself, so taking the time to perfect the cover, blurb, and content can itself have a significant impact on sales.

Most self-publishers rush their book out to the market only to regret this later. They don't regret writing the book. What they regret is not taking more time to perfect the book, getting feedback and help, learning more about marketing, and developing a plan. I see these kinds of comments on the community help forums (especially, at KDP) quite frequently:[6]

- "I got a bad review saying there were typos. Can anyone suggest a cheap editor?"
- "Sales are really slow. Please give me feedback on my cover."
- "My blurb doesn't seem to be working. Advice would be appreciated."
- "A review says there are formatting problems, but it looked great in the preview."
- "Does anyone have some good marketing suggestions?"
- "Is it possible to unpublish a book and republish it later?"

I sometimes provide my two cents in an effort to help them. I appreciate that they have realized that they need help and are trying to improve their books. However, it would have been wiser to seek this help before publishing their books. Don't wait for a bad review or slow sales to motivate you to improve your book. You can revise the book, but you can't remove the bad review and the history of slow sales will affect your sales rank after the revisions. The wiser course is to seek feedback and help – and properly invest the time to perfect the book – prior to publishing.

With your first book, you're establishing yourself as an author. Start out with the best product you can and create a positive, professional image for yourself as an author. Your image is part of your marketing.

Look at what traditional publishers do by example. They often have a whole team of people – who specialize in editing, formatting, illustration, marketing, etc. – work on a book for 6 months after it's written. They spend 6 months perfecting the book, and also use this 6-month period to build "buzz" for the book and develop promotional plans (the author is generally expected to do much of the promotion himself/herself, but the publisher may send out advanced review copies, press release materials, and a host of other things that we will consider in Chapter 8).

The indie author spends an average of one month doing these things all by his or her lonesome self, whereas publishers have a team of experts doing these same things for 6 months. Yet the self-published book is available online in the same search results as tradition-ally published books. If you want your book to be competitive, exercise the patience to spend more time perfecting your book, seeking and receiving valuable help and feedback, creating "buzz" for your book, and learning how to develop an effective marketing plan.

Sales usually don't come to you; you have to help drive sales through marketing efforts. Many of us enjoy the "art" of writing, but the reality is that selling books is a "business." Learn how to translate the passion that you have for your book into a passion for sharing your book with others – and you can use this to motivate yourself to learn how to become successful at marketing your book.

---

[6] These are not actual quotes from any particular users, but instead represent a variety of common questions.

Read Chapter 8 before you publish your book. Strive to create buzz for your book. Develop a marketing plan and motivate yourself to carry it out. Don't expect instant results. Train yourself to relax and exercise patience. Have you thought about the concept of pre-orders? You can learn about preorders in Sec. 7.1.8. You know that you were successful in creating buzz when you sell several copies of your book through preorders. This can give your book a good jumpstart. Instead of starting out with slow sales and struggling to make up for it, strive to start out with several early sales and meet the challenge of maintaining the sales.

One other thing you may want to do before you approve your proof is obtain copyright registration. This was described toward the end of Sec. 5.1.1.

5.1.10 Making Revisions to the Paperback

You can revise your cover and interior file as many times as you want prior to publishing your book; there is no limit. Simply click on your book on your Member Dashboard and click Interior or Cover in the Setup column. From there, you can upload a new file and submit your files for review again. You can't make changes to your file while they are in review; you have to wait for CreateSpace to complete their file review, and then you will be able to submit revisions to your files.

You can make other changes, too – such as modifying your description, about the author, keywords, sales channels, and browse categories. However, there are a few things that can't be changed without deleting your title and starting over: Your title, subtitle, author(s) and other contributors, and ISBN are locked after you make your ISBN selection. If you used the free ISBN option, you can delete your title and start over at any time prior to clicking Approve Proof (well, if your files are in review, you may have to wait for that). If you invested in an ISBN or other services, you probably don't want to delete and start over – and lose that investment. In that case, you should call support, explain your situation, and ask if they can make the change you need or if they can transfer the service(s) that you paid for onto another book so that you can start over. It shouldn't hurt to ask.

Think carefully before you click Approve Proof. Once you do that, you can no longer delete your book. However, if you want to unpublish your book, you can disable all sales channels. Although that will prevent CreateSpace and Amazon from selling new copies of your book, your book's detail page may remain on Amazon permanently – allowing any customers who may have a copy to sell their copies used. You can also retire your book after disabling all sales channels, but again that won't prevent Amazon from still retaining your product page. Once you enable the Amazon sales channel and approve your proof, you can expect your Amazon product page to remain there forever, even if you unpublish your book. Also, once you claim a book on AuthorCentral, it will remain on the list of books on your Author Page at Amazon indefinitely.

What if you want to make changes after you publish? Not a problem![7] The quickest way to update your book description or About the Author sections at Amazon are through Author-Central (see Sec. 6.1) – though you'll still need to revise your description through CreateSpace for Expanded Distribution outlets and your CreateSpace eStore. You can also revise your files, browse categories,[8] keywords, sales channels, etc. – just not your ISBN or title information.

Your book will be unavailable for purchase from Amazon during the time it takes to upload the new file(s) and approve the new proof. It can take as little as 12 to 24 hours for this, if you proof your book digitally. Check the digital proof (see Sec.'s 5.1.7-8) very carefully. Remember, a single small change can wreak havoc if that small change causes big adjustments to your page layout – e.g. through unappealing page breaks. Look carefully for formatting problems. If instead you order a printed proof, your book may be unavailable for a week or more, which can have a major impact on your sales rank.

Should you make a new edition? It's optional. You can update your book without making a new edition. If you made a change based on information posted in a review and wish to make it clear that your book has been revised, you can choose to include a note to this effect in the description (but don't make any reference to the review whatsoever; also, see Chapter 7 to learn more about customer reviews). Another thing you might do is make some change to the copyright page. It can be a subtle change that only you would notice (if you don't want it to be obvious that there is a new version), or you can write something like 2nd edition, Version 4, updated 3/14/13, etc. At the very least, this will be helpful for you. Why? For one, if you view Amazon's Look Inside, you'll be able to readily determine if the Look Inside has been updated yet (it may take several days for the Look Inside to match the revised files). Also, if you happen to see a customer's book, you'll be able to tell which version they purchased.

It's handy to keep records of your files in at least two different places so you know which files were the most recent. Also, backup your most recent files in at least two different places. Every once in a while, a computer pretends like a file isn't there when it is, and if you don't realize this, you could accidentally open a version that wasn't your most recent file and start revising that. Fortunately, CreateSpace shows you the filenames of the cover and interior files that you uploaded last time, which can help with this (but note that KDP does not do this).

A totally new edition can be made by adding a new title with a new ISBN, for example. This is common among textbooks, for which a new edition comes out every year or two (which publishers use not only to make improvements, but to help reduce the impact of used textbook sales). The previous edition can be unpublished by disabling sales channels (and it can even be retired by contacting support – but the listing may still remain on Amazon so that

---

[7] CreateSpace may charge a $25 for this if you have the Expanded Distribution. To find out for sure, you should contact support to see if they are presently charging such a fee, or if the fee has changed. Also, it can take several weeks for some changes to propagate through all of the Expanded Distribution channels.

[8] However, if you've already asked CreateSpace to add a second browse category to your Amazon page, you should make this change by contacting support.

customers can resell used books). The two editions may be linked together on Amazon (probably, with the old edition less visible – a customer may have to click a link to see all of the editions). Any reviews on the old edition may automatically show up on the new edition.

5.1.11 Getting Help with Your Paperback

You may be able to get free help and advice from fellow authors. One place where this is possible is CreateSpace's community forum. There are many authors and small publishers there who regularly share their expertise, and it's usually a friendly ambiance. You can also meet other authors like yourself.

CreateSpace offers professional editing and design services, and you can find many other options online (even some members of the CreateSpace community forum offer this).

5.2 Proofing Your eBook

5.2.1 Perfecting Your eBook

Much of what we discussed about perfecting your paperback cover, interior, blurb, and biography in Sec.'s 5.1.3-5 also applies to your eBook. In this section, we will focus on details and formatting that are exclusive to eBooks, so as not to repeat what we have already discussed regarding paperbacks; but we will save picture formatting in the interior file for the following section. When you proofread your paperback book and revised it, hopefully you also took the time to update your eBook file. It's important to remember to revise both files any time that you make changes.

Virtually everything that applies to designing a print cover from Sec. 5.1.3 also applies to the eBook cover – even the part about the cover looking good in large size. The majority of Kindle buyers shop for eBooks on Amazon's website on their PC. The cover must look nice as a thumbnail to attract attention, but once they click on the listing, many customers will click to see the large cover image (they will also see this when they use the Look Inside). I've seen many covers that looked nice as thumbnails, but then some imperfections (jagged lines, blurry, pixelated, text not crisp, or stray marks) showed up in the large image. Since this can deter sales, you want to ensure that it looks nice both ways.

Since your cover will automatically be included inside of your eBook, don't include the cover in your eBook file (you should, however, have a title page; what you don't want is a duplicate cover in your book). Also, use the maximum resolution allowed for your cover (up to 2500 pixels for the longest side) because many customers will be viewing the large image on a

PC. The width of your eBook cover should be shorter than the height. Almost all of the other thumbnails look like this, so if your eBook cover is wider than it is tall, it will really stand out – but not in a good way. This will likely hurt sales.

The two-space issue described in Sec. 5.1.4 has a greater impact on eBook formatting than it does on paperback formatting. Don't use two consecutive spaces in your eBook – not even following a period – otherwise one of the extra spaces will either show up at the end of one line or the beginning of the next if the two spaces happen to come at the beginning or end of a line displayed on the screen of the eReader (and you can't plan for where this will occur, since the device user can vary font size, line spacing, etc. – plus, screen sizes vary).

Don't use blank lines to separate sections in your eBook. Instead, place asterisks (* * *) or other symbols on a single, centered line (with a single linespace above and below it) – or do the same thing, but use a glyph. However, there is an important formatting issue with glyphs that we will discuss in the next section. Note that drop caps won't format perfectly on every device. A better alternative is to write the first three words of each chapter in CAPS.

There are some places where you should use Shift + Enter instead of just Enter in your eBook. This yields a more predictable blank line, which you may have between elements of your table of contents, copyright page, before and after images, etc. Hold down Shift and press Enter twice to create a single blank line. When you do this, the last line of the previous paragraph will look funny on your screen. Don't worry about this because eReaders should display it correctly (well, it would be wise to check this among other things as described in Sec. 5.2.3). However, don't create blank linespaces this way in your paperback book file.

The best way to make dashes is to use Alt codes. Hold down Alt and type 0150 to make the en dash (–) and 0151 to make the em dash (—). The dashes that Word makes via AutoCorrect as you type often don't work on some of the older Kindle devices, but do work using the Alt method. If you have numerous dashes to update, copy/paste one of your old dashes into the Find field in Replace and use the Alt method in the Replace field. You don't need to make any changes to hyphens (-) typed directly from your keyboard.

It's also safest to use the Alt codes for other supported characters, such as standard curly quotes (" and "). Be sure to angle the quotation marks correctly. You can find a table of supported Kindle characters by going to the KDP help pages and looking on the left column for Preparing Your Book > Formatting Your Book > Character Encoding. After pulling up this page, click the second "here" link to see an image of supported characters and their Alt codes. Note that Alt codes for characters not on this list won't work on Kindle (and other eReader) devices. Here is the current link for the page of supported characters:

https://images-na.ssl-images-amazon.com/images/G/01/digital/otp/help/Latin1.gif

Actually, there are other characters that you can use. You can't use them in Word, but there is a simple way to use them. When your Word file is complete, click Save As in the File tab and set Save As Type to Web Page, Filtered (don't pick Single File Webpage and make sure it says Filtered). Click Yes and wait for the file to fully save. Then open the file in Notepad (not Word). Now you can type the ampersand symbol (&) followed by the name of a supported HTML symbol and a semicolon (;). For example, ⊥ makes the perpendicular symbol (⊥) and ♦ creates a diamond (♦). A list of supported HTML symbols can be found here:

http://en.wikipedia.org/wiki/List_of_XML_and_HTML_character_entity_references

One problem with eBook design is that text can wind up anywhere on a screen, since users read eBooks with different size screens, font sizes, line spacing, etc. One way to gain some control over this is to use Ctrl + Shift + Spacebar to create a space between two words (or a word and symbol) that you don't want to be split. For example, you can do this if you want to type "4 lbs." in such a way as to prevent the "4" from being on the end of one line and the "lbs." from being on the beginning of the next line. This is called a non-breaking space.

Remember, the eBook can be in color even if the paperback edition is black-and-white; there is no charge for adding color to the eBook. However, don't overuse color in the text; the most important function of text is that it be clear and easy to read. Color is most effective as a highlight or to catch attention when used sparingly. Another consideration is that some colors that ordinarily contrast well sometimes don't contrast well in grayscale (they may even blend together), yet many readers have black-and-white eReaders. For example, where red stands out on a color screen, it looks gray on a black-and-white device. These are all important considerations, which you can judge by viewing a preview on a black-and-white device (see Sec. 5.2.3). It would be ideal to make preliminary a sample when you first start making figures.

Consider avoiding long paragraphs in your eBook. Some readers – so this may depend in part on your audience – are easily overwhelmed by long paragraphs. Long paragraphs can easily occupy the entire screen on small devices, which makes them seem unending.

We will now explore some details that are quite important for perfecting the formatting of an eBook. There are many common formatting mistakes that arise from eBook files that are typed in Word that can be avoided, and which you want to avoid in order to make your eBook appear professional. The problem has to do with the fact that an eBook is designed to function more like a webpage, whereas a word processor is designed to perfect the look of printed pages on separate sheets of paper. The natural language of a webpage is HTML. Ultimately, your Word file will be converted to a mobi file for Kindle, and at some point in the process your Word document will be interpreted as a set of HTML instructions.

What does this mean to you? What you see on your monitor – and what you would see on a piece of paper if you were to print your document out – can be quite different from what you see on the screen of an eReader. Therefore, you want to learn how to make Word produce an eBook file that looks just as nice on any eReader as it appears on your screen; and you want to preview your eBook very carefully on every device before you publish it.

The problem is that documents typed in Word can result in HTML instructions that one or more eReaders may interpret differently than you expect. The solution is to learn techniques to format the Word document in such a way as to make the HTML cleaner and unambiguous.

One way to do this is to use the Styles on the top right half of the Home tab. Format every piece of your Word document with one of these Styles so that Word will add tags to the converted HTML – like Heading 1. You need to use at least 4 different styles: Normal, FirstNormal, Heading 1, and Title. Modify the default Normal, Heading 1, and Title styles to suit your needs, and add a new style for FirstNormal (a different style for the first paragraph of each chapter and other paragraphs or stand-alone lines that you don't want to have automatically indented by eReaders).

Right-click a Style to modify it. Set the font style to Times New Roman (and note that the user will be able to set the font on his/her eReader), the font size to 12 for the Normal and FirstNormal Styles (which the user will also be able to adjust; this is the best size for paragraph text), and the font color to Automatic. The Heading 1 and Title Styles should use a larger font size than Normal. To add a new style – such as FirstNormal – click the funny icon in the bottom right corner of the Styles group on the Home tab – which looks like ⬑ – and click the bottom left button (New Style).

In each Style, click the single spacing button. Click the justified full button for the Normal and FirstNormal Styles, and the center button for the Title and Heading 1 Styles. If you want any left-aligned text, use justified full in the Style, highlight the text, and click the left align icon in the Paragraph group of the Home tab (don't use the left align button in the Style) – after the Style has already been applied (and remember, like FirstNormal, you need to set First Line to 0.01" to prevent this paragraph from being automatically indented). Adjust the paragraph options for each style by clicking the Format button in the bottom left corner (where you modify the Style). Choose Paragraph from the list. Set the Spacing Before and After to 0 and the Line Spacing to Single (not Word's default of 1.15). Exception: For Heading 1, set Before to 18 pts and don't create a blank linespace before it. In the FirstNormal Style, set First Line to 0.01"; in Normal, adjust Special to First Line and By to 0.3" (or so – we'll improve upon this later in this section); and in Title and Heading 1, set Special to None.

To save your Styles, click the Change Styles button at the right edge of the Home tab, select Style Set, and click Save As Quick Style Set.

Don't adjust the font size in the Home tab; instead, defined Styles that have both the font size and formatting that you wish to apply to the text (with the exception of how to make left-aligned text that we described previously).

To help Word produce clean, unambiguous HTML, Select All and click the Normal Style. Now go through your eBook file and apply the other styles to any text that you don't want to have the Normal Style – such as headings. Use the Title Style (large font, centered alignment) for pictures centered on their own lines. Apply FirstNormal to the first paragraph of each chapter (to prevent it from being automatically indented) and any other non-centered paragraphs or stand-alone lines that you don't want to have automatically indented (like lines from your copyright page and table of contents).

Sometimes, the table of contents bookmark hyperlinks can take the reader to the chapter, but not show the chapter heading at the top of the page. The way around this is to insert a blank line above the chapter heading, press the spacebar a few times (this is the one exception to the rule to never have two or more consecutive spaces), highlight these spaces, apply the FirstNormal Style, place the cursor at the beginning of this row of spaces, and insert the bookmark there (instead of at the beginning of the chapter heading).

Aside from pictures (which we will discuss in the next section), this is satisfactory to achieve fairly good (a relative concept) eBook formatting in the eReaders (you still need to check the preview carefully, as described in Sec. 5.2.3 – however, not by using the convenient online previewer – and then you may need to tweak things a little to perfect the formatting). However, your eBook may suffer from a few problems in the Look Inside.

The Look Inside is the most important part of your eBook, and even when the equivalent of the Look Inside may look perfect on any eReader, there are still frequently formatting problems on the Look Inside seen on Amazon on a PC (where most people buy their eBooks). That's right: There can be formatting mistakes in the Look Inside on Amazon that aren't present when the eBook is read on a Kindle. The Look Inside is the most challenging part of your eBook to format properly because it uses the strictest interpretation of HTML. At the same time, the Look Inside formatting is the most critical toward earning sales. Perfecting the Look Inside formatting can give you a professional edge over the competition.

After perfecting your eBook file – including pictures, which are discussed in the next section – and prior to inserting supported HTML symbols – as described earlier – save it as a filtered webpage (we described this in the discussion of supported HTML symbols). If you have pictures, make a compressed zipped folder (as explained in the following section). This filtered webpage (which, if your file has images, is inside the compressed zipped folder) contains your HTML code.

There are programs available online (even for free) that can help you clean the HTML file that Word produced. A cleaner HTML file helps to achieve a more professional Look Inside.

You can view and edit the HTML file by opening it in Notepad. Most other HTML editors are likely to mess up the HTML code (as far as using it for an eBook is concerned), so Notepad or Notepad++ are your best options.

Note that you don't have to be an HTML expert in order to learn how to tweak your eBook file. Rather, you just need to learn what to look for and how to modify it, which is far easier than learning HTML.

For example, you can tweak the HTML to make more professional indents. To do this, look through your HTML to see what your paragraph styles look like. The paragraph styles start with a <p> and end with a </p>, but there are usually statements inside of the first <p>, such as <p style="text-indent:0.3in;">. There may be other statements inside the <p> besides the text indent, and some paragraph styles may not even include the text indent. You can also find the text indent statements at the top of the HTML file in the style definitions. They will look like text-indent:0.3in; (the same as when it's included in the paragraph style). It's the text indent that you want to modify.

If you formatted your eBook properly, you should have two types of text indents: One set to 0.3 inches or so (for Normal) and another set to 0.01 inches (for FirstNormal). Use the Replace tool in Notepad to change 0.01in to 0 and 0.3in with a percentage or a measure in ems. Be careful not to remove any semicolons (;) or quotes (") when you do this. Publishers tend to set indents in terms of the em (the width of the uppercase M in the font style and size); in this case, 1.5em or 2em are common values. A percentage is useful because a reader may view the book on a cell phone or an iPad. Setting the indent to about 8% or so bases the size of the indent on the length of the line on the screen. In the former case, replace "text-indent:0.3in;" with "text-indent:2em;" and in the latter case, replace with "text-indent:8%;" (don't use the quote; do use the actual indent size that you had previously set in Word).

You can find a list of supported HTML tags in the KDP help pages. Look under Preparing Your Book > Types of Formats in the left column, and then click Supported HTML Tags. Once there, you can also see a shorter table of Common HTML Tags. The current link to this page is:

https://kdp.amazon.com/self-publishing/help?topicId=A1JPUWCSD6F59O

KDP also has a guide for HTML publishing experts:

http://kindlegen.s3.amazonaws.com/AmazonKindlePublishingGuidelines.pdf

Some Kindle publishing experts use special programs to make epub and mobi formats from their HTML. These include Sigil, Calibre, Kindlegen, and others. There are many guides available that describe how to tweak the HTML or use such software to create epub and mobi files for an eBook. If you're new to styles and modifying HTML for eBooks, there is a handy guide called *Formatting of Kindle Books: A Brief Tutorial* by Charles Spender that provides a good visual introduction to both using just Word's styles and also modifying the HTML.

Another important aspect of the Look Inside is the front matter, which is often neglected. The details discussed in Sec. 5.1.5 regarding how to perfect the front matter and Look Inside also apply to eBooks, but the formatting is a little different with eBooks. For one, if there is a table of contents, the eBook edition should have hyperlinks. The title and copyright pages of a paperback may have design marks, which might not appear in an eBook. Making front matter that appears highly professional can make a great impression. Browse through bestselling eBooks by traditional publishers and see what they do to make the front matter look very professional. This will give you ideas that you can apply to your eBook. But remember, you want to get into the action quickly – in Chapter 1, which hopefully has a captivating start – so you don't want too much front matter. For short eBooks, it's not uncommon to move some front matter (like an Introduction) to the back in order to increase the amount of Look Inside available to prospective readers.

Remember, there are a few differences between Kindle and other eBook publishing services. For example, using Page Layout > Breaks > Next Page to create page breaks (instead of inserting ordinary page breaks) will create page breaks that are recognized by PubIt's preview tool for the Nook. (PubIt was replaced by Nook Press.) Also, remember to modify your copyright page to designate the Smashwords edition if you publish with Smashwords.

5.2.2 Perfecting eBook Images

Here's a funny Kindle fact: It's possible to have a picture that measures 600 pixels across look small on a Kindle screen that's only 600 pixels wide! One way this could happen is if you insert the picture into Word and Word downsizes the image so that it only fills the available margin width in the page. Also, make sure to use Insert > Picture and not copy/paste to add images to your eBook file.

One way to fix this is to right-click the image in Word, click Size and Position, choose the Size tab, and adjust the Scale to 100% for the width (and the height will automatically change to 100% if the aspect ratio is locked). Ensure that the box is checked for Relative to Original Picture Size. If you check a few of your pictures and suddenly realize that you have a large number of pictures with the scale set below 100%, there is a very quick way to rescale many images at once: Open the HTML file in Notepad (as described in the previous section) and use the Replace tool in order to change the percentage. Check that the width="100%" statement is inside of the image style, as in <img width="100%" src="filename.jpg">. **Note**: If you want an image to **automatically fill the width of any screen**, insert the width="100%" statement into the HTML (not Word); delete the old width/height statements (don't make height 100%).

The common size of 600 pixels by 800 pixels will fill the screens of most devices with the width scaled to 100% except for screens that are larger than 600 x 800 – such as the Kindle Fire HD, Apple iPad, and a PC monitor. See 4.2.2, which has a table of screen sizes for a variety of eReaders. Full-screen pictures on these devices require higher resolution images.

Pictures should be placed on a line all by themselves, with Wrap Text set to In Line With Text in the Format tab. Apply the Title Style to pictures. It may help to place blank lines before and after pictures using Shift + Enter to create the blank lines (but don't worry if this causes strange formatting with the last line of the previous paragraph in Word – as long as it looks good in the downloadable previewer). Center pictures that may be less than full screen. For full-page images, a blank page problem on the Kindle may be prevented by using a Style with First Line set to 0.01" and then clicking the left align button on the Paragraph group in the Home tab.

For the Nook, if you want to see a page break prior to the picture show up on the previewer at PubIt (replaced by Nook Press), use Page Layout > Breaks > Next Page to do this.

Note that if a picture file size exceeds 127 kb, the picture file size will be reduced when the book is published to Kindle, which may affect how the image appears on a device. If you compress your images (see Sec. 2.2.5; an alternative is a picture compression program that you may be able to find online), this will help you not only reduce the size of your pictures, but also the overall size of the content file, which can affect your list price and royalty as explained in Sec. 4.2.5. Also, you should save your file as a filtered webpage and send it to a compressed zipped folder, as explained in the last paragraph of this section.

Pictures saved in the jpeg format with a "clear" background actually will have back-grounds that look white even if the user sets the device background to sepia or black. This can cause some images to look funny when the user uses a sepia or black background. It poses a problem with using glyphs for section breaks, for example. This is also why the KDP publishing guide states that GIF format should be used for line art and text images (instead of jpeg). Line art and text should be saved in GIF format with a maximum size of 500 pixels by 600 pixels.

When your Word file is complete, go to the File tab, choose Save As, and select Web Page Filtered (not Single File Web Page, and make sure that it says Filtered). Click Yes, then wait for the file to fully save. Next, clean and tweak the HTML as needed and as described in the previous section (you may also want to modify the image statements in the HTML using Notepad). Once your HTML file is fully prepared, close the file and find it in your Computer or Documents folder. Right-click the file, choose Send To, and select Compressed (Zipped) Folder. Find the folder with your compressed images (it has the same name as the HTML file) that this creates, copy it, and paste it into the compressed zipped folder. Look inside the zipped folder to make sure that it has both the HTML file (the filtered webpage) and the matching folder of compressed pictures. Saving your file as a filtered webpage is necessary in order to prevent gray lines from showing up on one or more edges of the pictures on the eReader.

5.2.3 Proofing Your eBook

The best way to publish on Kindle is directly with KDP so that you can take advantage of the downloadable previewer to see exactly what your converted mobi file looks like. If you use an aggregator like Smashwords in addition to publishing with KDP, be sure to disable the Kindle sales channel from the aggregator (if available) as soon as the option appears. Nook Press has a previewer for Nook. For Smashwords, you actually have to publish your book first, and then preview the result; you can make changes afterward, but your book has a brief period of high visibility immediately after publishing, so it may help to avoid mistakes on the first go.

First upload your book cover to KDP; the thumbnail that you see for your cover is much lower resolution than the actual thumbnail will be. When you upload the content file, KDP will automatically add the cover to the first page (in the past, this was an option, but not anymore). There are two previewers available in Step 6 of the KDP publishing process. The common mistake is to use the convenient online previewer. This is a mistake because there are often formatting mistakes in the eBook that don't show on the convenient online previewer that you can see right away with just the click of a button. Look closely and you will see that there is a downloadable previewer available in the same step. Use the downloadable previewer because it is more accurate.

Download the downloadable previewer by clicking the Windows or Mac link. Look carefully at which folder this is installed in on your computer and write down this path so that you can find it easily. You may also pin it to your Start Menu or add it as a shortcut. Then click the Download Book Preview File link. Also record the name and location of the downloaded book preview file. Once you have more than one Kindle tool for reading books on your PC (such as Kindle for PC and Kindle Previewer), the Kindle reader that you wish to use may not open by default; and if you open the tool you want (as opposed to clicking the book to read it), your book won't be on the history unless you've already read it with that tool. You may need to open the Kindle reader on your PC (either the Kindle for PC or Kindle Previewer), click File, select Open Book, and then find the downloaded book preview file on your computer.

First use the Kindle Previewer (not Kindle for PC). This is the Kindle reader that you installed when you clicked the Windows or Mac link in Step 6 of the KDP publishing process. Open your downloaded book preview file in Kindle Previewer. In the Devices tab, there are three options: eInk, Fire, and IOS. When you choose eInk, you will see three buttons – Kindle Paperwhite, Kindle, and Kindle DX. There are two buttons when you select Fire – Kindle Fire and Kindle Fire HD. There are two more buttons for IOS: Kindle for iPad and Kindle for iPhone.

Be sure to preview your eBook carefully with all 7 options. The Fire, eInk, and IOS devices format a little differently, so an eBook that looks perfect on one device may have major formatting flaws on another device. Customers who purchase your eBook may have any of these devices, and if there are formatting mistakes on any one of these devices, a customer is likely to point this out by leaving a 1-star review. You can prevent this by investing the time now to carefully preview your eBook on all 3 devices with all 7 options. Even on a single device, such as the eInk, the different eReaders can have significant formatting differences. For example, there may be serious problems with the Kindle Paperwhite even if the book looks fantastic on the Kindle. **The only way to be sure that you don't have any serious formatting mistakes is to view your eBook page by page with all 7 options.** This will take some time, but it is well worth it. You only need to read your eBook thoroughly once to proofread it, but you need to quickly browse through every page on all 7 devices to proof the formatting.

Don't browse too fast when you check the formatting: Maintain a slow enough pace that you see every page and are able to spot any formatting mistakes. Take breaks to rest your eyes and rejuvenate your brain frequently, and only check the formatting for one option at a sitting. Keep a pencil and paper handy to make a list of all of the formatting issues that you find and precisely describe where to find them in your eBook file. In addition to browsing for formatting mistakes 7 times, slowly and carefully proofread your eBook at least once.

There is yet an 8th option that you need to check: Kindle for PC. Find any eBook in the Kindle store on Amazon to find the option to download the free Kindle for PC to your computer. Make sure that you open Kindle for PC and not the Kindle Previewer (which you've already used to proof the first 7 options). Then go to File, click Open Book, and find your downloaded book preview file. Check the formatting of your eBook on Kindle for PC.

You're still not done! The most important way to check your eBook is on an actual device. If you have a Kindle, iPad, or iPhone, use it. If you know a friend or family member – or even an acquaintance – see if you can borrow their device. They might not want you to take their device to your home and use it, but they might be willing to upload your eBook on their device and allow you to quickly check the formatting in their presence – at the very least, they might be willing to let you put your eBook on their device and leave it there so that they can read it for free (that should get their attention).

Don't email the downloaded book preview file because this can apparently change the formatting of the eBook. Instead, use a USB cable to connect the device to a computer where you directly downloaded the book preview file to that computer from Step 6 of the publishing process (or download it again on a different computer, if needed). Now check the formatting of the eBook on that device. The greater variety of devices you can find, the better.

You need to check both the formatting and text. We already discussed how to proofread the text in Sec. 5.1.8. You should proofread your eBook (on one device of your choice) at least once even if you've already perfected the proofreading of your paperback. There are almost always some significant issues that are found this way. Also, reading the eBook instead of just quickly turning the pages will help you to see some subtler formatting mistakes that you might miss when checking the formatting.

When you check the formatting of your eBook with the 7 different options (plus Kindle for PC and actual devices), following are some issues that you should look for (in addition to the relevant formatting issues that were outlined in Sec. 5.1.8 regarding paperbacks):

✓ First inspect the cover on the first page. Check that the aspect ratio looks okay (no distortion) and that the image(s) and text look clean and sharp with good contrast.

✓ Most eBooks will look more professional with no space between paragraphs (or very little, like 0.1 pts), justified full (not left-aligned), and consistent indents. There are a few rare categories where non-indented block paragraphs with a linespace between are common, but most eBooks shouldn't use this format.

✓ Check for inconsistent indents. It's common to find occasional indents that are shorter or longer than the others. Very often, this is a sign of a tab that needs to be removed.

✓ A small space at the beginning or end of a line, which often results from having two or more consecutive spaces (especially, following a period when a sentence happens to end at the margin edge).

- ✓ Are there any unsupported characters? Look for boxes with question marks (?) inside them or streams of funny characters. Sometimes, characters that look fine on the Kindle Fire show up as ?'s on the Kindle and Kindle DX, for example. Look carefully for unsupported characters with all 7 (and more) options.
- ✓ Check that quotation marks are angled correctly. Also, check for consistency – don't mix the use of both straight and angled quotes.
- ✓ Test out the table of contents links, website hyperlinks, and links for email addresses (some of these may only function on the real devices and Kindle for PC, but not in the Kindle Previewer). Make sure that they work on the actual devices.
- ✓ If you used color, see if the colors look good on black-and-white devices.
- ✓ Are you satisfied with the size of the pictures on all devices? It's not too late to change.
- ✓ In Kindle for PC (and an actual device that has this option), go to View, click Show Display Options, and see how your eBook looks with White, Sepia, and Black backgrounds. Quickly browse through your entire eBook with each background to see how it looks. Check for images or colors that don't look nice on these backgrounds.

Also, use the convenient online previewer in Step 6. Don't trust the online previewer – trust the downloadable previewer, Kindle for PC, and especially the actual device. The convenient online previewer does mimic the device screen, which can help give you a feel for the aesthetics and check how large images look compared to screen sizes.

When proofing your eBook – with any of the options that we discussed – try changing the font size, switching between portrait and landscape, and other options. This will also help you gauge aesthetically the various ways that your eBook may appear to different customers.

Most formatting problems can be corrected by closely inspecting your original eBook file and making an adjustment. Other formatting issues can be resolved by tweaking the HTML (which we discussed briefly in Sec. 5.2.2). If you can't correct an issue that you see, try posting a question on the Formatting discussion in the KDP community help forum. There is a good chance that someone else has experienced a similar issue and found a solution.

After you upload your file to Kindle, you will see a list of possible spelling errors. Check this list, correct any mistakes, and ignore any that are actually correct until KDP tells you that there are now 0 spelling errors. (This does <u>not</u> mean that your book is free of mistakes.)

On page 2 of the KDP publishing process, look below the list prices in various countries to find the file size of your converted mobi file. If you wish to reduce this file size, the way to do it probably lies in picture compression, converting images to grayscale (small effect), or resizing or removing images.

It's very important to have your eBook perfected as much as possible prior to publishing. Mistakes in the Look Inside deter sales, and so do reviews that complain about formatting, spelling, or grammatical mistakes. If you take the time and effort to create buzz for your book, have a book launch party, send out advanced review copies, and succeed in having several sales when your eBook is first published, it will all backfire if it turns out that there are formatting or editing mistakes in the eBook.

The best time to submit corrections is prior to publishing. You can upload your cover and content files as often as you want. Once you publish, your original eBook will still be available for 12 to 24 hours (or more) after you submit revisions. So if you find any mistakes after publishing, they will be there for a day or so before the corrections take place.

After you publish your eBook, you should see what the published eBook looks like firsthand and check it very carefully.

Then there is one more thing that you have to preview: the Look Inside. First, view the Look Inside on your PC. If you have any mistakes in the Look Inside, you absolutely want to correct and update this. A common formatting problem on the Look Inside is an indented first paragraph of each chapter, even where you know you set First Line to 0.01".

Next, view the free sample on a Kindle device – or at least download the free sample file from Amazon and view the file on your PC (this is different from just clicking to Look Inside).

5.2.4 Making Revisions to Your eBook

You can revise your eBook after publishing. However, your original eBook will continue to be available until your submitted revisions go live – unless you first unpublish your eBook. Depending on where you publish your eBook, it may take quite some time to unpublish, also. If you have major issues, you should unpublish your eBook until you are able to resolve the issues so that no new customers experience those problems. (Obviously, the best course is to avoid the problems in the first place.) For minor issues, you just need to submit the revisions; don't worry about unpublishing. If you use an aggregator like Smashwords, once your eBook is distributed to various eBook stores, it may take much longer to submit revisions or unpublish. Therefore, you should check your eBook carefully as soon as it goes live with an aggregator and strive to correct any issues as soon as possible. When you submit revisions to just about any eBook publishing service, you will have to wait at least 12-24 hours for the revisions to go live before you can make any other changes to your eBook.

What if your files are fine, but you just want to revise your description, keywords, price, or other details? You still need to republish your eBook, unless you only want to change the description. For Amazon, the description can be changed using AuthorCentral (see Chapter 6).

Keep track of your files so that you always have a record of which version of the file is the most up-to-date. You'd hate to revise an older file by mistake, reintroducing old mistakes while correcting new ones. Save this list in at least two places in case you lose one (and when you update it, be sure to update both copies of the list).

Put some information on the copyright page to distinguish between the new and old versions of your eBook – such as "second edition," "updated on August 12, 2013," or "revised to include larger images." You can make this more subtle if you don't wish to advertise that minor corrections have been made. Either way, this information will help you determine if the Look Inside that you see on Amazon is the new version or the old one.

You may revise the interior file, cover file (for your thumbnail image), description, keywords, list price, DRM choice, and just about anything else (unless you have an ISBN, in which case you can't revise the title and shouldn't make drastic changes to the content) – in contrast to CreateSpace, where the title, subtitle, and contributors are locked after the ISBN option is selected. If you just want to modify your KDP Select enrollment, this can be done from your Bookshelf.

Note: **KDP now overrides the AuthorCentral description when you republish**. Save your AuthorCentral description (copy and paste the HTML into Word), then when your book goes live you can update it through AuthorCentral.

How do you notify customers of changes? For Kindle, go to the KDP help pages and click the yellow Contact Us button in the bottom left corner. Select Publishing Your Book > Making Corrections and enter the ASIN for your eBook (you can find this number on your eBook's Amazon detail page, and copy/paste it). Enter a subject and type a message explaining very clearly what corrections have been made and that you wish to notify the customers of this change. KDP will do one of three things (but note that their action may take 4 weeks):

1. If they decide that the changes are major, KDP will email customers to notify them that the book update exists (remember, this can take a month). Customers will be able to get the update at the Managing Your Kindle page on Amazon.

2. If they decide that the issues are minor, KDP will not email customers. However, customers can still obtain the update from Managing Your Kindle.

3. If your eBook has critical issues (this can happen if customers complain about your eBook, even if you didn't contact KDP), KDP will make your eBook unavailable for sale until you notify them that the eBook has been revised. KDP will then review the corrections and either ask you to make further revisions or notify customers by email that an update is available.

5.2.5 Getting Help with Your eBook

Try posting a question on the Kindle community forum. There are many authors and small publishers who frequent those forums and regularly share their expertise. You can also meet fellow authors. There is also professional eBook formatting help available. For example, go to the KDP help pages and click Preparing Your Book > Conversion Resources for a list of companies that offer such services.

Chapter 6

Creating Author Pages

Chapter Overview

6.1 Creating an Author Page at Amazon
6.2 Creating Your Own Websites

This chapter answers questions about the following topics, and more:

- ☑ How to create an author page at Amazon.[9]
- ☑ Advantages of creating an author page at Amazon, like being able to track sales.
- ☑ Creating a biography, choosing and uploading photos, monitoring sales information, reviewing feedback, and adding feeds to blog posts on your Amazon author page.
- ☑ Formatting your book's description with boldface, italics, and basic HTML.
- ☑ Developing a blog that can attract members of your target audience.
- ☑ Writing blog posts and feeding them into your Amazon author page.
- ☑ Setting up your CreateSpace[9] eStore.
- ☑ Creating a website for a personal author page or publishing company on the internet.
- ☑ Linking your CreateSpace eStore and Amazon listings from your website.
- ☑ Benefits of driving traffic to your book's Amazon page instead of your CreateSpace eStore or selling in person.
- ☑ Making effective use of social media, such as Facebook and Twitter.[9]
- ☑ Setting up an author page and Goodreads[9] and using free author tools there.
- ☑ Including your books on social websites, like Facebook pages.
- ☑ Driving traffic to your blog, author website, and social media websites.

---

[9] Amazon,™ CreateSpace,™ Facebook,™ Goodreads,™ and Twitter™ are trademarks and brands of their respective owners. Neither this book, *A Detailed Guide to Self-Publishing with Amazon and Other Online Booksellers*, nor its author, Chris McMullen, are in any way affiliated with any of these companies.

6.1 Creating an Author Page at Amazon

6.1.1 Setting Up Your AuthorCentral Account

You can and should create an Author Page on Amazon. AuthorCentral is an Amazon program designed especially for authors. You don't have to be a famous author to have your own Author Page. Sign up at

https://authorcentral.amazon.com

There are several benefits of joining AuthorCentral:

➢ It's totally <u>free</u> (even though many authors would actually be willing to pay to join).

➢ Get access to graphs for sales rank history for print books sold in the U.S. There is even an option to see where your print books are selling geographically. (Although the sales rank is for print books, everything else at AuthorCentral applies to print and eBooks.)

➢ AuthorCentral provides email and daytime phone support for authors who sign up.

➢ Edit your description using boldface, italics, blank lines, and even basic HTML.

➢ Add your biography and author photos to your Author Page. Your biography and primary photo will show up on your book's detail page on Amazon, along with a link to your Author Page.

➢ Customers can learn more about you as an author by clicking on the link to your Author Page. In addition to your photos and biography, customers will be able to quickly find all of your books, and you can also add feeds from your blog and Twitter, videos, and information about author events (like book signings or tours).

➢ See your author rank to discover how you compare with other authors.

➢ Add editorial reviews, About the Author, From the Author, and From the Back Cover sections (all are optional) to your book's detail page on Amazon.

➢ Visit Shelfari to add Book Extras to your book's detail page.

You're a professional author now. Therefore, you should have your very own Author Page at Amazon. Make your book's detail page look more professional by having AuthorCentral include your photo, the beginning of your biography, and a link to your Author Page on your book's detail page on Amazon.

You can add an AuthorCentral account for a pen name. If you write in your own name and a pen name, for example, you can create separate accounts for each. This is very common when an author writes in two quite different genres, or when an author writes some books specifically geared toward adults and others that may also be suitable for a wider audience. You may have up to three AuthorCentral accounts linked to one email address.

When you login to AuthorCentral (after you sign up), you can claim books that you have written by going to the Books tab and clicking the yellow Add More Books button. Search for your books by typing in your name, the title of the book, or the ISBN or ASIN number for your book. Sort through the list of books carefully because there may be books on the list that you didn't write. If the paperback and Kindle editions of a book are linked together, you should only need to add one of these.

Note that a book can't be removed from AuthorCentral once you add it just because it's no longer in print. Suppose, for example, that you publish a paperback book, then later decide to unpublish it. If it was added to your AuthorCentral account, it will remain there forever. Amazon's reason for this is to help customers find all of the books that each author has written. Even though the book may be out of print, customers may still be able to buy it used. An eBook won't be available used if it's unpublished (unless Amazon starts permitting the customer resale of eBooks), so if your book is only available as an eBook and you unpublish it, you should ask AuthorCentral if they can remove it from your account in this case.

If you find any of my books on Amazon, you can explore my Author Page from there. Try finding Author Pages of other authors, including successful top selling authors – both traditionally and self-published. This way, you may see a variety of ways that different authors use AuthorCentral and get some ideas for what you can do with your own Author Page.

The big publishers have special privileges. As a result, you'll see a few things on their product pages – even things that their bestselling authors can do on those pages – that self-published authors can't do. Nonetheless, self-published authors do have a great variety of helpful tools available at AuthorCentral. In Sec. 6.1.4, we'll see that self-published authors can improve their product pages using formatting tools at AuthorCentral.

As an example of what a bestselling, traditionally-published author can do, check out *The Eighty-Dollar Champion* by Elizabeth Letts. Obviously, you can't say *New York Times* Bestseller like Ballantine Books put in her description (unless, of course, your book actually becomes a *New York Times* Bestseller). If you look further down the detail page for her book – in her editorial reviews – you will see that she has an Amazon.com review, which is actually a letter from the author herself. You won't be permitted to post an Amazon.com review this way (or review your own book). However, there is a From the Author section on AuthorCentral that you can use, and if you have legitimate reviews that qualify as editorial reviews, you can include them in the editorial reviews section. You can also achieve professional formatting in the blurb and other sections available from AuthorCentral, such as Elizabeth Letts has on her book's detail page (see Sec. 6.1.4). We'll return to the subject of editorial reviews in Sec. 6.1.7.

You can make a highly professional detail page for your book on Amazon using features available on AuthorCentral. The main thing that will probably be lacking on your page compared to traditionally published books and bestsellers is the number of editorial reviews and the distinguished sources of those reviews.

To find authors who use AuthorCentral extensively, try visiting Shelfari (there is a link to it from AuthorCentral), since this is where authors go to add book extras to their Author Pages at Amazon. Search for those authors on Amazon to see what their Author Pages look like.

Also, AuthorCentral has a few example pages. After logging into AuthorCentral, click the Help tab and you will find a few samples of Author Pages illustrating what you can do with them.

Note that you must be at least 18 years old in order to use AuthorCentral. See other eligibility requirements when you read the terms and conditions presented during sign-up.

6.1.2 AuthorCentral in Other Countries

In addition to creating an Author Page at Amazon US, you should also add an Author Page through AuthorCentral at Amazon UK. The link for UK's AuthorCentral is

https://authorcentral.amazon.co.uk

Unfortunately, you must separately login to AuthorCentral at each country's AuthorCentral site; your US Author Page does not automatically show up at Amazon's websites in other countries. However, once you login (using the same account as in the US), your AuthorCentral account in each country will be able to locate your list of books from your US AuthorCentral account. At least, you won't have to individually add all of your books for each country.

Not every country offers AuthorCentral. For example, presently AuthorCentral isn't available in Canada; but this may change in time. As of now, only the following countries provide Author Pages via AuthorCentral:

https://authorcentral.amazon.com (United States)
https://authorcentral.amazon.co.uk (United Kingdom)
https://authorcentral.amazon.fr (France)
https://authorcentral.amazon.de (Germany)
https://authorcentral.amazon.co.jp (Japan)

I just have Author Pages in the United States, United Kingdom, and France. Although I do sell a book in Germany or Japan occasionally, the vast majority of sales come from the United States and United Kingdom.

You will need to add your author photos and biography for AuthorCentral in each country. You may even choose to customize your biography for each country. If your books are in English, there really isn't any need to translate your biography into French, Spanish, or other languages – since anyone who can read your book will be able to read your biography in English. However, for non-English speaking countries, you may need some translation help in reading the website to understand what you're doing. Google's free translation service is better than nothing (for trying to understand the instructions – but using this service to translate your biography is not recommended). Also, by comparing controls in Amazon US with the other countries, you can often deduce the correspondence. Finally, try searching online for how to setup an AuthorCentral account in non-English speaking countries. By using an internet search engine such as Google, you may discover that other authors who have figured this out have posted instructions in English.

Note that your books won't show up under the main search results in non-English speaking countries (unless your books have been translated to the relevant language), but will show up as books in a foreign language. Social media that can be fed into your Author Page at Amazon US may not feed into your Author Pages for other countries. For example, presently only Twitter can be fed into your Author Page in the United Kingdom.

6.1.3 Adding Your Biography and Author Photos

Think about your image as an author as you search for a suitable photo (or take some new photos) and prepare your biography. Strive to come across as likeable, credible, competent, and professional. Look for an image that suggests these qualities, and prepare a biography that suggests this, too. Realize that the photo and biography – like just about everything else that you do – relate in a small way (but every way counts!) to marketing. Your photo helps to establish your brand as an author. Recognition is important. The more often readers see your photo – on Amazon, on your blog, on your website, etc. – the more likely they are to recognize you. Products often sell from recognition (kind of like laundry detergent – most customers go with a brand they remember having heard before).

Select a photo of yourself – readers want to see the person behind the words. They don't expect you to look like a model; they are interested in reading your ideas, not dating you for your looks. You should present yourself well so that you appear professional. It can be a head-and-shoulders shot, but doesn't need to be close-up; go with what you feel comfortable with, and explore what other authors have done. You can have your photo touched up, if done so that it appears professional. The photo should definitely be well-lit, any red-eye must be removed, the photo needs to be cropped nicely, you should look good against the background, the photo has to be clean (no stray marks, for example), and the background must look appropriate. Using a quality photo does make a difference.

If you're particularly self-conscious, there are a variety of ways to get a nice image of you – like getting a professional, low-cost sketch (along with written permission to use the sketch for this purpose). Whatever you choose to do, make sure that you come across as likeable, credible, competent, and professional – and also look like someone who may write a book in your genre. You can get a little personality into your photo, but it will only work out well if you meet the aforementioned criteria.

Try changing your photo after a month if you have any doubts about it, and see if it seems to have an impact on sales. I've tried changing my author photo a few times, and observed that the sales of some of my books can be significantly affected by the author photo.

Get input about your photo and biography from family, friends, acquaintances, and – perhaps this is more important – complete strangers who can provide honest feedback. The more credible you appear as the author of the type of book you wrote, the better.

You may load up to four different photos for your Author Page. Only the primary photo will display on the book's detail page; the other photos will be seen if shoppers click to see them on your Author Page. Remember that you must separately add photos for your Author Page in the United States, United Kingdom, and any other countries where you have an Author Page.

Go to the Profile tab after logging in at AuthorCentral to add photos. Click Add Photo to insert photos. If you have multiple photos, click Manage to reorder them or delete them; just drag to reorder or drag down to the indicated space to delete. The leftmost image will serve as your primary author photo.

Write your biography in the third person so that it sounds like someone else wrote it. You can also ask someone else to write it, but that's only a good idea if they write biographies well; if you do this, be sure to get written permission to use the biography for this purpose.

Your biography can help to establish your credibility as an author in your genre. Don't brag, though: Let your work speak for itself. You may list relevant, truthful qualifications and expertise, if you have any. Readers don't expect you to have a degree in English if you're writing fiction; while qualifications are particularly important for most nonfiction. Do you have relevant experience? For fiction, life experience can be implied from your biography. What qualifies you to write this book? For example, if you are detective or police officer, this may be relevant for a mystery. Have you spent a noteworthy (above average) amount of time researching your book, or working with editors, for example? Such things may fit in as minor points in your overall biography, but one minor point can make a difference.

The biography is not just about expertise and experience, though – especially, in fiction. If you have relevant expertise or experience (or even awards), you want to mention it, but the biography shouldn't just be devoted to this. Some readers are curious to learn more about the author – what the author does, hobbies, background, etc. These things give the reader an opportunity to relate to you in some way, or to want to share part of your unique experience. For example, if you happen to mention that you grew up in Brooklyn, this can attract interest two ways: "Hey, I lived in Brooklyn for a few years," or, "I wonder what it would be like to grow up in Brooklyn." When you meet a stranger, do you appreciate it when you discover that you have something in common? How about when you discover something unique?

You can also get your personality into your biography and have a little fun with it. However, you must appear likeable, credible, competent, professional, and ultimately like an author in your genre; don't let your personality and fun betray these qualities. Biographies do have a tendency to come across as boring for many readers, so if you're able to present yours in a way that interests readers – while still meeting the above criteria regarding your image as the author – that can be a plus (it bodes well for the actual book being interesting, too).

It's important to proofread your biography carefully, get proofreading help, and receive feedback on it. This, along with your blurb, will be highly visible, so these are important for marketing. Any mistakes in these relatively short writing samples (compared to the length of the book) may suggest major editing and formatting issues in the book itself. Give readers every reason to Look Inside, and strive not to give any reasons for them to walk away.

Note that only a fraction of your biography will be immediately visible, while the rest will only be read by customers who click the Read More link (unless you have a very short biography). By viewing other Author Pages, you can get a sense for approximately how much will show up front versus what will be hidden. There will be customers who read the visible portion, but who don't click to read more; and what is included in the visible portion may also influence how many customers decide to read the rest. Therefore, you might consider which parts of your biography should appear in this visible portion, while also ensuring that your biography is well-organized.

Go to the Profile tab in AuthorCentral to add or update your biography. After you add your biography, note that the Read More link doesn't quite coincide with the position of the Read More link that will appear on your book's detail page (although it is pretty close). Furthermore, the Read More link will be in a slightly different position on your book's detail page compared to your Author Page (but again, it will be close).

Unfortunately, you can't format your biography with boldface, italics, or even basic HTML; but you can apply this formatting to the About the Author, product description, and other features available in the Books tab (as described in the following section).

Note that AuthorCentral and CreateSpace both allow you to enter an About the Author section that is different from your biography. If you submit both of these, they will both appear on your book's detail page. It might not look professional to have two copies of the same biography. The one to remove, if any, is the About the Author section. It's okay to have both if they aren't completely redundant. The About the Author section might be much shorter, with the biography more elaborate, for example. If you publish a variety of books, you might cater the About the Author section to specific books. There is another possibility for books that have coauthors: Describe each author briefly in the About the Author Section, while each author has his/her own Author Page (multiple author pages *can* show on the same book's detail page). If so, separate the About the Author into paragraphs using AuthorCentral.

6.1.4 Formatting Your Blurb

Go to the Books tab in AuthorCentral to format or otherwise revise the description for one of your books. Click on the book. If it's available in multiple editions – e.g. paperback and eBook – you'll have to click each edition and edit the descriptions separately. Click the Edit button next to Product Description.

AuthorCentral allows you to format your description and other written sections (like About the Author or From the Back Cover) with *italics*, **boldface**, numbered lists, simple bullets, and even some basic HTML. When you type a description at CreateSpace, it shows up as a single paragraph at Amazon even if you see separate paragraphs at CreateSpace (unless you use HTML at CreateSpace). Your AuthorCentral blurb can have up to 4000 characters.

Update: KDP now supports HTML blurbs (the same HTML as AuthorCentral, except that if you use the Enter key in the KDP description, it will add an additional linespace). However, KDP doesn't show a preview. Note that if you republish your book at KDP, the KDP description will override the AuthorCentral description (and your AuthorCentral description will be lost). Copy and paste the HTML from your AuthorCentral description into the KDP description before republishing. An advantage of using HTML in the description at CreateSpace is that it will propagate to Amazon UK, BN.com, and other retailers. The HTML for the CreateSpace description works just like AuthorCentral, except that you must use <br/> instead of <br />.

Don't copy/paste text directly from Word or most other programs into AuthorCentral; copy/paste from Notepad instead to remove hidden formatting that will cause problems and delays (but see how it looks in Word at some stage to help catch spelling/grammar issues).

Keep your paragraphs short in the description and separate them by blank linespaces. In Compose mode, use the Enter key to create linebreaks; in HTML mode, use
 (put a space before it – AuthorCentral's HTML has a few idiosyncrasies) to do this (use it twice in a row following a paragraph for a blank line). Note that the Enter key won't start a new line if you're in HTML mode. Don't end a line in mid-sentence to force the sentence onto the next line.

Only very limited HTML works in AuthorCentral. It's generally best to avoid paragraph <p> tags in AuthorCentral's HTML. Some basic HTML that works in AuthorCentral includes:

- ❖ **Boldface**: type bold phrase here
- ❖ *Italics*: <i>type italicized phrase here</i>
- ❖ Linebreak: Type
 (with a space first) precisely where you want the line to break.
- ❖ Numbered or bulleted lists, <ol> and <ul>. It may be simpler to do this with Compose.

Following is an example of the effect that formatting can have on a description. This description is for a chemistry book, and is much longer than most effective descriptions in fiction and entertaining or less technical nonfiction. First, see it unformatted:

OVERVIEW: This eBook focuses on fundamental chemistry concepts, such as understanding the periodic table of the elements and how chemical bonds are formed. No prior knowledge of chemistry is assumed. The mathematical component involves only basic arithmetic. The content is much more conceptual than mathematical. AUDIENCE: This eBook is geared toward helping anyone – student or not – to understand the main ideas of chemistry. Both students and non-students may find it helpful to be able to focus on understanding the main concepts without the constant emphasis on computations that is generally found in chemistry lectures and textbooks. CONTENTS: (1) Understanding the organization of the periodic table, including trends and patterns. (2) Understanding ionic/covalent bonds and how they are formed, including the structure of valence electrons. (3) A set of rules to follow to speak the language of chemistry fluently: How to name compounds when different types of compounds follow different naming schemes. (4) Understanding chemical reactions, including how to balance them and a survey of important reactions. (5) Understanding the three phases of matter: properties of matter, amorphous and crystalline solids, ideal gases, liquids, solutions, and acids/bases. (6) Understanding atomic/nuclear structure and how it relates to chemistry. (7) VErBAl ReAcTiONS: A brief fun diversion from science for the verbal side of the brain, using symbols from chemistry's periodic table to make word puzzles. ANSWERS: Every chapter includes self-check exercises to offer practice and help the reader check his or her understanding. 100% of the exercises have answers at the back of the book. LENGTH: The paperback edition of this eBook has 176 pages. COPYRIGHT: All rights are reserved by the author. However, teachers who purchase one copy of this book or borrow one copy of this book from a library may reproduce selected pages for the purpose of teaching chemistry concepts to their own students. FORMATS: This book is available in paperback in 5.5" x 8.5" (portable size), 8.5" x 11" (large size), and as an eBook. The details of the figures – including the periodic tables – are most clear in the large size and large print edition. However, the eBook is in color, whereas the paperback editions are in black-and-white.

Here is the same description with formatting:

OVERVIEW: This eBook focuses on fundamental chemistry concepts, such as understanding the periodic table of the elements and how chemical bonds are formed. No prior knowledge of chemistry is assumed. The mathematical component involves only basic arithmetic. The content is much more conceptual than mathematical.

AUDIENCE: This eBook is geared toward helping anyone – student or not – to understand the main ideas of chemistry. Both students and non-students may find it helpful to be able to focus on understanding the main concepts without the constant emphasis on computations that is generally found in chemistry lectures and text-books.

CONTENTS:
(1) Understanding the organization of the periodic table, including trends and patterns.
(2) Understanding ionic/covalent bonds and how they are formed, including the structure of valence electrons.
(3) A set of rules to follow to speak the language of chemistry fluently: How to name compounds when different types of compounds follow different naming schemes.
(4) Understanding chemical reactions, including how to balance them and a survey of important reactions.
(5) Understanding the three phases of matter: properties of matter, amorphous and crystalline solids, ideal gases, liquids, solutions, and acids/bases.
(6) Understanding atomic/nuclear structure and how it relates to chemistry.
(7) VErBAl ReAcTiONS: A brief fun diversion from science for the verbal side of the brain, using symbols from chemistry's periodic table to make word puzzles.

ANSWERS: Every chapter includes self-check exercises to offer practice and help the reader check his or her understanding. 100% of the exercises have answers at the back of the book.

LENGTH: The paperback edition of this eBook has 176 pages.

COPYRIGHT: All rights are reserved by the author. However, teachers who purchase one copy of this book or borrow one copy of this book from a library may reproduce selected pages for the purpose of teaching chemistry concepts to their own students.

FORMATS: This book is available in paperback in 5.5" x 8.5" (portable size), 8.5" x 11" (large size), and as an eBook. The details of the figures – including the periodic tables – are most clear in the large size and large print edition. However, the eBook is in color, whereas the paperback editions are in black-and-white.

You can apply boldface, italics, linebreaks, numbered lists, and bulleted lists to the About the Author, From the Back Cover, and other sections available in AuthorCentral, too – but note that you can't apply this formatting in the author's biography in the Profile tab. **Note**: KDP overrides AuthorCentral's description when republishing, so save it before republishing.

6.1.5 Monitoring Sales, Sales Rank, Author Rank, and Reviews

AuthorCentral is a convenient place to see the Amazon sales rank and reviews for all of your books – both print books and eBooks – at once. It also shows you your author rank and provides BookScan statistics for print books. The BookScan data even has an option to see how your books sell by geographic area in the United States.

One way to see the current sales rank for all of your books – including both print and eBook editions – is to select the Books tab. If you have paperback and Kindle editions linked together, you will have to click on the book and then select the other edition to see its sales rank. Another way to find sales rank is to choose the Sales Info tab and then click Rank Over Time below Sales Rank. Use the drop-down menu to view all of your books or to select one. There is even a third way to view your sales rank: In the Rank tab, click Sales Over Time under Sales Rank. These last two options also show how your sales rank is doing compared to the previous day: A number in green shows improvement, while a number in red shows a drop.

The lower the sales rank, the better. We will discuss Amazon sales rank in detail in Sec. 7.1.4, including the correlation between sales rank and sales frequency.

You can also find your BookScan data for print sales in the United States in the Sales Info tab. There are some sales that don't show in the BookScan data – like used books sales – as explained in the Help tab under Sales Information. Although it says "Books published through CreateSpace" under "Sales figures do not include," CreateSpace books sold through Amazon (at least) will show up in these reports if your books have the Expanded Distribution channel enabled (if not, then sales may not be reported here). The important thing is that BookScan data for sales does not reflect eBook sales.

You can click Weekly Sales or Sales by Geography under BookScan Data in the Sales Info tab, and you can also choose data from the last 4 weeks or up to all available data (from the inception of the program). Seeing your print sales by geography provides useful information about where your audience resides. Most of my sales are made in New York. I also have very strong sales support from California, which may be influenced a little by the fact that I was born and raised there. My Louisiana sales clearly reflect that I live and teach here, and this probably extends into my Dallas and Houston sales, too. In general, authors sell most of their books in major metropolitan areas like New York City, Los Angeles, and Chicago.

Of course, you can also see your sales reports for CreateSpace books by logging into your account at CreateSpace, and similarly you can login to KDP, Nook Press, Smashwords, and anywhere else that you may have published eBooks to see your eBook sales reports. One nice feature of the sales rank and sales info stats available at AuthorCentral is that you can corroborate sales (and sales spikes in the sales rank) with royalties that are reported.[10]

You can find your Author Rank in the Rank tab. Select as little as two weeks or up to all available data. As with sales rank, the lower the number, the better. See Sec. 7.1.4 regarding how to interpret you Author Rank.

If you have multiple books, you may appreciate that you can see all of the customer reviews at Amazon for all of your titles (at least, those registered to your AuthorCentral account) in the Customer Reviews tab. There is a noticeable delay between the time that the review first shows on Amazon and the time it appears on AuthorCentral, but the convenience for multi-book authors is easily worth the delay. We will discuss customer reviews in depth in Sec. 7.1.6.

6.1.6 Feeding Blog and Twitter Posts into Your Author Page

AuthorCentral allows authors to feed their blog and Twitter posts into their Author Pages. Do this from the Profile tab. All RSS and Atom blog feeds are supported.

If you have a blog that is relevant to your work as an author, feed it into your Author Page by clicking Add Blog beside Blogs. You should get a blog if you don't already have one (see Sec. 6.2.2). Two of the most popular blogs for writers are WordPress and Blogspot (or Blogger); I will discuss how to setup these feeds into your AuthorCentral account. For other blogs, you can learn how to do this by consulting their help pages or looking for the universal RSS feed icon (an orange square with white broadcast marks) where you run your blog.

For WordPress, simply add /feed/ to the end of your blog's url. For example, my Word-Press site is http://chrismcmullen.wordpress.com, so the feed for my WordPress blog is http://chrismcmullen.wordpress.com/feed/. The feeds for Blogspot (or Blogger) have the form http://yourblogname.blogspot.com/feeds/posts/default?alt=rss (or the same without the ?alt=rss). For example, my blog's name at Blogger is McMullen4D, so my Blogger feed is http://mcmullen4d.blogspot.com/feeds/posts/default?alt=rss.

You can actually feed multiple blogs into your AuthorCentral page. I have one blog at WordPress and another at Blogger, and feed both into my Author Page.

Your three most recent blog posts will show up on your Author Page. There may be a delay of up to about 24 hours after you post before it shows up at Amazon.

---

[10] However, there may be occasional inconsistencies. For example, returns and used books affect sales rank, but don't show on your royalty report. Rarely, Amazon chooses to source a new sale made directly from Amazon through a third party. When this happens, CreateSpace doesn't report the royalty until Expanded Distribution royalties are reported, which can be a delay of two months. At this time, CreateSpace will correctly report the royalty as being an Amazon royalty instead of an Expanded Distribution channel royalty. Remember, this is rare.

After you add your blog feed(s) to AuthorCentral, any new posts will show up on your Author Page within 24 hours of the post, but any that you posted prior to adding the feed to AuthorCentral will not show up unless you repost them.

If you encounter problems with the blog feeds, select the Help tab and then click on Your Blog Feeds under Your Author Profile. The last three paragraphs that begin with "if" discuss common issues and how to solve them.

To add a Twitter feed, go to the Profile tab and click Add Account beside Twitter. Simply enter your username. Your most recent Tweet will show in addition to your three most recent blog posts (if you have both blog and Twitter feeds).

Note that there are differences in AuthorCentral functionality between countries. For example, you can add Twitter in the UK, but not blogs.

6.1.7 More AuthorCentral Goodies

Here are some more things that you can do with AuthorCentral:

- ➢ You can add Book Extras through Shelfari.com. Click the Books tab, select a book, choose the Book Extras tab, and click the Visit Shelfari.com link (or the Learn More link to find out more about Shelfari). The Book Extras might only show up if several of these fields are completed at Shelfari. A spoiler alert should show at the top of any Book Extra that spoils the plot – like the Ridiculously Simplified Synopsis (if not, mark it as a spoiler). You can easily go overboard with the biography, About the Author, From the Author, From the Back Cover, and all of the Book Extras. Some of these features may be more relevant for your book than others. Also check out what other authors have done.
- ➢ Editorial reviews from **reputable sources** can be added from the Books tab by clicking on a Book and then the Add button next to Reviews. Quote just 1-2 sentences – but adhere to the "fair use" copyright guidelines – in quotation marks, then use a dash to cite the source (as in the example at the top of the window where you add the review). There is a 600-character limit. Remember only to copy/paste from Notepad (not Word) in order to avoid formatting complications and delays.
- ➢ Add events like book signings, appearances, and presentations that relate to your work as an author in the Profile tab. If you do a book signing, for example, get a photo that you can use (with written permission, if someone else takes it). That could be one of the photos on your profile to help establish your credibility as a professional author. Your events help to convey this, too – in addition to spreading word of the events to your fans and new readers.
- ➢ In the Profile tab, you can also add a video – a book trailer, footage from a book signing, or an author interview, for example.

> ➢ The Help tab may also come in handy. For one, you will find a Contact Us button. There is also handy information on the Help page, such as Reporting Copyright Infringement.
> ➢ Click the Profile tab and update your Author Page URL. Share this link to your page.

6.2 Creating Your Own Websites

6.2.1 Different Types of Author Websites

There are different types of websites that you can use to help market your book and establish your image and brand as an author. A very common type of website that most writers have is a blog. There are several free blog sites that allow authors (and others) to express themselves with images and text. Blogs can be helpful in a variety of ways, as we will learn in Sec. 6.2.2. Every writer should maintain a blog, and it's a simple way to get started online.

The next step beyond the blog is to have an author website. Some authors refer to their own website and really mean their blog site; a blog essentially is a website, and the url for it can even be www.yourname.com – just like a major website. However, in this book, when I refer to an author website, I will mean more than just a blog. The distinction that I have in mind is offering much more content on the author website than is available on a typical blog. We'll discuss maintaining a website for the author, book, and/or imprint in Sec. 6.2.3. I recommend having both a blog and a separate website with additional content; the blog can also be fed into the website (and AuthorCentral, and elsewhere). It's a good idea to first develop the blog site, and then develop a website (as we'll see, you can do this for free, and get hosting with free tools so that you don't have to do any technical "developing" by yourself) with additional content.

Your online presence may also extend into your CreateSpace eStore (Sec. 6.2.4), Goodreads (Sec. 6.2.5) and similar websites, social media (Sec. 6.2.6), and elsewhere. We'll consider some of the "and elsewhere" in Chapter 8, such as making a video for YouTube and writing articles online (which can be highly effective).

6.2.2 Start Out By Blogging

A blog is a great way to begin developing your online presence as an author because it's easy to get started and maintain, and you can do it mostly by writing a little bit here and there – exactly the kind of work that writers enjoy doing. Starting out with easy things that lie in your comfort zone is a good way to get the ball rolling.

Two very popular blogging sites among writers are WordPress and Blogspot (or Blogger). There are several others, too, such as Posterous and Tumblr. There are many advantages of using the two main blog hosts – WordPress and Blogspot – when you start out. For example, they are free, highly regarded, include many helpful features, and because a large number of writers and readers already use them, this can help your beginning blog get noticed.

You don't have to choose just one blog. Presently, I have two: I blog about writing at WordPress and math at Blogspot. My writing blog relates to my self-publishing books and my recent fictional works – *Romancing the Novel* (soon to be released) and *Why Do We Have to Go to School?* – while my math blog relates to my math workbooks – the *Improve Your Math Fluency Series* – and general science books – *Understand Basic Chemistry Concepts* and *An Introduction to Basic Astronomy Concepts*. I feed both of these blogs into my Author Page at Amazon. I update my writing blog more frequently than my math blog.

I recommend starting out with WordPress or Blogspot (aka Blogger), then once you get the hang of that, you should have both – widen your market this way. Differentiate between the two blogs, at least a little bit. Use the same author image and show the same book covers – recognition and repetition are important for establishing your brand. What you might do differently is develop your writing and pictures (other than your author picture and covers) around different concepts. You can widen your presence by adding more blogs, but then it becomes more challenging to juggle your blogs, writing, social media, and other marketing activities. Successful writers are very busy doing many other things besides just writing.

WordPress and Blogspot share some similarities, but do have some important differences. Personally, I like WordPress's system of Likes and Follows, which shows a little icon with the person's avatar. At WordPress, underneath each post, you see a table of photos of people who Liked that post; it's very easy to follow a blog, and when someone follows your blog, you see their avatar and can easily click to check out their blogs. Blogspot, being Google's blog, features Google's Plus button and also has a system of following blogs; I guess I just find WordPress's visual layout for Likes and Follows a little more appealing. On the other hand, Blogspot has a few other features that I like better; each has its benefits.

I will discuss WordPress first, Blogspot second, and offer a little more blogging advice toward the end of this section.

Note that there are two WordPress sites – www.wordpress.com and www.wordpress.org. The .com site is free and provides free web hosting, whereas the .org site requires web hosting (which means you either need experience as a web developer so that you can provide your own hosting, or you need to find a hosting service). Using the .com site is free and easy; the .org site allows for greater flexibility and a much wider variety of options, but is essentially just like developing your own website (see Sec. 6.2.3). I will describe the free, easy .com site.

The first step is to choose the name for your blog's web address. My blog's name is my name, so the url is www.chrismcmullen.wordpress.com. You can get a domain without the "wordpress" in it if you're willing to invest a little money; WordPress offers free blog hosting, but they also provide several add-ons that bloggers can invest in. The free services are actually pretty good. If you plan to have an author website in addition to your blog, as described in Sec. 6.2.3, then it might be preferable to leave the "wordpress" in your blog's url. In my case, my website is www.chrismcmullen.com, which is different from my blog site, which has the "wordpress" in it. Both domain names feature my name – reinforcing my brand as an author – while the "wordpress" distinguishes the author website from the blog site.

Once you have already signed up, when you login to www.wordpress.com, there are Reader, Stats, My Blogs, and Freshly Pressed tabs at the left, and New Post, a notifications icon, and your author picture (once you add one) at the right. Place your cursor over your author picture (or the placeholder for it at the far right) to find Settings. Be sure to update the information under Public Profile, including your Public Display Name, About You, and Current Gravatar (place your image here).

Three very useful places to go after you login to WordPress's .com site are the My Blogs, Stats, and Reader tab.

Compose and edit posts in the My Blogs tab. From there, you can quickly edit posts or view and approve comments. Click on the number of posts to see all of your posts and also find options for changing the appearance of your blog, for example. Clicking the Add New button from this page is the best place to add a new post – better than clicking the convenient New Post button at the top of just about every page. The workspace is larger and you can easily add tags and keywords this way. Just to be clear, go to My Blogs, select the icon that shows how many posts you have, and click Add New next to Posts at the top of the page; don't click the New Post button from any page.

There are many formatting options available, and you can add images and videos, too. Click the Preview button before you publish your post. Don't underestimate the importance of editing anything you post online. If you want to establish your credibility as a writer, it's important for all of your writing to look well-edited. Be sure to select a handful of relevant categories and tags for your post. On subsequent posts, you can check categories that you've used previously and click a link to choose from your most frequently used tags. Check the boxes to show likes and sharing buttons at the bottom of the page. At the bottom right, you can set a featured image, which could help with your image branding (see Sec. 8.1.6).

From the page that shows your posts (click the My Blogs tab and then the button that shows the number of posts), you can find other helpful options, such as Appearance. Select a theme that fits with your image as an author and the types of books and blogs that you write. You can find several valuable tools in Widgets. Following is a list of some handy widgets. Find them when you click on Widgets in Appearance. Drag the Widget to the Sidebar on the right side of the screen. Reorder the Widgets in the Sidebar by clicking and dragging. Place your cursor over your name/photo in the top right corner and select your domain on the bottom of the list to see what your site looks like. First, I recommend exploring a variety of other blogs to see what other bloggers do. This might give you some helpful ideas (but don't be a copycat).

- ➢ Follow Blog allows readers to follow your blog by email.
- ➢ My Community makes a table of avatars from your blog's community.
- ➢ Gravatar shows your author photo and About Me description.
- ➢ Recent Posts provides links to your latest blog articles, images, and videos.
- ➢ Top Posts & Pages highlights your most popular blog posts.
- ➢ Blog Stats displays a counter for the total number of views on your website.
- ➢ Search allows visitors to find specific information in your posts.
- ➢ Archives is a nice way to consolidate your older posts.
- ➢ Twitter feeds your Tweets into your blog.
- ➢ Facebook Like Box connects readers to your Facebook page.

The Stats tab provides a nice analysis of pageviews, both numerically and geographically. See how many followers your blog has at the bottom of this page.

In the Reader tab, you can choose just to view blogs from those you Follow or in your favorite categories, for example. Check this out each time you login to see what writers you Follow have recently posted. One way to get noticed is to click Like when you read a blog post that you enjoy and click to Follow blogs that interest you. A few writers expect everybody to reciprocate to every Follow, but this is unrealistic. There are a couple of good reasons to just Follow blogs that truly interest you. For one, people will know that you really like their posts, and aren't just hoping for reciprocity. Also, what you choose to Like and Follow is part of your brand. If you Like something controversial, for example, this can impact your image. It's okay to Follow several blogs, and a wide variety of blogs, including many far outside of your writing interests – like photography or investments. Just have your image in mind with all of your online behavior because the internet has a very long and far-reaching memory.

The notifications icon near your name at the top right will light up when someone Likes one of your posts, Follows your blog, or makes a Comment. Simply click on the notifications icon when it lights up. It will also show you when you reach new milestones, such as 50 Likes, 20 Follows, or 10 Likes in one day; this gives you something to look forward to even if things progress slowly at first.

When you click on the notifications icon, click on the notification, and then click on the user id to go to that person's blog. If you like their blog, you can easily Follow it by clicking the Follow link next to their user id that appears next to the notification.

Now let's turn our attention to Google's Blogspot, also referred to as Blogger.[11] You'll get the most benefits by signing up for Google Plus (it's free). After you sign up with Blogger and create your own free domain, when you login you will see your blog site and your reading list for blogs that you follow. Click on the domain name for your blog to see stats, change the

---

[11] Whether you search for Blogspot or Blogger, you wind up at the same website. The technical distinction is that Blogspot provides the domain service, which has to be used with the publishing platform Blogger, while it's possible to use a different domain service with Blogger.

layout (the option for this is on the left), and find other helpful tools and information – like the links under Blogger Guide (on the right). When you click Layout, you will find a list of handy Gadgets that you can add, such as:

➢ Profile (at the bottom of the list) displays your photo and About Me section.
➢ +1 Button is Google's version of the Like.
➢ Google+ Followers lets readers follow your blog and also highlights your Followers.
➢ Follow By Email provides a convenient way for people to keep up with your blog.
➢ Google+ Badge shows others that you're signed up with Google Plus.
➢ Translate is handy for potential readers who don't speak English.
➢ Popular Posts collects the links of your blog's best content.
➢ Blog's Stats displays the total number of times that your blog has been viewed.
➢ Search Box makes it easy for others to search your blog for specific information.
➢ AdSense allows you to earn a little money by displaying advertisements. This may be viable if and when you become fortunate enough to develop an extremely popular blog (e.g. if it goes viral). Otherwise, advertisements may deter readers and followers.

Don't be surprised if your blog develops very slowly; this is very typical of many very good bloggers. You may receive just a few Likes and Follows with each of your first several posts. It takes time for your blog to be discovered and for your following to grow. Similarly, don't expect the blog to drive instant sales or to drive many sales. Your blog isn't a tool that, used by itself, will reap many instant rewards. However, blogging does play a valuable role in your overall marketing campaign, offers some important indirect benefits, and helps to establish your brand and credibility as an author. It's also easy to do and a comfortable way to get started with your online marketing.

What you choose to do with your blog can be quite significant. Posts about your upcoming book, interviews, contests, and other direct marketing should be infrequent – no more than 10% of your posts. Blogging about yourself or what you're doing like a daily journal probably won't attract new readers and may not even interest your current fans (but you should do this occasionally to appear human) – unless you happen to be a celebrity. Using your blog as a fan page also probably won't work well until you become a famous author. Fans can learn more about you at Goodreads, follow you on Twitter, and Like your Facebook author or book page, for example, so you really don't need to use your blog that way.

Identify your target audience. Which people are most likely to read your book if they discover it? Answering this question and finding your target audience is the key to marketing. Your blog isn't the most effective way to reach them, but everything ties together and it's a start. You should be blogging with your target audience in mind. Prepare content that will interest your target audience; this same content should be of interest to your present fans.

Spend some time thinking about content that is relevant to the books that you write, which will attract your target audience. Avoid duplicating content from your books; a little crossover is okay. You want to develop useful content in your blog, with the hope that some readers who appreciate this will want more and check out your book. A typical post should be about 300 to 1000 words in length. Most readers aren't looking to read more than 1000 words in a blog. An occasional fun short post is okay. If you post poems, you may have shorter posts.

Nonfiction blogs have an advantage – these pull readers in who want to learn how to do something or are curious about a topic. If you write fiction, you might consider what nonfiction posts you can write that relate to your topic or genre and are relevant for your intended audience. Poets can post short poems, but don't give away too much for free if you also want to sell collections.

Look at what expertise or special knowledge you have, which others in your target audience may want to know and relates to the books that you write. If you write fiction, at the very least you have knowledge and experience that relates to the genre that you write in and the topics involved in your books.

Fiction writers can occasionally post some fiction. This can be a very short story, a very short piece to work on character development and solicit feedback, or a chance for you to explore a different type of writing. If you're hoping for feedback, respectfully ask for readers to please post some comments, explaining that you would appreciate some feedback. At the same time, if you receive brutally honest criticism, absolutely do not sacrifice your image as an author by retaliating, making any negative comments, or showing any poor behavior. If you react this way – which can be natural, because your work is personal and we tend to take pride in our work – take a couple of days off from the computer before responding, and then only respond with a brief thank you note. An author who exhibits any form of bad behavior online can find a quick end to his or her writing career; see Sec. 7.1.6. Keep in mind that it's difficult to develop an audience by writing exclusively fiction on your blog.

Your blog should have a main theme, which is relevant to your writing. It's okay to have some fun, show some personality, and offer some variety, so long as you keep a main theme that relates to your writing and maintains your author image. You want to appear knowledgeable in your genre, credible as a writer, and professional. Since your blog is your territory, you can and should be personal – interact with people who post comments, but be courteous and professional.[12] See how other authors do this on their blogs.

Keep in mind that your last three posts will feed into Amazon (provided that you activate this feature at AuthorCentral – see Sec. 6.1.6). Ideally, you should always have one post with valuable content for your target audience in these last three links. Your blog doesn't just help a little to drive sales; customers from Amazon may also discover your blog. Include the url for your blog in the About the Author sections of your books. Post a link to your blog at Facebook, Twitter, and your author website. Feed your blog into your Author Page at AuthorCentral, Goodreads, and elsewhere. Everything ties in together, and traffic can go both ways.

---

[12] Commenting on customer reviews at Amazon or Goodreads is a different story, and can cause many problems, as we will explore in Chapter 7 and Sec. 6.2.5.

Choose a name for your blog that's easy to spell and remember, and use the same author photo that you use elsewhere to help establish a recognized image – your brand of author and book. Develop a theme that fits in with your writing.

It's the content that may attract a readership and maintain a following. Remember, not everyone who reads your blog will purchase your book. When you start out, you will have a very small following, which may grow rather slowly, and only a small fraction of your readership may actually buy your book. But everything is multipurpose, and indirect benefits often outweigh the direct ones. Your blog serves many functions:

- ✓ Attracting a small number of new readers from your target audience.
- ✓ Providing additional content for customers who have already read your book.
- ✓ Helping to establish your credibility as an author and develop/reinforce your image.
- ✓ Feeding your posts to other websites, including Amazon and Goodreads.
- ✓ Pulling a few customers from Amazon and Goodreads to your blog.
- ✓ Adding information to your Author Page at AuthorCentral through the RSS feed.
- ✓ Giving you a chance to explore new writing and request feedback on it.
- ✓ Letting you express yourself creatively with words, images, and videos.

Ideally, you should begin blogging before you publish your first book. This helps you develop a small following and stir up a little more buzz before its release. If you missed this opportunity with your first book – as most new authors do – then there is always the next.

A successful blog may lead to other possibilities. Publishers, for example, may be more interested in your work after you establish a large following. Also, advertisers tend to favor popular websites. However, if you want to maintain a large following once you build it, keep any advertising to a bare minimum so that it doesn't seem intrusive.

Let's look at a few examples. One of my favorites is www.kelihasablog.wordpress.com. What I love about this blog is the combination of imagery and content. Her poetry is, in my humble opinion, quite a treat, and it is always accompanied by the perfect artwork.[13]

Here is a short blog dedicated toward self-publishers who need help formatting their eBooks: http://notjohnkdp.blogspot.com. This blogger is very active in the KDP community help forums, and had this blog up long before his book was released. The content is effective as the resources are of interest to a wide audience, and his credibility and following had been established well in advance of the book release. Observe that the simple theme matches the content of the blog site.

As I already mentioned, my WordPress site is http://chrismcmullen.wordpress.com. This may be of interest to you as there are many free self-publishing articles on my blog. For

---

[13] If you use images, get permission to use them; or use your own photos or drawings; or use pictures that are in the public domain (e.g. over 90 years old or created by the federal government). Consult an attorney with your legal questions – including the use of photos, plagiarism, and even possible copyright infringement when quoting or citing the source (search "fair use" online – and speak with an attorney – to learn more about this).

example, the first link is for an article on cost-benefit analysis as it applies to book marketing. The second article below describes the art of branding and its importance in marketing. Not all of my posts are strictly about self-publishing, though. For example, the third link below is a fun post that may be of interest to anyone who appreciates books, as it is about both reading and writing with passion.

http://chrismcmullen.wordpress.com/2013/04/16/cost-benefit-analysis-for-marketing-books/
http://chrismcmullen.wordpress.com/2013/03/15/marketing-the-4-rs-of-branding/
http://chrismcmullen.wordpress.com/2013/01/05/reading-writing-with-passion/

6.2.3 Creating an Author Website

As explained previously, in this section I mean something separate from and in addition to your blog site. There are many places online that allow you to create an author website for free, such as Wix, Weebly, and Webs.com. Free is great when you're on a low budget or have no idea how much you might make in royalties.

The main problem with the free domain services is that your url will contain an extension. This extension makes it more difficult for people to remember the name of your website, and also shows that the website is part of a free domain provider.

It's possible to buy a domain name for a long period at a very affordable price – like $10 per year or less. If you purchase your own domain name – from a site like Go Daddy – and find a free web hosting service, this will be a great way to keep your costs very low while also eliminating the problems of an automatic url extension.

Most of the websites that sell domain names also offer paid web hosting and other services. If you draw hundreds of dollars per month in royalties, then investing $10 per month or so for web hosting and other services might make sense; but if you publish a single book and sell less than one copy per day, any monthly fee will gobble up just about all of your royalties. A compromise might be to start out with a paid domain name and find free web hosting, then when you achieve modest success, switch to a paid web hosting service.

Go Daddy and other sites that sell domain names and provide web hosting and other services are very clever with their marketing strategies. They tempt you with add-ons. Also, the costs always seem cheaper until you go to checkout – when all of the little things add up, plus they hit you for the total cost up front (it sounds like X dollars per month, except that many of these websites don't bill you monthly – they bill you up front for a year or more). Many of the services are also discounted when you book them for a longer period of time.

Don't get me wrong. I use Go Daddy myself and am quite pleased with the services. I'm just warning you that if you're on a low budget, you have to exercise self-control and buy just the services that you actually need and can modestly afford.

The first step is to get your own domain name. As I already mentioned, it's worth investing about $10 per year for this in order to avoid having an extension added to your url. You can search for a domain name on Go Daddy or similar websites to see what's available. Get a .com website; they'll try to sell you .net, .info, .co, and so on, but most authors really just need .com. Although one year is usually quite affordable, they usually provide a large discount to entice you into buying several years. If you can afford a few extra dollars, this is a good deal. However, it's only a good deal if you'll still be using your website so many years from now. Are you ready to make this commitment?

Next, you need web hosting. Paid web hosting can come cheap – as little as a few dollars per month for the most economical service, even with a big name like Go Daddy. There are also free web hosting providers that you can find online. I suggest going free or economical at first. When your monthly royalties start to show at least modest success, then you can think about upgrading to better services.

Unless you have HTML or web design expertise, what you need is web hosting. Go Daddy and similar websites provide both website building or design and website hosting; the former is for HTML experts or web designers, while the latter is for the rest of us. Unfortunately, some of these websites don't make it clear that you don't actually need both. For most writers, I recommend a domain name and web hosting, which means you don't need website building or design (you'll be able to "build" and "design" your website with the tools included in the web hosting package). Hosting may come with free stock images that you can use on your website without copyright infringement (see the web hosting site for details about this, and contact an attorney regarding your legal questions).

You should have an author website, preferably with a domain like www.authorname.com, if available. Using the author name in the url helps with branding. The url should be both easy to spell and easy to remember. In addition to an author website, there might be a separate website just for the book, perhaps www.booktitle.com. For authors who write numerous books, this can become a challenge to keep up with. If you publish using an imprint, you can also help establish the imprint's credibility and brand with a publisher website, of the form www.imprintname.com. Using a single imprint for all of your books, you don't need to have a separate website for each book. In this case, you only need to register two domain names – one for the author and another for the imprint (it would be wise to see what is available before locking in your imprint name – in addition to what imprints are already in use).

A photo and information about the author should appear on the author's website, and this should match other branding efforts across the web (e.g. using the same photo). The author's website also needs to include pictures of the front covers. You can sell your book directly from your website, include a link to your CreateSpace eStore, or link to your book on Amazon. As we will discuss in Chapter 8, although you can earn a greater royalty in the first two cases, there are many incentives for promoting sales directly through Amazon. In this case, you can also use Amazon Associates (see Sec. 7.1.8) to earn a commission for this.

You can also provide a forum for customer discussions or comments, a form for people to provide feedback, or an email address. If so, you'll want a web hosting service that can help filter out potential spam, and you might want to create an email address (there are many places to sign up for free email accounts, such as Yahoo and Gmail) specifically for this purpose (but if you do, you must then remember to check it periodically). A page on your website can even be dedicated to a fan club, although this may fit better on the book's website (or the book's page on an imprint's website), if you have one. Feed your blog into your author website. Link to your social media pages, your author pages at Amazon and Goodreads, and other related websites where you have an author presence.

Amazon does not allow content to be copied onto your website. However, you can link to books using thumbnail images. You can't copy reviews – in whole or in part – but you may be able to link to an excerpt that pulls up the full product page (including the reviews) when clicked. Again, consult an attorney for all of your legal questions. Sign up for Amazon Associates (as explained in Sec. 7.1.8) and use this program to create links to Amazon pages.

As with your book, blog, and everything else, be sure that you only use images that you own, are in the public domain (e.g. over 90 years old), that the web host provided for your use on the website, or otherwise do not infringe on copyrights. Also, be sure that any para-phrasing or quotes adhere to "fair use" (it's worth searching for this on the internet to learn more about it). I'm not an attorney; contact an attorney to ask about copyright infringement and what does or doesn't constitute fair use.

Even if the author website is www.authorname.com, it shouldn't be just about you. The website will be much more effective if it includes valuable content that may attract members of your target audience. People probably aren't going to discover the website because they happened to search for your name and wanted to learn more about you (although this might happen rarely), unless of course you are or you become famous.

Identify your target audience. Strive to think of what content you can provide on your website that would be of interest to them, which relates to your writing. Make significant content the main theme of your author website. Your presence should be visible, but let the parts about you be on their own pages or off to the side, with the homepage featuring the valuable content. Other valuable content that you may add is supplemental content for readers who have finished reading your books. Include your web url on the About the Author pages of your books, and let them know what they can find of value – e.g. supplemental content for readers who want more, or a fan page. People are more likely to go to a website when they know that something interesting or helpful is waiting for them there.

Be sure to announce promotions – giveaways, contests, freebies, discounts, etc. – on all of your different websites, including your blog, social media sites, and so on. Include a way for potential booksellers to contact you about the prospects for buying books wholesale. You could just provide a link to CreateSpace Direct or mention that your book is listed with Ingram (if you have the Expanded Distribution), but most booksellers will probably want a greater discount than those options offer along with the option to return them. Therefore, they may be more likely to buy and resell books if they can buy them directly from you (and you can afford to provide this discount because author copies are quite inexpensive). We'll discuss this further in Sec. 8.1.16.

If and when you can afford to upgrade and may be considering this, here are a few of the add-ons that web hosting services may try to sell you: A malware scanner to help protect customers who may download your content, programs that help with search engine optimization, a seal to certify your domain name, tools to sell books and accept payments directly from your website, or an SSL certificate for secure transactions.

Search for author, book, and publisher websites to see what options may be available and to generate ideas, but note that some of the cool things out there may not be possible with all web hosting services. If you visit the author websites of popular authors, such as Stephen King (www.stephenking.com), you'll see that their websites are usually not just blogs. On the other hand, because they are very popular, their websites are all about their books and related merchandise. (Sure, even you can sell t-shirts and bookmarks on your website, if you want.) These professional websites often have striking imagery and interactive features. They will also show you a lot of ideas that you probably hadn't thought of, which may be useful to you. But remember, the main thing you need to do differently compared to the popular authors is provide valuable content – since you don't have the same name recognition, you need another way to drive traffic to your site (as described in Sec. 6.2.7).

Most indie author websites are either essentially the same as blogs or mostly feature themselves and their books. Sadly, even mine does this presently (www.chrismcmullen.com). I did this because it was easy to do, whereas I must set aside some time soon to provide the type of content that I've been suggesting. For example, I want to provide some free self-publishing resources on the page for my self-publishing books and handy math resources on the page for my math workbooks. I hope to make some progress on this in the next few months, at which time my website might provide a better example of how you might use content to your advantage (but my blog serves to illustrate this). Like me, if you're short on time, at least put your books, photo, and biography on your website as a starting point – but eventually make time to improve your website so that it may be more effective.

A website for a book should feature the book. Use striking imagery from the front cover for the background. Feature the front cover on the website. Include a free sample (but not more than the Look Inside available on Amazon). Ideally, the website should be developed before the book's release and help you to build "buzz." In this case, you can add a countdown counter for the coming release date. If it's available for preorder (see Sec. 7.1.8), make this clear and include an Amazon Associates link.

The book's website should also include supplemental material for readers who want more. Give people reasons to visit the website. Include links to the author's website, blog, publisher website, social media sites, Goodreads, the Amazon page, etc. Of course, you can offer bookmarks, t-shirts, etc. here. Anyone coming to the book's website expects the website to focus on the book and must have already heard about it (or read it) to be there. If you're already adding content to your author website to draw readers from your target audience, you don't need to do this for the book's or publisher's website, too.

Check out a variety of publisher's websites, both big and small, to see how they look – they are significantly different from author or book websites. For big publishers, look at Random House and Simon & Schuster, for example. A couple of smaller publishers include www.booknook.biz and www.barefootbooks.com.

While having a publisher website might help give a little credibility to the imprint (ask yourself this: if you see a publisher you don't recognize when buying a book, do you search for that publisher's website?), the other side of the coin is that it might look odd if the imprint only features one book or only features books by one author. One way to have books by a few different authors is to also publish with a couple of pen names, but then you may lose many sales from customers who enjoy your book and would have bought some of your other titles. If you know a few other upcoming authors in similar genres, you could get together and use a common imprint. Some experienced indie authors advance to become small indie publishers.

6.2.4 Setting Up Your CreateSpace eStore

Activate your CreateSpace eStore simply by selecting this sales channel when you publish your book with CreateSpace. The eStore is then automatically setup; there isn't much to do with it, but there are a few options. From your Member Dashboard, click on the link for your book to open the project page and select Channels in the Distribute column. Click on eStore Setup to explore the very limited options:

➢ Add a banner image to your eStore. Ideally, this will be a JPEG picture that is 760 pixels wide by 75 pixels high. You can use a similar banner on Twitter, your blog, etc. You want a banner that is consistent with your other visual branding, or a different banner that specifically relates to each book.

➢ Click the Use Custom Colors button to choose a standard color or upload an image to use as your background. Set the text colors at the bottom. Look up the web color codes online to enter your own colors. Click the Use Standard Colors button to abandon the custom color scheme.

➢ Set a password if you wish to restrict access to purchasing your book. (There must be an exceptional circumstance for this. Otherwise, make it easy for customers to buy your book, and accept any sales that you can get. If you prepared a book specifically for a small group or just your family, for example, the password restriction may apply.)

➢ You can enter your author website in the Continue Shopping URL (start with the http://www part).

> ➢ If you enter Continue Shopping Text, then customers will click on this text in order to access the corresponding url. Otherwise, customers will see the actual url and click on that instead (which makes it clear where the link will take them).
> ➢ Select the Sales Region from the drop-down menu. If you have previously published and only own the rights in the United States or if your book conflicts with laws in any other country, you may need to use this option. International shipping and handling may be expensive for customers outside of the United States, but I would make it available worldwide unless an exception dictates otherwise.
> ➢ Copy the url for your CreateSpace eStore; you will need this to help direct traffic to your eStore. The url has the form https://www.createspace.com/4172624, where the numbers at the end (presently 7 digits) form the CreateSpace title ID for your book.
> ➢ Click the Save & Continue button to save your changes.

A nice feature of the CreateSpace eStore is that you can create discount codes. The discount codes only work with your CreateSpace eStores (they don't work on Amazon). From the same page where you clicked eStore Setup, you can also click Discount Codes. Look for the Click Here link in the middle of the paragraph to create a new discount code. Once you create a discount code, you can apply it to multiple books (i.e. any books in your own CreateSpace account), if you wish – this can be useful for giving a reseller an across the board 15% discount, for example. Copy/paste the discount code that you created into the table, select Dollars Off or Percentage Off, and enter the discount. Be sure to save these changes.

Unfortunately, if you have multiple titles, they can't be combined into a single eStore. However, customers can find all of your books quickly on CreateSpace by typing your name in the search field in the top right corner of CreateSpace's website and – this is very important – also changing Site to Store. If customers leave this set to Site instead of changing it to Store, they won't find your books.

CreateSpace fulfills all of the eStore orders, including processing, payment, shipping, packing slips, and customer service. You're not involved at all except for seeing the royalty show up on your reports (unless a customer who already has your contact information – or discovers it in your book, if it's available there – happens to contact you directly).

Unlike Amazon, customers will not discover your books and buy them on CreateSpace. In principle, they could visit CreateSpace, change Site to Store (very nonobvious), and search for books on CreateSpace.[14] However, in practice, virtually nobody is doing this.

Therefore, you must drive traffic to your eStore if you wish to sell books this way. You can include a link to your eStore from your author website or provide the link to potential customers by email (perhaps a friend or relative, or you may have a client list). Print the url on your business cards.

---

[14] That's a great way to discover books by self-published authors. If you're looking for a book, consider searching on CreateSpace to see if any of your indie colleagues have written one similar to what you're looking for.

The first question to ask yourself is whether or not you prefer to have customers purchase books through the CreateSpace eStore. If yes, then you want to try to market your eStore and drive traffic there. One advantage of the eStore is that you make a 20% higher royalty (off the list price) for eStore sales compared to Amazon sales. However, there are many advantages of selling directly on Amazon, such as its effect on sales rank and customer reviews showing as Amazon Verified Purchases. We will return to this point in Sec. 8.1.16.

Even if you do drive traffic to your CreateSpace eStore, customers may themselves prefer to purchase your book on Amazon. The only way to prevent this is to not sell your book on Amazon. Most CreateSpace published paperback books sell far more on Amazon than anywhere else, so disabling your Amazon sales channel is probably not a good idea. However, if you tour the country giving presentations and sell the majority of your books to people you personally interact with, then Amazon may just make a small fraction of your overall sales (there are businessmen and lecturers in this situation, for example). Once the customer reaches your eStore, they will see your book's title, author, and ISBN – so nothing prevents this customer from going over to Amazon and buying your book there instead.

Why will customers prefer to buy your book on Amazon instead of CreateSpace?

➢ First, they need to sign up for a CreateSpace account (if they don't already have one) before they purchase a book on CreateSpace. Some customers are reluctant to do this.

➢ Even though CreateSpace is an Amazon company, customers trust Amazon and feel comfortable buying books there.

➢ Many customers have Amazon Prime, which gives them free two-day shipping when they purchase qualifying products on Amazon.

➢ Customers can qualify for Free Super Saver Shipping (if the total comes to $35 – which they can reach by adding other books, if necessary) on qualifying Amazon purchases.

➢ Your book may be discounted at Amazon (if so, you earn the full royalty).

➢ There might be other books or items that they want to buy on Amazon, and they would prefer to buy everything together in a single transaction.

If you really want customers to buy your book through CreateSpace, one way to give them an incentive to do this is through a Discount Code. However, a discount code of 20% defeats the purpose of driving traffic to CreateSpace, since you only make 20% more in royalties through eStore sales compared to Amazon sales. If you offer a 5% to 15% discount, this is a bit of a compromise – the customer receives a discount and you earn a higher royalty than you do from Amazon sales. On the other hand, a discount of 20% or less might cost the customer more money: Customers have to pay shipping and handling for eStore purchases, but might be able to qualify for free shipping at Amazon. Also, sometimes books are discounted on Amazon, so the CreateSpace discount must compete with that.

You can probably see that customers will be unlikely, in general, to purchase your book from CreateSpace unless you offer a really good discount, like 35%. A large discount like this gives you less royalty than you would have made from Amazon sales. However, some customers may not buy your book at all at the list price. In this case, a large discount like 35% might get customers to purchase your book who otherwise wouldn't have bought it.

The Discount Codes may be more useful when working with resellers than for customer sales. You may be able to get local bookstores and small online booksellers interested in purchasing copies of your book to resell. If so, they might not want to buy through Ingram or CreateSpace Direct because those bookstore discounts are not too deep and CreateSpace doesn't allow books to be returned by bookstores. However, they might be willing to buy books from your eStore if you offer them a sufficient discount. You can also sell books directly (i.e. in person or through your own website); this gives you the best royalty, but many people are wary of buying online at unknown sites and buying in person doesn't seem as professional (but it is more personal, which has its own merits). We'll discuss this again in Sec. 8.1.16.

If you want to draw a greater royalty than Amazon provides, there is a way to do it: Buy author copies – which are very inexpensive – and sell them directly. This is a great option for people you know or meet in person – friends, relatives, acquaintances, and resellers that you visit. Instead of driving them to your CreateSpace eStore and earning 20% more than you do from Amazon, sell the book in person and you can make much more. You can also make this mutually beneficial by offering a discount. Since author copies are very cheap, you can easily offer a substantial discount for in-person sales and still make a much greater royalty than when customers buy the book from Amazon. Set a consistent price – you don't want Mike to find out that Bill got the book for less, for example.

However, when you sell a book in person, it doesn't boost your Amazon sales rank and if that customer reviews your book, it will show as an unverified purchase. If you expect to sell most of your books through Amazon, there are strong incentives for directing as much traffic as possible to Amazon, rather than selling on your eStore or in person.

If you want to see an example of a CreateSpace eStore, you can visit one of mine at https://www.createspace.com/3384656. I haven't modified the color scheme or added a banner because I prefer to sell my books through Amazon. I don't mind selling through CreateSpace; I just know that I'm not likely to sell books that way because I don't provide any links[15] to my eStores (I provide links to my books on Amazon instead).

Here is an eStore (not mine) that uses a banner https://www.createspace.com/3406206. This eStore uses the default color scheme.

6.2.5 Author Pages at Goodreads

There are reading-oriented websites like www.goodreads.com that allow you to create an author page, and which provide many helpful tools. First sign up as a reader. While you are

---

[15] Except for this one, of course. ☺

signed in, search for yourself on Goodreads. Click on your published author name in the search results. Toward the bottom of the page, look for the link that asks, "Is This You?" Within a few days, you should receive an email notifying you of your upgrade to an author account. You can also manually add a book before it is published. Click the Author Program link at the bottom of their website to find the instructions for this. Goodreads can help you create "buzz" for your book and generate early reviews by having your book manually added prior to its release.

If your name gets associated with someone else's book(s), or if not all of your books are added to your author account, you will need to consult the help pages and read the instructions carefully to resolve this. Also, note the Email Us link on the page that describes the Author Program.

When you sign in, note whether you are looking at your reader or author account page. Your author page shows you recent activity from friends (if you've added any). Visit your author dashboard to see your book ratings and customer reviews on Goodreads, and to find a variety of helpful tools. Add friends you know who use Goodreads. As a reader, add books, rate books you've read, review books you've read, mark books as to-read, identify yourself as a fan of your favorite authors, and follow authors who interest you.

Here are some helpful tools available from your author dashboard:

➢ Add an Author Widget to your website to let fans quickly add your book at Goodreads.
➢ Read the author newsletter for news, tips, and advice.
➢ Feed your blog posts into your Goodreads author page. You can also write blog posts at Goodreads, but it might seem more professional to feed your blog into Goodreads.
➢ Make your eBooks available on Goodreads.
➢ Display Goodreads ratings and reviews on your Facebook Fan Page.
➢ List your book for a Giveaway to help create buzz for an upcoming or recently published book; this may also help stimulate a few early reviews. It's recommended that you give about 10 free copies with this promotion – if you strongly believe in your book's success and have good marketing motivation and plans; if you're a little more tentative, try a smaller number. Order your books from CreateSpace at your author price and mail them out professionally with careful packaging. Note that shipping can be quite expensive if you allow international participation. This advance review copy option only applies to print editions of your book (not eBooks).
➢ Create a Q&A group to interact with fans and answer questions for a brief period. This is intended to help you create buzz for an upcoming or recently published book. If you use this, be sure to behave very professionally.
➢ There are some advertising options available. Advertising isn't magical – if you think you can just throw money to advertisers and reap instant success, it just doesn't work so easily. See Chapter 8 regarding free and low-cost marketing options. Even if you advertise, you still have to market actively; advertising doesn't relieve you of this need.

There are many horror stories floating around from authors who have made the mistake of responding to reviews on Goodreads (as well as Amazon) – especially, replying defensively to negative reviews, getting into discussions with reviewers, and displaying unprofessional behavior. I strongly recommend <u>not</u> commenting on any review at Goodreads for any reason whatsoever. If a customer wants to interact with you, there are many ways for the customer to initiate this – email, commenting on your blog, using a fan page, etc. Don't thank customers for positive reviews, don't ask Goodreads reviewers to also review your book on Amazon, and definitely don't respond to negative reviews at Goodreads. If they point out mistakes, don't ask which mistakes (I realize this would be helpful, but think about it – when you read a book, you notice mistakes, but you don't get out paper and make a list of them, so the reader doesn't have such a handy list to give you; therefore, don't ask for it). We'll discuss customer reviews in much more detail in Sec. 7.1.6 (but know that Goodreads "police" are more strict).

Don't engage people who add your book to their to-read list, rate your book, or review your book. Authors have been flagged as spammers for doing this, and can actually get their accounts suspended. At Goodreads, the best policy is to completely not interact with readers. The sole exception is the limited interaction with fans in a Q&A group specifically designed for fans to interact with authors for a brief period – and just in that author's group setting.

Note that almost all of your activity on Goodreads – including comments, adding books as to-read, or even just liking a review – is publicly displayed on your author page. So, for example, suppose a group on Goodreads says something bad about you or your book. That group itself is fairly invisible, but if you make the mistake of commenting in that group, now your behavior has turned an insignificant problem into a very public ordeal – which does not look good for you. The best thing you can do is nothing at all. Try to exercise restraint.

Read all of Goodreads' policies and recommendations carefully, as they provide good advice. For example, read the Author Program FAQ. A related point to note is that after you send out books to the giveaway winners, you're not permitted to contact those readers ever again. Some readers will report you if you send them material again, which will get you banned from doing giveaways and can get your account suspended or terminated.

If you want to see samples of author pages at Goodreads, try searching for your favorite authors. If you wish to find my humble Goodreads author page, search for Chris McMullen.

6.2.6 Author Pages at Social Media Websites

The two main social media networks are presently FaceBook and Twitter. Authors also get some use out of Pinterest, Google Plus, and LinkedIn. These are the main places to start, but there are other sites like these if you're looking for more. I will focus on FaceBook and Twitter.

Some authors swear by social media, and others claim that it's not really effective. Part of the difference may be your target audience. The first rule of marketing is to identify your target audience, then gear your marketing toward increasing your book's visibility among them. Who is most likely to read your book? What age group is this? What interests do they have? How many of them are likely to be using Facebook and Twitter actively? Are they mostly using these to interact with friends and family, or to follow celebrities? What are your prospects for connecting with them through Facebook and Twitter?

You don't necessarily need to connect with them directly. Especially, if you're an adult, while your target audience is minors, you want to find ways to spread the word without direct contact. Certainly, don't add minors as friends to your personal Facebook account. There is a distinction between fans following the posted activity of celebrities, and celebrities who interact directly via personal accounts, emails, or text messages.

Teen fiction, for example, can have a huge market on Facebook and Twitter. Just imagine the buzz among teens on social media that was generated before, during, and after the release of the books in the *Harry Potter* and *Twilight* series. There is potential to tap here. The question is how to tap into it.

If you simply create an account, who will look for it and start following? Unless you're a celebrity, you need to market your following; people aren't likely to just show up on your page. Of course, you can provide links to your social media pages in your books, but those readers already have one of your books. You can link to Facebook and Twitter from your blog and website, but again, it's like you're going in circles. What you really want to do is increase your visibility among people who don't already know about you. Think about this.

Let's start with the easy way to use social media. Some people already have a large following on Facebook and Twitter. If you already have hundreds or thousands of followers on a personal account, make use of this popularity. These are your relatives, friends, and mostly acquaintances. Seek input on your title, cover, and blurb before publishing, post an occasional note about how the writing is going, and let everyone know when your book becomes available. **But only mention your book very occasionally!** Most of your posts must be the usual things that Facebook friends tend to do; only a very small fraction can relate to your book, otherwise you'll get tuned out. Don't be a commercial or a salesman. If you do it just once in a while, you can use your following to help build buzz, and if you just send out one message projecting the release date and a few weeks later post another short, "Ta-da! I did it," kind of message – that lets everyone know your book is live, rather than asking for sales – then you're much more likely to generate early sales.

The next easy way to use social media is to develop a following among your readers. For this, create fan pages – or author pages, book pages, and/or publisher pages. People who read your book and enjoy it, and who also check out your About the Author section and decide to visit your social media sites may Like or Follow your social media author presence. You need separate personal and author accounts, so that your fans and readers are joining your author (or fan, book, or publisher) pages. You need to have one personal account for friends, family, and acquaintances, and a separate account for you as an author.

This fan following may be interested in your subsequent books. You can similarly create some buzz with your established fan base by allowing fans to vote on a choice of covers, for example, or announcing contests. Provide content or other material that will attract readers or fans to these pages; it's unlikely that people will follow pages that simply advertise or showcase the author's books, for example. What would draw your interest if you were a fan? Explore how other non-famous authors successfully utilize their fan pages.

These are the two easy ways to effectively use social media – the established connections in your personal account help you spread the word about your new book, while readers and fans added to your fan pages help with the marketing of follow-up books.

It's not as easy to use social media as a marketing tool to reach a large number of people in your target audience who don't know about you or your book, but there is some potential here. The first step is identifying your target audience (see Sec. 8.1.9). Then think about how these people use social media and, ultimately, how to make them aware of your book. You don't want to be a salesman advertising your book. Marketing isn't about salesmanship, but about discoverability. Advertisements and requests to purchase a book tend to turn people away. It's different when they briefly discover a book that interests them, or when they happen to discover that someone whom they've interacted with personally is an author.

If you're socializing online with members of your target audience and have a profile that they can check out if you attract their interest, this is one way to get discovered. Everybody has hobbies, interests, passions, etc. Most people spend a little time once in a while – not necessarily everyday, but perhaps once a week or so – pursuing these interests online. They could be reading blogs or articles, or they may be engaging in discussions with others. Spend some time writing down interests that people in your target audience are likely to have that relate to your book. Search online to see where people can pursue these interests online – the big sites have forums where people can interact with others with similar interests, plus there are many niches online for this. People like to buy books by authors who have personally interacted with them, and people are more likely to buy books that they "discover." Keep this in mind, but don't expect instant success. Sometimes you discover a product you like, but don't get around to buying it for many months. It can take a year for all of your marketing efforts to really start paying off. Twitter hashtags, which will be discussed shortly, provide a more direct way to reach your target audience (yet you still need to operate indirectly through discovery).

Another way that social media can be highly effective is when word-of-mouth about your book spreads from John to Jennifer to Jerry to Jenny to Jim and so on. Word-of-mouth sales can be invaluable, but aren't easy to generate. First, you must have a book that is not only very good, but which also elicits powerful emotions, has memorable characters, or features an impressionable plot, for example. Next, you need people in your target audience who tend to socialize – both online and in person – to find, read, and enjoy your book. The part you have the most control over is writing such a book and perfecting it. If you have such a book, all of your marketing efforts will help to stimulate word-of-mouth sales.

Gifting books to social people in your genre might help to create such a spark, but you must have the right book to increase your chances. This requires meeting people socially – online and in person – in your target audience. The Goodreads giveaways are geared toward this, and holding your own online contests – on your blog, website, or fan pages – may help. If your main audience is highly social – especially, with Facebook and Twitter – that's a plus.

To make author and related pages on Facebook, first login. At your Facebook Home, find and click the Like Pages link in the left column. Click the + Create Page button. In Artist, Band or Public Figure, select Author or Writer to create a Facebook author page. In Entertainment, select Book for a Facebook book page. In Company, Organization or Institution, select Media/News/Publishing for a Facebook publisher page. Read the terms and conditions carefully as there is plenty of material there about what is or isn't allowed regarding advertisements, contests (under promotions), etc. You don't want to violate any policies and lose your privileges (or worse, violate any laws). Remember to use images that help with your branding.

At Twitter, add a banner (wide, but short) that fits with your author brand. Explore hashtags and find those that are most relevant to your genre and the probable interests of your target audience, which relate to your book. Relevant hashtags can help you reach people in your target audience. Research hashtags at www.hashtags.org before you use them.

One key to Twitter is to first follow people that appear successful in areas that interest you and also follow top selling authors in your genre. For the first couple of months, just follow the posts and check out Twitter pages. Don't post content yourself during the first month. Develop and refine your Twitter page and learn what successful Twitter users do. There is an art to using the limited character count effectively. You want to master this and learn the secrets. Try to build a humble following and master the craft before you begin Tweeting yourself.

What you really want to learn is how to use the limited character count to provide useful content for people in your target audience. Very often, the useful content is a link that is likely to be of interest to people in the author's following or the assigned hashtags. People are much more likely to pay attention to your Tweets when the content that you Tweet – or reTweet – has proven to generally be helpful. Also, don't over-Tweet.

Authors who frequently advertise their own books and sites tend to get ignored. At least 90% of the time you should be providing valuable content that doesn't involve your own books or websites. Direct advertising and salesmanship often doesn't work; marketing in such a way as to provide valuable content and potentially have your work discovered is usually much more effective. Remember that you can feed your Tweets into your AuthorCentral account at Amazon in addition to your blog – and both will show separately.

Don't provide links to your Facebook author, book, or publisher pages or to your Twitter page until your sites are up-and-running with regularly updated content that will attract interest from your target audience. Fans will be disappointed if they discover a link that you provided to a social media site and take the time to visit it, only to find that the page isn't finished or hasn't been updated in a long time; the same holds for your blog, author website, and other online marketing efforts.

On the other hand, if these pages aren't listed in the About the Author section at the time of publication, when you finally get them together, you've missed some potential traffic. Still, this is better than driving traffic into dead-end streets. When your sites become ready, you can update your books to include them.

Ideally, you would have all of your online pages running when your book is released, and you would actively maintain all of these pages. However, there is a great deal of work involved in this and each page that you add carries a large long-term commitment. Unless you are really motivated and diligent regarding your blog, social media, website maintenance, etc., you probably need to be somewhat selective and choose wisely. Authors tend to choose what's easiest and most natural for them to do, and not necessarily what will be most effective with their target audience in mind. But it's the latter point that's far more important. To be successful, you must be willing to market outside of your comfort zone. You don't have to market every way imaginable; but you do need to use tools that may be effective at reaching your target audience. Very often, the most effective tools are the ones that lie outside of our comfort zones. So try to choose based on potential effectiveness, not based on what you feel most comfortable doing.

I have two blogs which I update regularly. I put together a website that appears complete and functional, but I would like to add much more content so that useful resources outweigh the presence of my books; there is something there in the meantime. I feed my blog posts into Twitter and Facebook, rather than posting separately to each. If you do this, don't also feed Twitter into Facebook and vice-versa (even though you will be prompted to do so; be sure not to select this option), otherwise you'll wind up getting double-posts on Twitter and Facebook. This allows people who prefer Twitter and Facebook to follow me without using my blog, and saves me from having to post separately to three different sites. I try to visit Facebook periodically to keep up with comments. Because you can only do so much (and you definitely want to save time for writing), you must choose wisely what you can do and which commitments you can make.

Commitments are important. If you drive traffic to a website that you haven't maintained for quite some time, this dead-end leaves a negative impression and affects the author brand that you're striving to establish through marketing.

6.2.7 Driving Traffic to Your Websites

There is a great deal of cross-linking among your various online sites – i.e. one site includes links to all of your other sites. Once someone discovers one of your sites, this helps to drive traffic to your other sites – some of which, like your Amazon detail page, offer your book for sale. Of course, you don't just want to create a circle where every site drives traffic to every other site – ultimately, you want new members of your target audience to discover your sites. All of these sites are like a giant net: The larger the net, the greater the chance that they will catch new traffic. First establish and expand your net, then work on finding new traffic.

One way to receive new visitors is through your choice of keywords and tags. For example, you choose keywords and tags when you post a blog, Twitter has hashtags, and some website tools allow you to associate words and phrases with each of your webpages. There is a high volume of web traffic, and you hope to direct a tiny fraction of this traffic to any and all of your websites.

You can type words and phrases into a search engine like Google to try to gauge what is popular and see what the results look like. There are also many tools out there to help with keyword selection; Go Daddy, for example, offers search engine optimization (SEO) tools. You might search online to see if there are free tools of this sort available. There are three issues to consider: (1) Which keywords are most relevant to your content? (2) Which relevant keywords are used most often? (3) How visible will your page be in search results? You must decide on the first point, while SEO or keyword selection programs can help with the second. Then you have to balance the second and third points: Would you rather have your page higher up on a less popular search, or further down on a more popular search? Relevance is very important – nobody will stay on a page that fools them into clicking on a link that doesn't actually relate to what they are looking for.

You also need to have valuable, regularly updated content on each of your sites. It's the content that can attract new visitors to your sites. Without the content, you just get the same small group of visitors circulating among your sites. Since the ultimate goal of marketing is to find new customers for your book, you need valuable content that relates to your genre and book to attract them.

If you just blog about yourself and your book, have a website that just shows your books, have a Facebook fan page for your book, Tweet about your book, get a few bloggers to interview you, and have a Goodreads author page… then let me ask you this: What is attracting new people to any of these websites? **Nothing!** That's a great deal of work to do for very little gain. Sure, a few new readers may discover your book or blog and add to the traffic, but these are small apples.

Compare that to this: Write an article that may interest your target audience and get it published somewhere online that has modest traffic, post content on your blog that is relevant for your readers, include free resources on your website to attract potential customers, and provide relevant and useful links with your Tweets. Do you see the difference? This has so much more potential to bring traffic to your "net" of websites.

Here are a few tips to help improve the visibility of your websites in search results:
➢ Older websites with a history of visitors are favored as they are more established.
➢ Unique content with relevant links and references looks good to search engines.

> ➢ Relevance of the content to the keywords is critical for good visibility.
> ➢ Specific keywords that are used frequently tend to better than general keywords.
> ➢ When other sites link to your content, this helps.
> ➢ Search engines favor pages that are easy to navigate and visually appealing.

There are other highly effective ways to market, too, such as through personal interactions (which tend to make a more lasting impression than online interactions via social media). We'll explore marketing in much more detail in Chapter 8. Those techniques not only help you market your book, but also to market all of the websites in your online "net." The more traffic in your net, the more customers will discover your book.

The primary key to driving more traffic to your marketing "net" is to post free content that will help attract your specific target audience. The free content is generally nonfiction, even for fiction authors, that relates to the content of the book and will interest most of the readers. One of the latest trends in marketing is less use of social media with much emphasis on creating a content-rich website. It's valuable content that can attract new readers; you don't simply want to direct current readers to new sites, so creating valuable content that will attract your target audience and posting it on your websites is an effective marketing tool at your disposal.

It's also important to go beyond your "net" to reach new customers. So don't just post content on your own websites. Write articles and make videos that will interest your target audience and submit them to high-traffic websites, newspapers, and magazines. Too many authors don't realize the value of posting an article where there is much traffic from the target audience, for which the target audience will be interested in the article. Just imagine hundreds of potential readers seeing Your Name, Author of Book Title at the bottom of the article. You can't do it if you don't try. Find ways to go beyond your "net" to effectively reach your target audience and you can get yourself a significant marketing advantage.

Chapter 7

Useful Tips about Amazon and Other Booksellers

Chapter Overview

7.1 Understanding Amazon's Website
7.2 Exploring Other Online Booksellers

This chapter answers questions about the following topics, and more:

- ☑ Information about sales rank in Amazon books and Amazon Kindle.[16]
- ☑ Interpreting sales rank and author rank at Amazon.
- ☑ What determines the order in which books appear in Amazon's search results.
- ☑ Various ways that customers will be able to find your book on Amazon's website.
- ☑ How add-ons help your sales, and when similar books can actually improve your sales, rather than compete for them.
- ☑ Information about used and new paperback books sold on the internet.
- ☑ Information about Amazon's browse categories, keywords, and tags.
- ☑ Using Amazon Advantage[16] to arrange for preorders of your book.
- ☑ Customer book reviews on Amazon and other online booksellers.
- ☑ The best and worst ways to deal with bad reviews of your book.
- ☑ Earning money through affiliate links with Amazon Associates.[16]
- ☑ Finding your paperback and eBook on other booksellers' websites.
- ☑ How to find the online booksellers that have picked up your paperback book through CreateSpace's expanded distribution.[16]

---

[16] Amazon,™ CreateSpace,™ Amazon Advantage,™ and Amazon Associates™ are trademarks and brands of their respective owners. Neither this book, *A Detailed Guide to Self-Publishing with Amazon and Other Online Booksellers*, nor its author, Chris McMullen, are in any way affiliated with any of these companies.

7.1 Understanding Amazon's Website

7.1.1 Your Book's Amazon Detail Page

After you click Approve Proof, your book will go live to all of your sales channels. It won't show up on Amazon instantly, but usually appears within 2-5 days (although there are occasional exceptions). When your Amazon product page first shows up, it may look relatively empty; it will continue to grow as features are added to it over a period of time:

❖ You might not see anything but the title and it may not even appear to be for sale when you first find your book on Amazon. Don't worry; this will change.

❖ Check the title, subtitle, author, and all other information on our book's detail page carefully. You can make revisions to the blurb or Author Page from AuthorCentral, and you can change the cover, interior, keywords, and categories at CreateSpace or KDP. If there are other mistakes that aren't your own fault (e.g. if you type your title incorrectly, that's your own fault) then contact CreateSpace or Amazon, explain the problem clearly, and politely ask if they can please resolve it for you. Amazon has over twenty million books listed, so there may be a rare issue. Don't contact them if a feature simply isn't showing yet; exercise patience, as some features take time.

❖ The first items that will appear on your book's page are the cover and description.

❖ It can take weeks for the Look Inside to be activated.

❖ If you update the description through AuthorCentral, it may take several hours for the revision to show up.

❖ The tagging system appears to have been phased out. There were both authors and customers abusing this system, which is probably the reason for this. However, you can still add keywords to your book (see Sec.'s 4.1.3 and 4.2.6). If the tagging system happens to be available for your book, it allows customers to associate tags with it.

❖ You may not see Likes. It appears that the Like feature is being phased out, perhaps from authors who have abused it. If the Like feature happens to be available for your book, it allows customers to show that they like it.

❖ Check your list price. If Amazon discounts the price, you should be happy ☺ about it. Why? Because they pay you the same royalty whether it's discounted or not. If anything, the discount may stimulate sales. On the other hand, if it is discounted now, it may just be temporary, so enjoy it while it lasts; you can't count on it. It's also possible that your price will never be discounted. You have no control over this.

❖ After the price, above the words "In Stock," it will probably say, "…& FREE Shipping on orders over $35." Above the Add to Cart button on the right, it will probably indicate that Amazon Prime is an option. These are incentives for customers to buy your book.

- ❖ CreateSpace books with a list price of $9.99 or less used to qualify for the 4-for-3 program. This program appears to have been discontinued in February, 2013. On the other hand, Amazon had rarely been discounting CreateSpace books in the 4-for-3 program, but recently CreateSpace books in this price range are sometimes put "on sale." Amazon changes its practices and programs periodically, in their effort to maximize their profits. You can't count on any discounts or programs – you can just be aware of what there is and enjoy them while they last.

- ❖ If you have paperback and Kindle editions of your book with the exact same title and author(s) – spelled exactly the same way (if you have a subtitle at CreateSapce, this means that you have to include the exact same subtitle at KDP, too) – they should automatically link together within a couple of days. If the title or author(s) do not match and you would like to have the two editions linked – or if they don't automatically link within a few days – sign into KDP, click the yellow Contact Us button in the bottom left, click Product Page, select Linking Print and Kindle Editions, fill out the form (you can copy/paste the ISBN and ASIN from the books' detail pages), and submit it online.

- ❖ When there are two or more paperback editions of the same book – such as regular and large print – linked together, one edition may be "hidden" by a + sign where it shows available editions. For example, if you have a large print edition linked with your regular edition, only the regular edition will appear in search results unless large print is specifically searched for, but customers will be able to discover it by clicking on the + sign. If the large print (or other) edition is newer than the regular edition, you can request Amazon to add a link at the top of the regular edition book's detail page indicating that a newer edition is now available.

- ❖ You won't have Frequently Bought Together or Customers Also Bought lists until you have several sales – and then it takes time for this to be added and updated.

- ❖ Customer reviews may not appear until you have hundreds or thousands of sales, but once in a while one of the first customers may review the book quickly.

- ❖ There may be third-party sellers offering your book for sale new or used. We'll discuss this in the following section.

- ❖ For paperbacks, the publisher will be listed as CreateSpace Independent Publishing Platform unless you used an ISBN option that allowed you to use your own imprint.

- ❖ Your cover will automatically show up in a few days; there is no need to upload customer images. The Look Inside will also appear in a few weeks or so.

- ❖ There probably won't be a discussion forum about your book. I do <u>not</u> recommend starting one because this will look unprofessional. We'll talk about Amazon discussion forums in Sec. 7.1.7.

- ❖ You will probably see a few sponsored links beneath the customer review area. This is normal and you have no control over this.

Next, look for your book's detail page in the United Kingdom and any other of Amazon's international websites that may interest you. In the non-English speaking countries, your book may show up under foreign authors (and you may need a translator to help understand these websites). Following are Amazon's current websites (you can also find a link to each at the bottom of Amazon's homepage):

www.amazon.com (United States)
www.amazon.co.uk (United Kingdom)
www.amazon.ca (Canada)
www.amazon.es (Spain)
www.amazon.fr (France)
www.amazon.de (Germany)
www.amazon.it (Italy)
www.amazon.cn (China)
www.amazon.co.jp (Japan)

You should know the short link to your book's detail page. This will be very handy when you want to provide someone a link to check out your book. The first step is to find your book's 10-digit ISBN (for paperbacks) or ASIN (for Kindle) as it appears on your book's detail page. The short link has the form http://www.amazon.com/dp/ASIN, where you must replace ASIN with the numbers of the ASIN or ISBN. For example, if the 10-digit ISBN for a book is 1479134635, the short link to it on Amazon is http://www.amazon.com/dp/1479134635.

The wrong way to make the link is to search for your book on Amazon, then copy/paste the link from the top of your browser. The problem with that is that the link is then much longer than it needs to be. It looks much more professional when you use the short link instead of a longer one.

You can shorten it down to http://amzn.com/ASIN if you want, but this isn't a whole lot shorter, and some people might wonder if "amzn" is some third-party site imitating Amazon. Therefore, I recommend using http://www.amazon.com/dp/ASIN.

In other countries, change the .com to the extension for Amazon's homepage in the other country. For example, in the United Kingdom, Amazon's site is www.amazon.co.uk, so the .com gets changed to .co.uk. Thus, the short link to your book in the United Kingdom has the form http://www.amazon.co.uk/dp/ASIN.

7.1.2 Third-Party Sellers on Amazon

For your paperback book, you may notice third-party sellers listing copies of your book new and used in addition to new books sold directly by Amazon. This may happen immediately if you opt for the Expanded Distribution, and will probably occur at a later time otherwise.

If you have the Expanded Distribution, you will probably see several sellers offering your book for sale both new and used almost as soon as your book goes live. You might be wondering how on earth they already have copies of your book. The answer is very simple: They don't! If they don't have your book, how can they sell it? If your book sells, they will place an order for it at that time. After all, your paperback book is print-on-demand.

In Sec. 4.1.7, I provided a few compelling reasons why customers may prefer to purchase your book new directly from Amazon instead of one of the third-party sellers. You may sell an occasional book that way, but unless they offer a significant discount (which is unlikely if they are getting their book through the Expanded Distribution – except in the case of a very high list price), most of your sales are likely to go through Amazon. Also in Sec. 4.1.7, I explained that in many cases, these third-party sellers may help more than they hurt.

When your book sells through a third-party seller who orders your book through the Expanded Distribution, you earn the lower Expanded Distribution royalty instead of the higher Amazon royalty. Also, the royalty appears in two months (or more) when your Expanded Distribution royalties are reported, whereas royalties for new purchases from Amazon are reported when the book is printed – very often, within one or two days.

Every once in a while, for whatever reason, Amazon chooses to fill an order for a new purchase directly through Amazon from one of their third-party affiliates. When Amazon does this, they report it to CreateSpace when Expanded Distribution royalties are reported. However, at this time CreateSpace will correct the mistake and report it as an Amazon royalty. The problem is that, in this rare event, the royalty is not reported within one or two days as usual, but a couple of months later like the Expanded Distribution sales. Those of us who have been using CreateSpace for a few years and who have sold several books through the Expanded Distribution know this because CreateSpace used to send out an email about this to us every month about these adjustments. They used to report it as an Expanded Distribution royalty and then make an adjustment, but now it just shows up as another Amazon royalty when the Expanded Distribution royalties are reported. If you monitor your sales spikes carefully, but don't see a royalty report within a few days, this is one possible explanation.

A peculiar thing about these third-party sellers is that a few will list their books for outrageous prices – way above your list price. It's absurd to worry that these booksellers are making tremendous profits and that you're missing out on the deal: What customer will pay much more than Amazon's price to get their book from some unknown seller? Those overpriced sellers don't actually expect to sell any copies (but if anyone is foolish enough to buy their books, they won't complain). It may be some scheme for them to try to improve their SEO rankings, for example; if they are way overpriced, they have some other agenda besides selling books. Don't worry about them – they're not affecting your royalties.

Eventually, a few customers may resell their books used on Amazon. You don't earn any royalty when this happens. Only a small percentage of customers will probably try to resell their books used this way. If there are several customers doing this, it's a good sign that your sales have been mildly successful. Customers can qualify for free shipping by purchasing directly from Amazon, but have to pay shipping when buying used or from third-party sellers (except for the rare Fulfillment by Amazon, which costs them more money to do), so customers have incentives to buy your book new from Amazon. In most cases, these things are not worth worrying about.

Third-party sellers usually list the book by ISBN so that their book shows up on your book's detail page as one of the used or new options. Rarely, a seller will create a separate listing for your book, using their own cover image and a title as they enter it, which will only show their own book for sale. It's to their own disadvantage to do this, which is why it's rare. Theoretically, they should only do this for editions of books that aren't in Amazon's system. There is a slight chance that you will notice such a page. If so, it should appear further down in the search results than your book's main detail page. If you find such a page, don't click on it (or you might inadvertently make that page more visible).

7.1.3 Finding Your Book on Amazon

With twenty million paperbacks and two million Kindle eBooks showing in search results on Amazon, you may be wondering how in the world anyone will ever discover your book. If you expect your book to show up on the front page of its category or broad searches (like "mystery"), that's quite unreasonable. Amazon wants the most relevant, top-selling, likely-to-be-purchased books to show up on the front pages. When your book is released, there are already tens of thousands in their search results that already have an established history of (at least) mildly successful sales frequency. Your book won't leapfrog past all of these titles without good cause.

But don't despair: There are ways that your book can be discovered in search results. This doesn't mean that it will be discovered and purchased; just that there is potential. Most books don't sell by simply being discovered in search results. Most books sell because of good marketing, great covers, great blurbs, great Look Insides, great beginnings, and good content. The better you do at these things, the more your book will also be discovered in search results and purchased that way. The let's-just-throw-it-out-there-and-see-what-happens approach (i.e. zero marketing) usually doesn't pan out – what it generally does is establish a history of low sales frequency, which makes it more challenging for marketing to help later. This is, unfortunately, a common approach from new indie authors.

My point is this: Although I will show you a few ways that your book may be discovered initially, most books won't sell much this way unless you also market your book effectively and have done a good job with the cover, blurb, etc. Don't rely on your book selling through discovery in search results; rather, foster sales through marketing and improve the potential for your book to sell this way, too.

Obviously, if you enter the ISBN or ASIN into Amazon's search, your book should be the first and only search result. However, the only people searching for your book with these numbers are those who already know about your book.

Similarly, if your book has a long title or unique words in the title, your book may show up at the top of search results where customers enter the title. Again, only someone who knows about your book is likely to enter most or all of the title into a search. On the other hand, if your book's title is short, this may pull up hundreds or thousands of search results, and your book may not even be on the first page of the list (and there may even be books on the first page with titles that aren't even direct matches with your search). This is kind of like searching for keywords, so hold this thought for a moment.

Your book will also be searchable by the names of the authors (and other contributors) as they were listed when the book was published. If you happen to have a name like Robert Jones, this can pull up a large number of search results, but if your name is much less common, your own book may be the only search result. Some people who know you will search for your book by your name, so you should go to Amazon and see how far down the search results your book is when you try this.

But you're not interested in searches by ISBN, ASIN, title, or author. What you really want to know is how potential customers might discover your book through category or keyword searches. So we'll focus on this now.

Suppose, for example, that you have just published a romance. If you go to Amazon and search for "romance novel," for example, your book might be a hundred pages down the search results. If instead you browse by categories and select, for example, the Contemporary Romance category, your book will still be very far down the search results.

So how will anyone ever discover your book? Surely, nobody will browse through a large number of search results to find your book.

The answer lies in filtering. Many customers don't want to sort page by page through thousands of search results, so they usually filter the results in one or more ways.

One way to filter books is to check out the new releases. After searching for a keyword or browsing in a category (or both), once the customer has selected Books or Kindle eBooks (as opposed to All Products), in the top left corner they will find links for New Releases – Last 30 Days, Last 90 Days, and Coming Soon (this last is for preorders – see Sec. 7.1.8).

The New Releases links provide you a window of visibility. Take advantage of it by marketing your book actively before and during your book's release. If you wait a few months and then decide to start marketing because sales aren't what you'd hoped for, you will have missed this golden opportunity.

For the first 30 days after your book's publication date,[17] if a customer clicks on the Last 30 Days or Last 90 Days link, your book will suddenly be part of a much shorter list of search

---

[17] If you back-date your book's publication date – instead of using the date when you click Approve Proof – then you may miss out on this opportunity.

results.[18] These links greatly enhance your book's prospects for being discovered. The more customers you drive through marketing to search for your book on Amazon and purchase it shortly after its release, the more visible your book is likely to be – both within the Last 30/90 Days search results and other search results. If you just let your book "go-it-alone," you're squandering this wonderful opportunity.

Another way that a customer may filter the search results is by using the Sort By drop-down menu on the right side of the page. One option that may help your early sales potential is Publication Date. There is also New and Popular; your book is new when you publish it, but it will have to earn the popularity part.

Some other filters (these are on the left side of the page of search results) that may help your book include FREE Super Saver Shipping, Amazon Prime, New (as opposed to Used – not as in recent), unchecking Out of Stock, and Paperback or Kindle Edition.

Success can help bring your book more success. A history of a high sales frequency can help your book attain greater visibility; especially, the more customers search for your book by keywords or in browse categories and then purchase it. More sales get your book added to the Customers Also Bought lists. If your book has amazing success it can get featured on the top 100 bestseller lists in a category or subcategory.

The 30-day and 90-day periods are short. After that, your book needs to have developed different legs to stand on. Creating "buzz" for your book prior to, during, and shortly after its release can help. Sending out advance review copies can help. Launching a successful marketing campaign when your book is released can help your book not only thrive during the first three months of sales, but also gain long-lasting visibility in other ways.

When the 90-day period ends, your book needs to have developed strong relevance for a variety of searches so that it shows up on the first pages for some keywords, and it needs to have maintained a strong sales rank in order to be highly visible within its subcategory. A large number of sales may lead to a modest number of reviews, which is another way to help your book's visibility. Customers can order search results by the total number of reviews (this is a new feature) or by the average review (strictly highest to lowest, regardless of number).

Your keywords should be relevant to your book – not just kind of related. Customers use keywords because they are looking for specific types of books. If your book shows up high in the search, but isn't the type of book that the customer is seeking, it will almost certainly be passed over.

Broader keywords tend to be more popular searches. For example, "sci-fi" is a very broad and extremely popular search, whereas "sci-fi alien romance" is much more narrow and not

---

[18] Obviously, the customer must first do a search or browse in a category where your book is somewhere on the list to begin with (even if dead last) in order for it to be in these filtered search results. If the Last 30 Days and Last 90 Days links are not active for your book, contact support (CreateSpace, AuthorCentral, or KDP) for help. Explain clearly what you would like and make your request polite. Amazon doesn't have a responsibility to put our books here (and hasn't always done so); we hope that they do this and should be grateful when they do.

searched for nearly as often. While it would be great to have your book show up on the first page of a very broad and popular keyword, it's also highly unlikely because there is so much competition for it. If you have a sci-fi alien romance, for example, the narrower keyword will probably net more sales even though the search is far less popular – because your book (if that's what you wrote) would be a better fit for the results (i.e. it is more relevant). On the other hand, if the narrow keyword is really unpopular – only used by customers a few times per month, then such a keyword isn't too helpful. Remember, you get 5 to 7 keywords (7 at KDP, 5 at CreateSpace) – you could have both "sci-fi" and "sci-fi alien romance," along with three others. The "sci-fi" would help with some filtering, such as Last 30 Days (i.e. when a customer chooses two or more filters). So you should have a broad, popular keyword and a narrow, highly relevant, and not too infrequently used keyword as two of your choices.

Including your keywords in your blurb may affect your book's positioning in search results. It's not reasonable to expect this to make the difference between page 1 and page 100, but there may be a noticeable effect. The trick is including your keywords as less than 15% of your description while still writing it effectively (and without just ending the description with a list of keywords, which is rather tacky); it's more challenging for fiction.

Remember, you can have your book added to a second browse category by contacting CreateSpace. First, visit Amazon and browse the categories to find one relevant for your book.

What determines the order in which books appear in Amazon's search results? That's the million dollar question. Amazon isn't publishing their algorithm – in order to try to prevent people from taking advantage of it. Nonetheless, we can observe the visibility of different books and see which factors appear to affect this. The following may affect search results. Keep in mind that Amazon does change its algorithm periodically. Obviously, they want to fine-tune their algorithm to maximize their profits, and they will revise it as they see fit.

- ❖ The search term must match your keywords, or a combination of words from your title, subtitle, author, and imprint.
- ❖ A history of customers clicking on your book after using the same or similar search may improve your book's visibility – especially, if they purchase the book after performing the search (on the other hand, if several customers click on your book in the search results and don't purchase it, this might establish lack of relevance).
- ❖ Sales rank plays some role in determining relevance. The lower the sales rank number, the better.
- ❖ Reviews also affect relevance to some extent. Having more reviews and a higher review rating both help.
- ❖ Some traditionally published books appear to have special privileges. You can hardly blame Amazon if they give some traditionally published books a little boost. Even so, there are many cases of self-published books showing up very high in search results.
- ❖ Tags and Likes appear to have been phased out. These may have affected search results, but also were abused by authors (and even customers, to some extent).

❖ A book that suddenly finds itself with very high placement (or winds up on a bestseller list, or gets featured on the Customers Also Bought list of a hot seller) has a limited window of opportunity – to run away with it or fall back off the map. If a book gets promoted to a special position and doesn't seize the moment, this may quickly affect its placement (and the chance of this recurring). If your successful marketing gets your book onto such lists, step up your marketing even more.

❖ Returns may have some effect. Obviously, it's in Amazon's best interest to offer better placement to books that have a lower return rate – all other things being equal. Customer satisfaction is very important to Amazon's future.

❖ Sales history in the last 24 hours, week, and month is also important. A book that is usually ranked in the millions, but presently has a sales rank of 200,000, may not be as visible as a book that's usually ranked near 40,000, but is presently at 200,000 – again, all other factors being the same. Also, the latter book's ranking will climb much more slowly than the former book.

It's easy to see the importance of creating buzz for your book, sending out advance review copies, and marketing to try to get early sales and, hopefully, a few reviews to go with those sales – these things impact your book's visibility and discoverability at Amazon.

Another thing that's significant is where and how you attempt to drive sales through your marketing efforts. You make a greater royalty when you sell books at your CreateSpace eStore or in person, but those sales don't affect your Amazon sales rank. If you expect to sell most of your books at Amazon, then any book that you might have been able to sell in person or at CreateSpace which you instead sell at Amazon helps to improve your sales rank.

Furthermore, if you provide a link to your book, or if customers search for your book by ISBN, title, or author name and then buy your book, that doesn't help your book's visibility in keyword searches. Ideally, you would like your customers to search for your book with some popular keywords and then purchase your book. On the other hand, it's most convenient for customers when they can simply click on a link to your book; they might not buy your book at all if finding your book proves to be inconvenient. So it's tough to promote the ideal situation.

Meeting people in person and word-of-mouth sales can help improve your chances that customers will click on your book in keyword search results and then buy your book. They might remember what your book is about – but forget the title or author name – and try searching for it that way.

However, the most probable way that your book will get sales through keyword searches is when your marketing efforts yield good results – frequent sales and some reviews, especially in the first three months – can help to improve your book's discoverability among new customers who are just performing searches on Amazon.

A very significant percentage of customers actually buy books by browsing the 100 bestseller lists in their favorite genres. It's not easy to get on these lists – and can take dozens of sales per day (or many more, depending on the list), on average, to get on these lists – but if you can get your book there, sales can really skyrocket.

Remember, Amazon.com isn't Amazon's only website. There are also many English-speaking customers at Amazon.ca and Amazon.co.uk, for example.

7.1.4 Sales Rank and Author Rank at Amazon

At Amazon, sales rank is a number with 1 to 6 digits that provides a measure of how frequently a book is selling. A lower number represents more frequent sales.

The sales rank for your book is a number that is constantly changing. You can't look at a book's sales rank just once and pinpoint precisely how well it is selling. Rather, you must monitor sales for a longer period, such as a week, and see what its average sales rank is.

You can monitor your sales rank by checking your book's detail page at Amazon or by logging into AuthorCentral (see Sec. 6.1.5). A handy feature at AuthorCentral is a chart that shows how well each of your books has sold over a period of time.

When a book sells, the sales rank drops down to a significantly lower value. Sales rank then starts to climb until the book sells again. The following numbers are for **print** books.

Sales rank is a combination of how frequently a book has sold in the past 24 hours, week, and month. A book that has no sales rank hasn't sold yet.[19] When a book first sells, its sales rank will start out at around 200,000 and quickly rise upward, reaching 1,000,000 if it doesn't sell again in the next couple of days. A book with a sales rank of 1,000,000 or more hasn't sold for a few days or more; if the sales rank is well over 1,000,000, it may not have sold for weeks.

A book's sales rank climbs more slowly when it has a history of frequent sales in the past 24 hours, week, and month; a book's sales rank climbs very rapidly when it has sold only rarely (or not at all) in the past month.

The following table provides an approximate correspondence between average sales rank and frequency of sales. These numbers change with time. Every year, a million new books are added and there are changes in the economy, so you can't interpret this table literally and expect to know *exactly* how many books you've sold just by looking at your sales rank. However, these numbers should hold approximately true for a long period of time.

Average Sales Rank (Print Books)	Approximate Sales Frequency
around 100	100 per day
1,000 to 5,000	10 per day
around 200,000	1 per day
around 500,000	1 per week
1,000,000 to 2,000,000	1 per month

---

[19] It could have sold recently; sales rank isn't always quite up-to-date.

First note that this table is for physical books sold on Amazon. Kindle eBooks form a similar pattern, but with slightly different numbers, and have different ranks for paid and free.

There is some room for error in this table – don't take it too literally. For one, it depends on Amazon's overall sales figures, which can fluctuate greatly and have seasonal effects. Also, there can be a marked difference between a sales rank of 1,000 and 5,000, so the 10 per day figure can't apply to both ends of this range. These rough figures do help to give you some indication, and others have observed similar numbers. Remember also that this table involves average sales rank, whereas the sales rank itself can change considerably in just a few days.

My own books have been ranked anywhere from around 5,000 to the millions; I usually have multiple books in the 30,000 to 200,000 range at any given time. The sales frequency for a sales rank of around 100 is a figure that I've heard from multiple sources; the other sales frequencies I can corroborate with my own experience. The sales frequency in the top 100 is sensitive – it could easily be 500 per day instead of 100 per day depending on various factors.

Sales rank is based on the sale of one book relative to other books. The bestselling book at any given time has a sales rank of 1. A sales rank of 100 means that only 99 other books have a better sales frequency (the actual formula used weighs sales from the past 24 hours, week, and month together to make the sales rank; there are 99 other books selling better according to Amazon's sales rank formula).

Since sales rank is relative to other books, this means that sales rank can actually drop a little without a sale. Suppose that several books with a sales rank in the millions suddenly sell. Their sales ranks climb very quickly. Other books that generally sell once a day but haven't sold recently will have a sales rank that climbs more slowly. As such, the quickly climbing sales ranks can actually cause the slowly climbing sales ranks to drop a little even though they haven't sold. I've been talking about overall ranks; there are also ranks within categories.

Sales rank includes both new and used books, including direct sales from Amazon as well as those by third-party sellers. Note that different editions receive separate sales ranks. Unfortunately, this is one disadvantage of making regular and large print editions, or color and black-and-white editions – if you just have one edition, all of the sales improve the sales rank of the only edition available. (On the other hand, a few customers may not buy the book at all if the edition they prefer isn't offered.)

It's nice to know that if someone buys an Expanded Distribution book on Amazon that it still improves sales rank – so although the royalty is less than Amazon's royalty, we still receive this benefit. Also, if you ever have so many sales that many customers are selling your book used for cheap, all of these used sales will be helping your sales rank, which might help to get more new sales. There are often ways to find a silver lining. Almost all sales have a positive effect, even if we don't receive a direct royalty payment. (In addition, every sale widens the awareness of your book and improves your prospects for word-of-mouth sales.)

Occasional returns do not appear to affect sales rank (i.e. the sale seems to still improve the ranking – but might impact visibility in search results); cancelled purchases do not affect sales rank (i.e. it doesn't have the effect of a sale). Customer reviews do not improve sales rank. If a single customer places a large order for your book on Amazon, it has the exact same effect as a customer who purchases a single copy. However, if the same customer places multiple orders for your book, each separate order does improve your sales rank.

Beware that at any time Amazon may revise their algorithm for computing sales rank. Therefore, these practices are subject to change with time.

The sales ranks for Kindle eBooks are similar to print sales ranks, but the correspondence between sales frequency and sales rank is a little different. In addition, there is a separate sales rank for free and paid sales. If you have a book enrolled in KDP Select, when you run a free promo, it doesn't have a paid rank during that time (in contrast, a Countdown Deal has a paid rank). When the free promo ends, it reverts back to a sales rank for paid sales – except that at first the sales rank is worse because no paid sales occurred during the free promo period (so the sales rank has steadily climbed). However, if the free promo is successful, there may be a flurry of sales two or three days after the free promo period ends. Such a sales flurry is what authors hope for when they run a free promo, but not all books are successful at this.

In addition to overall sales rank in books – and separately in Kindle eBooks – there are category and subcategory ranks. Your book will receive a splendid dose of additional exposure if it reaches the top 100 in a subcategory. It's very difficult to reach the top 100 in overall sales rank or the top 100 in a category, but the top 100 in a subcategory is much more viable. Since the top 100 sellers in a subcategory get nice exposure, this is one more incentive to try to create buzz for your book and market your book actively before, during, and after its launch. It also provides a compelling incentive to try to drive traffic to Amazon, rather than sell in person or on your own website.[20]

Amazon has recently introduced a new type of rank called author rank, which you can view at AuthorCentral (see Sec. 6.1.5). Like sales rank, the lower the number the better for author rank. The overall bestselling author will have an author rank of 1. If you have an author rank of 20,000, this means that 19,999 authors have a better author rank than you.

All of your books affect your author rank. Authors who write multiple books in the same name have a distinct advantage when it comes to author rank. For example, a writer who has 3 books that each sell an average of 40 copies per day will have a better author rank than another writer who just has 1 book that sells an average of 100 copies per day. The second writer in this example has the more successful book, yet the first writer has a better author rank by having more books. A book that sells poorly doesn't hurt your author rank. Both print books and eBooks help your author rank; even audio books help. Also, note that author rank just depends on the number of books sold, and not on list price or royalty.

---

[20] It does depend on your circumstances. Some authors sell the majority of their books in person or through their own websites, in which case the Amazon sales rank isn't as important. If you're in this position, then you should strive to earn the higher royalty by selling in person or on your own website – or your CreateSpace eStore. For those authors who will sell most of their books on Amazon, there is good reason to prefer Amazon sales.

An author selling an average of 10 books per day may have an author rank of about 20,000. Selling 30 to 40 books per day results in an author rank of about 5,000 to 10,000. Just a couple of sales per day will lead to an author rank of about 50,000 to 100,000.[21]

As with sales rank, these numbers can fluctuate. Since most authors write multiple books, every time an author writes a new book, this helps improve his or her author rank. With the large number of new books being released each month, these new books may affect the correlation between author rank and sales frequency in the future. Other factors, like the current state of the economy, can also affect these numbers.

At AuthorCentral, you can view your author rank in specific categories, just in books, just in Kindle eBooks, and your overall author rank.

Customers will only be able to see your author rank if you sell enough books to make the top 100 overall or the top 100 in a browse category. If your goal is to be a top seller, you should be marketing with the goal of getting on as many top 100 lists as possible. Books and authors that get on these lists get amazing exposure.

It would be useful before you publish – even before you choose your book idea – to be familiar with the top 100 bestsellers and bestselling authors overall and in genres that interest you. If you're wondering which genres sell best, the answer is readily available. These authors and books are successful. Studying them can help you understand what works – and whatever they are lacking (i.e. features that you don't find in their books, covers, blurbs, etc.) might be things that don't work. You can experiment with your own writing by just putting your book together and publishing it, or you can look at the results of experiments that other writers have done. One might even search to see what these authors have done in the way of marketing. Some hints for how we might succeed are right before our very own eyes.

It's not just about what's hot. You also have to weigh what you're a good fit to write (in terms of knowledge, experience, and writing style), as well as what has a need and how much competition there is in that genre. If there happens to be a genre with very hot sellers, not much competition, and tailor-made for your writing, then you should be in Heaven. That's unlikely, but it gives you some goal to strive toward.

Not all book ideas will sell well, and not all writing makes for good reading. There are limits to what research and marketing can do for you, but these can be very helpful tools. Join a writing club to help gauge how well you write and learn what you might improve.

Your sales rank in the United Kingdom and at other Amazon websites works the same way as in the United States, but the correlation between sales frequency and sales rank is somewhat different. You can monitor your sales rank at the UK AuthorCentral, but presently they don't show a UK author rank.

---

[21] I've published books in my own name and a pen name, and have also published books for fellow authors, so I have a few different author ranks ranging from 5,000 to 120,000 to judge by. You can also find screenshots that other authors have posted on the internet. Your research may come up with somewhat different numbers, as these figures do vary with time.

7.1.5 Complementary Versus Competitive Titles

Two books are competitive if customers will probably buy one book, but not the other. Two books are instead complementary when many customers who purchase one book will also purchase the other book.

Most authors think of other books similar to theirs as being the "competition," but this instinct is false. Almost all similar titles are more complementary than they are competitive. Think about this: Similar titles will most likely help stimulate sales for your book rather than take them away.

Every book on Amazon that has any sort of regular sales frequency has an extensive Customers Also Bought list. The first books on this list are almost always similar books. That's because customers often buy several similar books together when they make a purchase, and over the course of several purchases, many of the books belong to the same genre. It's extremely common for customers to purchase similar titles – either all at once, or over the course of time.

Other titles similar to yours will actually help market your book. (It won't be a substitution for the many things you should be doing to market your book, but it can be a big help.) Once enough customers buy your book together with similar titles, your book will show up on their Customers Also Bought lists. It works both ways – their books will also appear on your book's Also Bought list. At first, your book might not be on the most popular books' Also Bought lists, and when it is, it might be buried far down the list; but it's a start. The better your sales, the more exposure your book will receive. This way, your marketing efforts may be doubly re-warded. It takes time for the Also Bought list to show up and grow. Be patient.

Your book also receives this kind of exposure when a customer adds a title that is similar to yours to the shopping cart. After a customer views or buys a similar title, your book may appear on their Amazon homepages – with the Customers Also Viewed or Bought lists.

Occasionally, a cutthroat author conspires to "eliminate" the competition by giving bad reviews to similar books. What he/she doesn't realize is how adversely this will affect his/her own sales. If the author actually succeeds in hurting the sales of similar books, this will in turn hurt the sales of his/her own books – those Customers Also Bought lists only help when the similar titles are selling frequently. Also, if the image of all of the similar titles deteriorates, many customers may search for a different kind of book all together.

When you wish your colleagues good luck with their books, you should *really* mean it – because it may very well have a positive impact on your own sales. To carry this idea a little further, there are a few authors who have achieved success who disparage other self-publishers for their writing and formatting mistakes. Think about the contradiction that occurs when they're trying to market their own positive image while at the same time they are marketing a lousy image for indies in general. If eBook sales drop as a result, this hurts their own sales. Sell a positive image for yourself, other writers, Kindle, Amazon, etc. It all helps.

You should have been **outraged** when I suggested that an author would consider blasting the competition. Unfortunately, on occasion this has been done. It shouldn't happen for the simple reason that the author is shooting him- or herself in the foot by doing so. But obviously they don't realize this. You could also argue that it shouldn't happen for the simple reasons of integrity and scruples – but, alas, we know that everyone doesn't behave this way.

However, there is an even better reason that it shouldn't happen – **it's against Amazon's customer review policy**. Authors are not allowed to review other books in the same genre (good or bad – so giving 5-star reviews to similar titles isn't permitted either). Authors who violate Amazon's policies are looking for serious trouble – they shouldn't bite the hand that feeds them. These unscrupulous authors risk suspension, loss of privileges, and termination.

7.1.6 Amazon Customer Reviews of Your Book

Customer reviews are important, hard to get, often not what you expect, agonizing once in a while, and even occasionally entertaining. Anyone can review your book – and it shows in a wide variety of reviews – yet only a small percentage of customers actually review books.

The major problem that indie authors face is that books with only a few reviews are quite vulnerable. One lousy review right off the bat can be a huge hurdle. Everybody who reads 100 customer reviews knows that he or she will personally disagree with many of them. However, if a book has a single one-star review, hardly anybody will check out the book in search results. This is sort of contradictory, but that's the way it is.

Check out your favorite bestselling author and you'll discover that everybody gets bad reviews. Not everyone will like any book – no matter how good it is. If people give bad reviews to the most highly respected books – and they do – you can bet that some people will do the same with your book – and once you have enough reviews, it will, unfortunately, happen.

If you have dozens of reviews, one bad review isn't going to hurt – rather, it will help provide balance if most of your other reviews are good.

But if you only have a few reviews, a bad review can really hurt. Not all bad reviews hurt; much depends on what is said and how. However, when there are only one or two reviews, a low-star review may prevent several potential customers from even clicking on the book to read the reviews. There is a way around this problem. Try to stimulate early sales and reviews by sending out advance review copies – such as through the Goodreads program described in Sec. 6.2.5 – when your book is released (but note that those won't be Amazon Verified Purchases). Also, try to stimulate many early sales by creating buzz for your book and actively marketing: The more books you sell, the more reviews you're likely to get.

Once you have a handful of good reviews, one bad review probably won't hurt. Your book becomes far less vulnerable to the effect of a single low-star review once it receives a handful of good reviews.

Too many good reviews is also a problem! **Customers are suspicious of a book that has just four- and five-star reviews.** A number of authors who abused the system in the past have aroused this suspicion in customers. No writer *wants* to receive a bad review, but an occasional low-star review is needed to achieve a sense of balance.

It's not just the number of stars that matters – what is written can actually carry more weight. Reviews that simply say, "This was the best book ever," or, "It was awful," will be ignored by most customers unless they also describe what they did or didn't like about the book. Similarly, reviews that describe the author instead of the book aren't helpful. There are many such reviews out there – they just aren't helpful to customers.

Good reviews that explain specific features that made the book worth reading tend to carry more weight, and bad reviews that describe spelling, grammatical, formatting, writing, plot, and storyline mistakes tend to get more credibility. Unfortunately, unscrupulous individuals who may be out to shoot a book down can easily lie about such mistakes to create a false impression (and Amazon will do absolutely nothing about them – unless it can be proven that the reviewer is an author in the same genre, which is unlikely to happen unless they actually used their own name). However, the vast majority of such reviews do have merit.

The problem is that there are many self-published books that do have several spelling, grammatical, and formatting mistakes, so most of the reviews that point this out are correct. Customers are aware of this, so they tend to believe such a review and usually don't even bother to check the Look Inside to see if the review is correct (especially, since the mistakes might come after the Look Inside). If you happen to have a book that is virtually free of mistakes and you receive such a review that really is false, then I feel your pain. As I said, a book with very few reviews is quite vulnerable. Advance review copies and early sales give you good prospects for getting some early reviews that can help offset any such nonsense.

Although there are a few books that have been attacked with malicious reviews, **most books are not**. I didn't mean to scare you with this. Chances are that it won't happen to you unless you do something to provoke it. It does happen to a few books: Some authors have sworn enemies or jealous rivals, plus there are a few anti-self-publishing people out there.

You also want to try to keep clear of the self-proclaimed "behavior police." There are such "policemen" and "policewomen" on Goodreads and several discussion forums – like KDP – where indie authors frequently participate. They like to give "citations" – i.e. bad reviews on Amazon or Goodreads – when they see self-published authors comment defensively on a review, post bad things about reviewers on the KDP discussion forum, etc. Strive to maintain a professional image as an author and you can greatly reduce your chances of being targeted by the Goodreads and KDP forum "police."

At some point, every author who sells enough books will get some bad reviews. **Most of these bad reviews are <u>not</u> malicious like the few that I've already described.** No book can please every reader, people like to disagree with others, readers have many different interests, and so on. Eventually, you will receive a "legitimate" bad review. Brace yourself.

Authors need to develop a thick skin. Successful writers don't let reviews get to them. A bad review may hurt – even those authors who don't show it. Successful authors analyze the bad reviews for possible areas of improvement as a writer. If a review complains of poor writing, assess to what extent this review may have merit. Should you invest in an editor, read a book on writing style, and strive to develop further as a writer? The author who becomes a better writer because of a bad review grows and has the promise of a more successful future.

You can't do everything that every review tells you that you should do. Customers will come up with all kinds of ways that they believe a book could be "better." You can't please everyone. Therefore, some reviews you just have to shrug off and ignore. Don't try to make a change in your writing based on *every* comment you read.

The important thing is not to let your emotions provoke unprofessional behavior on your part. Replying to reviews emotionally has cost some authors their writing careers. If you tend to react emotionally, maybe it's best not to read your reviews at all – or to shut your computer off after reading the review and not turn it back on for a few days. Give yourself a chance to cool off first.

Our books are our babies, so it's easy to take any criticism personally. We put so much time, thought, and effort into our books; we're very attached to them. We worked hard to do our best. Thus, hearing that a customer didn't like the result of our hard work can really hurt.

But customers are reviewing the book; they're not reviewing you as a person. Remember that. The purpose of customer reviews *isn't* to provide feedback to the author. Nope. The purpose is to help other customers decide if this book is for them. A reviewer isn't writing a note to the author, but to other customers. The review isn't directed at you, so don't take it personally. Even if a review does attack you personally, still you just have to shrug it off.

A bad review isn't necessarily an instant sales killer, unless perhaps all of the reviews are bad – if the book has an average rating of one to two stars, then customers may not even click on the link. A bad review mixed with good reviews doesn't tend to kill sales. First of all, every review increases the total number of reviews, and more reviews make the book seem more popular – books that sell more tend to have more reviews. A few bad reviews provide some balance and differing opinions for potential customers to consider. I've seen some books' sales improve significantly after receiving a low-star review, so bad reviews are not all bad.

The most important thing about a bad review is how you handle it. Don't let it get to you. Try to see if there is anything useful that you can extract from it. Try not to take it personally. Don't dwell on it. Strive to grow a thicker skin so that it doesn't bother you. Everyone is entitled to his/her own opinion. You're not going to like everybody's opinion. You want people to review your book, you want to receive a diversity of opinions, and you want your reviews to be balanced. Nobody wants a bad review, but having just five-star reviews arouses suspicion.

The self-published author's initial reactions to a bad review are often (1) to try to get it removed, (2) to downvote it with No votes, and (3) to post a comment on the review. Amazon almost never removes a bad review (there must be a very clear violation to their review policy from Amazon's perspective – not the author's point of view – for this to happen), so any effort to get the review removed probably won't pay off. We'll discuss Amazon's review guidelines later in this section.

Resist the temptation to downvote the review by pressing the No button to vote that the review wasn't helpful. Why? Before you react emotionally, think about how it will look. Especially, if there is a No vote shortly after the review was left, customers will assume that the author did this. It doesn't look professional. It's possible that other customers will vote No, indicating that the review didn't help them; if so, there's nothing you can do about it. But what you shouldn't do is vote No thinking, "How do you know it wasn't a customer?" Even if it was a customer, they may still believe it was the author. It's how it looks in the eyes of the potential buyer that matters, now what actually happened.

Suppose that you make the mistake of voting No. What might happen? The customer might see that – or the "review police" might take notice – and they can send their friends (or army) over to your product page and vote Yes to the bad review and No to any of your good reviews. It would have been far better if the author didn't vote at all.

Sometimes, when this happens, the author recruits his/her own posse of friends to vote the good reviews up and the bad review down. Now how will this look to potential customers to see reviews with 16 Yes votes and 9 No votes, for example? **Unprofessional!** The reviewer and his/her friends have nothing to lose by looking unprofessional; the author has a reputation and image at stake. The way to avoid this problem is to not vote at all.

If a random customers votes No, the same chain reaction probably won't occur because – unlike the author – that customer will only vote No once and be done with it.

Commenting on a bad review out of frustration is another common mistake. Very often, the author's emotions show through, the author appears defensive, or – worse yet – the author attacks the reviewer. This looks highly unprofessional and creates a poor image for the author. It's far better to have a bad review with no comments or No votes, as this looks much more professional. Every book will have bad reviews once enough customers have reviewed it, and ideally the reviews should be balanced. Accept that everybody won't like your book.

Some authors jeopardize their writing careers by commenting on a review in a negative way and then letting it get out of hand. Once you comment on a review, the reviewer is likely to reply to your comment – very often, in such a way as to entice you into posting another comment. This quickly turns into a long discussion in the comments section, which discourages sales and may catch the attention of the "review police."

If the "review police" feel that an author has misbehaved, they may recruit their friends to post a series of negative reviews. That's far worse than having one bad review with no comments or No votes.

Don't be tempted to get your own posse of friends together to downvote reviews or comment on reviews. It will just look unprofessional. An occasional customer will comment on a review, and there's nothing you can to prevent it; but it will just be occasional.

I've been describing possible problems because you need to be ready for it and prepared to deal with it professionally. Don't do anything rash. Don't do anything to jeopardize the potential success of your book. I hope I haven't misled you to believe that there will be several bad reviews. If your book is good, there should be a good balance with several good reviews, a few neutral reviews, and a few critical reviews. I didn't mean to make you worry that there might be loads of bad reviews or that many customers are out to get you.

The vast majority of customers who leave reviews provide honest feedback, which is helpful to both other customers and to authors. Many customers try to find good things to say about the books they read. Many customers make wise purchase decisions and tend to be happy with the books that they buy. We wouldn't sell any books if not for customers, and we wouldn't have any reviews if not for the customers who take a few moments to post them. Take a moment to be thankful for customers and reviewers. We absolutely need them.

On the other side of this, a good review isn't an instant sales booster. When an author's first review – or even first handful of reviews – is glowing with five stars, very often sales don't pick up; sometimes they even slip a little. Many authors find this surprising and frustrating. In the customer's mind, it's suspicious when every review just has great praise for the book – they wonder if maybe all of the reviews were written by friends and family. Some authors have abused the system in the past, and many customers have heard about it, which makes them wary. **Fake five-star reviews are a much greater problem than fake one-star reviews.**

If you read the reviews of any book that has a hundred of them, you'll surely see some crazy remarks. A few have nothing whatsoever to do with the book. Some reviews will outright contradict others. A review with three spelling errors may complain about mistakes. There may be a couple of reviews that don't seem like they're describing the right book. Customers will even admit to not having read the book. If you can dream of it, someone has probably written such a review.

With this in mind, you can't take any single review too seriously. Most customers know this, too. The total number of reviews you have and the kinds of remarks therein outweigh the number of stars received. What you hope for is that some of the good reviews will outline specific things that made your book good (like a memorable character, a great plot, or suspenseful writing) and that the bad reviews won't be too bad. Customers won't be swayed by a review that attacks you or says the book is awful without giving a credible explanation – so just disregard those. In fact, when the bad reviews don't look bad or credible, they actually make your book look good. Another thing you hope is that the low-star reviews will come in moderation; nobody wants to receive these in high frequency.

Just as reviews show a wide variety of comments, customers analyze the reviews in many different ways. Some look just at the bad reviews. Others ignore the first handful of reviews, assuming that they come from friends and family. A few only trust neutral three-star reviews. There are customers who just look to see if anyone has complained about formatting and editing. Many ignore the stars all together and just look for statements that explain what they did or didn't like about the book (this might be one of the wiser practices). Fortunately, there are also customers who mainly look at the cover, blurb, and Look Inside, virtually disregarding the reviews (this may be the wisest practice of all). Although I've identified two practices that I believe are wisest, most customers apply a different method. Everybody has a different method of making decisions that they feel comfortable with; we just have to accept this.

Note that customers don't have to buy a book in order to review it. According to Amazon's policies, a customer doesn't even have to read the book in order to review it. Don't shoot the messenger; that's Amazon's decision. (We'll get to their review guidelines later in this section.)

If a customer does buy your book, when they review your book they can check a box to mark the review as an Amazon Verified Purchase (if bought at Amazon). They may also choose to review using their Real Name. Remember, customers can review your book even if it's not an Amazon Verified Purchase. For print books, customers may actually have the book even if the review doesn't show that the purchase is verified: They could have borrowed it from a library, received it as a gift, bought it from a different bookseller, etc. Even if they bought it from Amazon, they may have unchecked the box so that it doesn't show as an Amazon Verified Purchase. For a Kindle eBook, they might have bought the eBook elsewhere (if available that way). Amazon doesn't care if it's an Amazon Verified Purchase. Amazon doesn't care if they even have the book. They're still allowed to review it.

On the other hand, reviews declared to be Amazon Verified Purchases tend to have more credibility among potential customers than those that aren't. Another way that customers can check on credibility is to check out the reviewer's profile and other reviews. When the reviewer only has one review or a small number of reviews, or if most of the reviews are not for books, customers tend to be suspicious – if it's a good review, it could be a friend of the author, and if it's a bad review, there may be malicious intent. Many reviews are actually legitimate even though the customer has reviewed just one book and it's not identified as an Amazon Verified Purchase; the problem is that many similar reviews in the past have abused the system, so this creates suspicion – legitimate or not. You're going to have some legitimate reviews that look suspicious – that's just the way it is (so authors who abuse the system have an inordinate number of these). You should also have many that don't seem suspicious.

Don't worry about what you have no control over. You don't have any control over what reviews customers might post, how customers may vote on other reviews, what comments they might make, how many other products the customer has reviewed, or whether the review will show as an Amazon Verified Purchase. So don't sweat these things.

You do have control over some things. You can try to create buzz for your book, you can send out advanced review copies (such as through Goodreads), and you can most definitely refrain from downvoting or commenting on reviews in order to maintain a professional image as an author. You have control in writing, editing, and formatting your book as well as possible. You control how much time and effort you are willing to put into marketing, and whether or not you will utilize effective marketing techniques. Focus on perfecting your book, creating buzz, attempting to stimulate early reviews of your book, and marketing your book – since more sales tend to lead to more reviews. Do your best and the reviews will take care of themselves. Statistically, reviews should average out once you get enough of them.

Since many customers understand that the reviews are inherently limited in their potential helpfulness, it's very important to have a great cover, blurb, and Look Inside. Some buyers will judge how professional these elements are in lieu of reading the reviews; others will check these things out to try to corroborate what is written in the reviews. Perfecting the cover, blurb, and Look Inside, as well as marketing effectively to achieve and maintain a good sales rank and earn steady reviews are more important than the reviews themselves. Professional appearance, sales rank, and the total number of reviews tend to influence buying decisions far more than any specific review – good or bad.

Customers are more likely to review a book if they feel strongly about it – really loved it (great characterization or plot) or hated it (not their style or found something to complain about) – or if it moves them emotionally (made them cry or giggle). Most customers don't review books. For some books, it can take hundreds of sales to get a review; for others, every few dozen or so sales spark a review. Some genres receive more reviews than others.

A free promotion through Kindle Select can sometimes have interesting effects. Authors intuitively expect to receive some great reviews by customers who receive the book for free, but it often doesn't work this way. First of all, most of the customers who download the book for free never even read it; they tend to download many more free books than can be read in several lifetimes. Some who read it won't start it for months – it will sit on their Kindles until they eventually get around to it. Others will start it right away, but spend months reading it. Only a few will start reading it immediately and finish it soon. So if you give away a thousand books, there might only be a few customers who finish reading it within a month. It's not reasonable to expect a large number of reviews shortly after giving away your book for free.

Back to the point where authors might think customers are grateful to get a very good book for free and will therefore leave a great review: The other side of the coin is that many customers believe that you get what you pay for. That is, some customers have a prejudice that free books must not be worth paying for. Sometimes a free promo results in bad reviews, not good ones. It happens.

Another thing to consider is that the free promo attracts readers from outside of your genre who may not understand what is typical of the genre. As a result, they may have unreasonable expectations. Sometimes this shows up in low-star reviews.

Finally, there are a few authors and publishers who loathe the free giveaways and believe that these free books are hurting everybody's paid sales. A few of these people are mean enough to go around blasting freebies with one-star reviews, unleashing their frustrations at fellow authors. Unfortunately, this practice hurts the image of eBooks in general, and may have a negative impact on their very own sales. However, this is rare. Most of the reviews are by actual customers. **The vast majority of one- and two-star reviews come from customers who just weren't happy with the book**, and are not malicious reviews from people who have an agenda. There are such people in the world, but fortunately most people aren't like that.

Amazon doesn't police reviews to prevent spiteful or malicious reviews. This makes it all the more important to behave professionally and establish a positive image as an author. Refrain from making any comments that may spark an attack from the "bad behavior police." Amazon won't remove their reviews, votes, or comments (except in very extreme cases). All you can do is try not to attract the attention of people who may leave malicious reviews.

On the other hand, Amazon does police suspicious four- and five-star reviews. Since many authors and publishers have abused the review system, Amazon does strive to prevent this. Amazon is far more likely to block or remove a suspicious five-star review than it is to remove a one-star review. Amazon isn't publishing exactly what data they look at to determine whether or not a good review is legitimate because they don't want people who know too much to try to game the system. If an author asks why a review has been removed, Amazon won't disclose the specifics. From all of the authors who have complained about the removal of good reviews, we have some ideas for what Amazon may look at in order to judge which good reviews to block or remove. This may include the following:

- ➢ The author has reviewed his or her own book. This is not allowed.
- ➢ The author's spouse or immediate family member has reviewed his or her book. If Amazon determines that the reviewer may have a financial interest in the book, the review will be removed.
- ➢ An IP address that a reviewer has used at least once matches an IP address that the author has used at least once. If a reviewer and the author have ever used the same computer or IP address, the review will be removed.
- ➢ Multiple reviewers have a correlation with at least one IP address. To Amazon, this looks like one person has created multiple accounts to give the same book multiple reviews. These reviews may be removed.
- ➢ A reviewer has the same last name as the author. Amazon may suspect that this is a family member. If Amazon removes reviews based on this, that's bad news for authors whose last names happen to be Smith or Jones. Maybe they also look at location. Again, there is no guarantee that Amazon uses this criteria; it's speculation based on what Amazon might do combined with stories that authors have told.
- ➢ A reviewer and the author appear to be friends. Amazon may be able to judge this based on Facebook or Goodreads' friends lists, for example. Or someone who believes that a reviewer is a friend of the author may contact Amazon to report this. There are some authors who believe Amazon may do this, but only Amazon knows for sure.
- ➢ Two authors exchange reviews – i.e. they agree to mutually review each other's books. In Amazon's eyes, this may look like two authors are trying to game the system.
- ➢ Anything else that Amazon deems to be suspicious.

Thousands (perhaps millions) of four- and five-star reviews have been either removed or blocked by Amazon. Most of these are reviews where Amazon suspects that the author or someone who may have a financial interest in the book's success may have written the review. If you have a good review that disappears, one of the reasons listed previously could be the cause. Another possibility is that the customer removed his/her own review; nothing prevents a customer from doing this.

Unfortunately, Amazon may occasionally remove a legitimate review in their effort to prevent and remove reviews that truly violate their policies. Amazon would rather remove a few legitimate reviews by mistake than allow a few authors to abuse the system.

At the same time, Amazon almost never removes a bad review. A one- or two-star review has to be a very clear violation of Amazon's review policy in order to trigger its removal. Following are some types of reviews that are not allowed:

- Authors can't review their own books.
- People who may have a financial interest in the book's success – including household family members or the publisher – are not allowed to review the author's book.
- Authors are not allowed to pay or compensate (except for mailing out free, legitimate advanced review copies) people for their reviews.
- Reviews may not include advertisements, personal information (like contact info), external links, or requests for helpful votes. However, it's okay if the review includes a link to another book on Amazon (provided that the reviewer doesn't have a financial interest in the sale of the linked book).
- A review shouldn't mention the price, availability, or shipping. Nonetheless, there are thousands of reviews that describe the shipping time or condition of the package.
- Authors are not allowed to review books in a subject or genre that is similar to their own books, or to review books with content that is similar to their own. Authors are not permitted to review complementary or competitive titles.
- Obscenity, profanity, and spitefulness are not allowed. However, Amazon does not remove *all* reviews that have some measure of spitefulness. Some authors have mildly (or even moderately) spiteful reviews that Amazon has elected not to remove.
- Reviews are not supposed to comment on other reviews on the product page.

If you see a review that you believe may be a violation of Amazon's review policies, you may report it to Amazon. Make a polite request. Reviews are removed at Amazon's discretion. They will look into it, and may choose to let the review stand. Amazon will not offer any explanation for their decision. You just have to accept it.

Although the customer review system isn't perfect, all in all it serves a valuable purpose: It offers potential customers some opinions from previous readers. The number of reviews is often far more important than any single review. It's only a rare occasion that a low-star review has an agenda. It's unreasonable to suspect every low-star review of having malicious intent. Very many customers leave positive reviews and provide helpful suggestions. When customers do offer criticism, they usually have a valid point.

Compared to independent movies, indie authors should be very happy with Amazon's customer review system. Many independent films – and even some major productions – get streams of one- and two-star reviews at websites like Redbox. Fortunately, there don't appear to be nearly as many harsh book critics as there are harsh movie critics. That's good for indie authors; the image of indie authors in general is nearly as important as each author's individual reputation. Like I mentioned before, the authors who sell a bad image regarding self-publishing with negative comments contradict their own efforts to market their own books. In addition to marketing your own books, help to rebuild a positive image of indies.

Don't focus on the shortcomings of the review system or the occasional abuse of the system. Focus on the fact that customer reviews – both the good and the bad – can serve as a helpful tool for potential customers.

Let's return to the controversial issue of whether or not it's okay to comment on reviews. The vast majority of authors and customers feel that authors should generally not comment on customer reviews. That alone should tell you that if you do it, it's going to upset a large number of customers and potential customers – not to mention the "review police."

Not commenting on a review is never a mistake. Not commenting on a review will never be interpreted as bad behavior. Not commenting on a review won't lead to retaliation from a customer or the "review police." Not commenting on a review will look professional.

Commenting on a review carries a great risk. It risks looking unprofessional. It risks possible retaliation by the customer and their friends (but only your image is at stake). It risks your image as an author. It risks future sales. It risks your writing career.

However, there are some authors – who are in the minority with their opinions – who believe that there may be occasions in which it is okay to comment on a review. This may include when the reviewer asks the author a question, to provide notice of updates, or to post that a new edition is available. In the former case, including some means of contacting you in the About the Author page may be the better option. In the latter cases, it's really not necessary: You can place this notice in the blurb, where it will be far more visible.

Other authors feel that replying to reviews offers customers that personal touch. Their feeling is, "What traditional author will take the time to reach out to his/her readers this way?" There are, however, many other ways to interact with readers who want the author to be personable – such as a fan club, the author's blog, or a temporary author/fan forum on Goodreads. Many reviewers don't want the author commenting on their reviews.

The majority of reviewers claim that customer reviews are their space, not the author's space, and don't want authors to invade this space. Whereas the author may feel that a simple, "Thank you for reading my book and taking time to share your thoughts," provides a personal touch, many reviewers feel that this is tacky – and something only a self-published author would do. When you thank a reviewer, other customers suspect that you are friends.

I recommend not commenting on reviews. Before you do some research and accuse me of being hypocritical, let me point out that I have commented on a couple of my reviews. I have done this, rarely, with my own books thinking that this experience may be useful prior to advising other authors – in this book – about commenting on reviews. By doing so, for example, I discovered that you can remove your comment afterward, but if anyone else has commented, too, when you remove your comment, it will say, "Deleted by the author on..." Here, the word "author" really means the customer who commented, but potential customers will interpret this literally as the author (so if a stranger posts and removes a comment – and there are other comments showing – that might create a little confusion; however, customers rarely comment, except when the author's comments provoke their participation).

If you do comment on a review, you must absolutely do so tastefully, politely, tactfully, and respectfully. Your image is at stake, and a negative author image can have a brutal impact on sales. No comment at all is more professional than a tasteful comment. Don't attack the reviewer; don't accuse the reviewer of anything; and don't be defensive. This behavior can lead to catastrophic results. Even tasteful comments place your image at stake and can get the attention of the "review police." Better to not comment and better not to thank customers for their reviews than to risk this.

Responding to bad reviews is even riskier, and takes a great deal of tact. First read the review carefully. If the writing suggests the possibility that the person could react quite negatively to your response, then your comment will likely attract negative attention. If the person has only reviewed your book, this person probably has an agenda. Commenting on reviews where the reviewer may have an agenda or may react emotionally is like playing with fire – and only you can get hurt. Part of the problem is that you can't always tell from a short writing sample that the person has an agenda or might react negatively, and it might be an onlooker who reacts this way – not the reviewer him- or herself. No wonder the vast majority of authors will advise you not to comment on your reviews.

You don't want to look needy, whiny, or defensive. You don't want to look like you sell so few books that you need to respond to your reviews. The cons of commenting far outweigh any pros.

Another thing you must avoid is blogging or posting on a forum (or anywhere online, like Facebook or Twitter) anything negative about any reviewer. It's tempting to want to blow off steam and/or seek some comfort and support by describing a bad review on your blog or a forum. However, this is unprofessional and very likely to attract the "bad behavior police." Your image as an author takes much time to establish, but can very quickly be ruined in just a heartbeat. Don't risk it by saying anything bad about reviewers or customers.

There are many mistakes that indie authors frequently make regarding reviews. A common one is to post a question online – such as at a discussion forum – asking for reviews. This looks tacky and unprofessional, and again tends to attract the "review police." Even worse is asking other authors to exchange reviews – i.e. review each other's book (providing feedback privately to each other is useful, but mutually exchanging public reviews is frowned upon). A few authors have even gone so far as to ask how they might buy reviews (and, believe it or not, some have actually done this). Paying for reviews is a violation of Amazon's policy. Amazon will remove a review if they believe that compensation has been provided for it (other than a free review copy). Furthermore, such behavior risks account suspension or termination.[22] Begging for reviews isn't good either – that also hurts your image as an author.

The proper way to get reviews is to send out advance review copies to people who are allowed to review your book (Goodreads, for example, has a program that can help with this), offer a relevant blogger (start small, as major bloggers are likely to get numerous requests) a free copy to read if they may have an interest in reviewing your book (as with advance review copies, there is no guarantee that your book will get reviewed or that the review will be good – it's a chance that you take), and market as best you can because the more books you sell, the greater the chances that your book will get reviewed.

If you explore Amazon UK and other international websites, you may find reviews on your books there that don't (presently) show up on Amazon US. If you have good reviews there, you will be wishing that the reviews showed up on all of Amazon's websites; but if you have bad reviews internationally that complain about differences between American and British English or customers who didn't understand what they were buying because of language differences, you may be glad that those reviews don't show up in the United States. This may change in the future. It's possible that all of Amazon's websites' reviews will be consolidated. If so, it is generally the case that having more reviews is better.

I've been fortunate to receive multiple reviews on several different books, including many good reviews. No amount of good reviews can make me appreciate them any less; every good review that I receive brings a smile to my face. I have a few critical reviews, too. I realize that these help to provide a balanced picture. I have even revised a few of my books, making improvements based on these suggestions. Some critical reviews help us write better books.

As a reader, my review policy is different than that of many other reviewers: I only review books that I believe merit five stars. For one, as an author myself, I understand how much time and effort goes into all of the stages of writing and publishing a book, and I know what it's like for an author to be very passionate about his or her work. I don't feel comfortable writing a review for which I would give less than five stars. So rather than review every book that I read – which would be very time-consuming – I only take the time to review those books that impress me the most. Some will argue that it may look biased that I don't give any bad reviews. On the other hand, this balances those reviewers who only give bad ones.

Also, I don't review books by request; I find my own books and review only those.

---

[22] Some of the people "selling" good reviews on Amazon actually leave nasty one-star reviews! Those are people who are appalled by the thought of authors paying for reviews and who are taking matters into their own hands, trying to "teach" such authors a lesson. If you see an advertisement offering to leave a good review for payment, don't think, "So that's how some authors are doing it." This unscrupulous tactic probably isn't working.

Do you review books that you've read? If you're hoping to have your book read and reviewed, it's kind of hypocritical if you're not taking the time to review books yourself. One way to help foster a better image for indies is to occasionally read indie books and review indie books that you like. Giving great reviews for bad books won't help our image, but giving good reviews for well-written indie books will help in a small way; if a great number of indies do this, the effect will be more significant.

In conversations and blogs, speak positively about indie authors; refrain from complaining or making disparaging remarks publicly. When you hear a negative comment about indies, take a moment to briefly and tactfully respond with a statement of the form, "Actually…" Keep it brief, sound positive, don't be defensive, and don't get in an argument. The small things we might do to help our image impact every one of us. If you have a friend or acquaintance who is self-publishing, provide some honest feedback. If you can tactfully persuade them to improve some aspect of their books, this also helps to improve our image.

Also, if you review books by other indies, remember that you're not permitted to review books that are similar to yours in content, subject, or genre.

7.1.7 Customer and Author Discussion Forums

If you participate in Amazon's customer discussion forums or the KDP community's forums, you have a choice of doing so anonymously or you may choose to reveal your identity in your profile. If you reveal your identity in your profile (or if your profile is anonymous, but you reveal your identity explicitly or implicitly in any of your posts), do so with your image as an author in mind. Be professional. Appear knowledgeable, trustworthy, and likeable. Write well. Proofread your posts because they are samples of your writing. Don't post anything that may attract negative attention, create controversy, or otherwise adversely affect your image as an author. You especially don't want to attract the self-appointed "bad behavior police."

Self-promotion is not allowed in Amazon's customer discussion forums. You're not permitted to say, "I wrote a book called __," for example, or to include the title of your book at the end of your posts. Customers will become very irate if you self-promote in forums where this is not allowed, and a moderator may edit or remove your post. It paints a bad image, too.

You can be a helpful, thoughtful participant in the discussions. If someone likes your writing or ideas, they may click on your user profile. If your profile reveals your name and indicates that you're an author, they may indirectly learn about your book this way. Most customers are not clicking on many profiles and buying books from authors this way. It's probably not the best place to promote – especially, since you're not allowed to include a signature line, and few people will indirectly discover your book by clicking on your profile. Also, most other indie authors are promoting only on Amazon, and most customers are weary of the self-promotion that occurs from thousands of authors who didn't know better.

When you visit your book's detail page at Amazon, you'll see a place where a customer could begin a discussion about your book. This is highly unlikely except for very popular traditionally published authors. Don't start your own discussion here, as customers may perceive it as tacky and unprofessional.

The KDP community forum is a good place to meet other authors, exchange ideas, get help with your Kindle eBook, and help others. You can benefit from these things anonymously. If you reveal your identity – even through a hint in a single post – remember that your author image is at stake. Always behave professionally. If you simply support others who are complaining – say, about a bad review – there is a possibility that you will be targeted by the "bad behavior police" indirectly just through your association (this has happened).

Some authors request feedback on their blurbs, covers, etc. on the KDP community help forum. Ideally, one would do this prior to publishing – you only get one chance to make a great first impression. You can get some honest feedback there, but beware that sometimes it's brutally honest. That's the most useful kind of feedback, but you have to be prepared for it and put on a thick skin. At the same time, not everyone who participates there is necessarily an expert on the subject, so you have to sort out the good advice from the bad; on the other hand, customers will have a variety of opinions, so hearing a variety of opinions from fellow authors might be helpful. Obviously, sharing your blurb or cover will reveal your identity, so remember the importance of appearing professional.

There are better places to promote your book than the KDP community forum. Almost everyone there is an author like you, busy writing and marketing their own books. A few authors there do occasionally buy books from other authors – especially, when they like the writing style and character displayed in the posts – but many other authors simply aren't looking for books to read while they are in author help forums. The more effective way to market online is to figure out where your target audience is likely to engage in conversations, and try to get discovered through your helpful participation at those sites.

7.1.8 Preorders and Affiliate Links

Go to Amazon's homepage, scroll down to the bottom, and find the Make Money with Us list. As a self-published author, you will probably be interested in Amazon Advantage and/or Amazon Associates. The links under Make Money with Us include – some of these won't be relevant for you – Sell on Amazon (you can make products or buy them wholesale, then sell them in a store on Amazon; you can sell your used books online as a third-party seller; or you could sell the books you've published as a third-party seller, but I don't recommend this last option), Become an Affiliate (earn a commission for any sales you generate by referring customers to Amazon via product links), Advertise Your Products (if you have any goods or services to advertise), and Independently Publish with Us (on CreateSpace and Kindle).

Find both Amazon Advantage and Amazon Associates by clicking the See All link under Make Money with Us. Amazon Advantage allows you to ship books (or other products) to Amazon to stock them in their warehouse and let Amazon sell them on their website. If you want to make your book available for preorders, use Amazon Advantage to do it. This allows you to create a listing for your book before it is published, and allows customers to buy your book in advance of the release date. A couple of days before your book will be released (i.e. when you will click Approve Proof and enable the Amazon sales channel at CreateSpace), go to the Amazon Advantage control panel and submit a request that Amazon Advantage switch control of your Amazon orders over to CreateSpace.

You have to be very clear and precise about what you want in your request to Amazon Advantage, and you may need to exchange a couple of messages with them. You don't want them to close your book; you want it to remain open until the release date. This shouldn't be a problem because it's only available for preorder – you listed the date that it will be available, and it's not available yet. If they tell you that they've closed the book, you want to respond and explain that you want it to remain open, and remind them why this should be okay (because it's not yet available – you set a release date which hasn't come to pass). You want a smooth transition so that CreateSpace can simply fulfill the orders that have already been placed and for Amazon to fulfill future orders through CreateSpace, too.

If Amazon Advantage tells you that you can't source orders through both Amazon Advantage and CreateSpace, explain that this shouldn't be a problem because it's a preorder. Again, you need to tell them that you would like it to remain open until the release date so that customers may preorder it, and then have CreateSpace take over when it's published.

Once you have suspended (not closed – at least, not prior to the release date) your book at Amazon Advantage, you can ignore Amazon's email alerts about stocking your title – since you have requested Amazon Advantage to have CreateSpace fulfill your orders.

The important thing is to check your book's Amazon detail page. You want the preorder option available prior to the release date with the Add to Cart button live, and you want this to change to being available and In Stock once your book is published. Your title should remain open at Amazon Advantage until the release date, and change to Closed when Create-Space takes over fulfillment.

At some point in the process, you may need to go to your Amazon Advantage control panel, click on Purchase Orders, and mark them as Cancelled: Not Yet Available. If done correctly, this shouldn't cancel the order completely, but should hold the orders until the book is available. You want the orders to be transferred to and fulfilled by CreateSpace.

If you have questions, contact Amazon Advantage to explain what you are trying to do (and if they misinterpret your intentions, try to clarify). You might also search the CreateSpace community forum for discussions about preorders or post a question there.

Note that preordering is presently only available for books, but not for eBooks. (However, you may notice that the big publishers have special privileges.)

Join Amazon Associates in order to earn commissions from sales that you refer to Amazon's website through an affiliate link. You can get an affiliate link for specific Amazon pages from Amazon Associates and then use it at your own website. You can also link to a book or product using a thumbnail image. The commission applies to any products that customers may purchase at Amazon after clicking on the affiliate link. This only works from websites – it doesn't work when the link is included in an email or an eBook (you're not permitted to include affiliate links in an eBook; you can include relevant links in an eBook, but you can't use affiliate links to earn commissions on referrals from an eBook).

Beware that a new limit on affiliate links to free promo books has been imposed by Amazon. If you use your affiliate links primarily to link to free promo books or if customers download 20,000 or more free promo books in a month after clicking on your affiliate links (of which 80% or more of the free downloads are attributed to your affiliate links), then you will not earn any commissions for that month. Some websites were avidly promoting free books through affiliate links, hoping that the customers would also buy others products while at Amazon. These program changes are evidently directed toward this practice.

If you use your real name or a pen name as your Associates name, the address bar will reveal this name when the affiliate link is clicked. This is something to keep in mind if you want to use affiliate links from a website without revealing your identity.

7.1.9 Changes in Amazon's Website

Amazon's website, programs, policies, and practices change periodically. These changes can seem scary at first, especially once you've achieved some level of success. Amazon strives to improve. Like all business, their goal is to maximize their profits, and like all consumer-driven businesses, this means optimizing the quality of the products and customer satisfaction. When you think about it, improvements that Amazon may make regarding the quality of their products or customer satisfaction benefit all of us – not only as customers, but as authors, too. Customers are more likely to buy books when they are generally pleased with the products and services. So we shouldn't fear possible changes at Amazon.

A couple of years ago Amazon began removing and blocking reviews – mostly with four and five stars – that they suspected of violating their policies. A small number of these reviews may have been legitimate, but overall this has improved the customer experience by helping to prevent review abuse that had been previously occurring. Customers and authors should generally view this change as for the better.

Recently, the 4-for-3 program was discontinued. I was concerned about this at first because most of my books had been in the 4-for-3 program, and frequently sold by the fours. However, Amazon now periodically discounts some of my books that had previously not been discounted. If anything, this change seems to have improved my sales.

There will surely be other changes, too. It doesn't help to worry about them. The changes usually provide improvement, which help both customers and authors. We should welcome this type of change.

Sometimes, there are temporary changes or glitches in the system. Once a year or so the sales rank feature seems to disappear for a day or two. Sales often plummet in such cases, and can take a while to rebuild afterward. However, this is very rare and doesn't last long. If this happens and you notice it, remember that it probably won't last long and it probably won't occur again for another year or so. Occasionally, there is a glitch in the detail page for a book at Amazon. These glitches often resolve on their own, but if you notice a glitch, you should report the problem to Amazon.

7.1.10 Contacting Amazon

If you have an author-related issue, you can contact Amazon from AuthorCentral. After logging into AuthorCentral, select the Help tab and look for the yellow Contact Us button. For issues that relate to a book that you've published with CreateSpace, you can contact support from your Member Dashboard. You can also receive much help from the CreateSpace community forum. For issues that relate specifically to your Kindle eBook, you can contact KDP from the KDP community help pages: Click the yellow Contact Us button in the bottom left corner. One way for customers to contact Amazon is to look for the small Help link at the bottom of their homepage and then find the yellow Contact Us button on the right side.

7.2 Exploring Other Online Booksellers

7.2.1 Online Paperback Booksellers

Most self-published authors are primarily interested in the nuances and subtleties of Amazon, many of which we have discussed in detail. Most other booksellers have much simpler websites, and most self-published authors sell only a fraction of their books there. For these reasons, I will focus on listing a variety of online booksellers and only mention a few pertinent details about them (and for another reason – that this book would be extremely long if I described each of these booksellers in as much detail as I have described Amazon's website).

If you've enabled the Expanded Distribution channel with CreateSpace, you may want to check where your paperback book is available. Visit http://www.gettextbooks.com and enter the ISBN for your book to see where it's for sale online. Of course, it takes time for online booksellers to learn about your book, decide whether or not to add it to their catalog, and, if so, make a product page for your book. Some sellers will do this very quickly, others very slowly. If you search for your book on this site shortly after you publish, there might not be any matches. Give it time, and you should see a variety of online booksellers listed. With even more time, you may notice many more sellers. Some books have a very large number of online sellers listed. If you want to verify this information, simply visit any of the websites (you don't have to click on the links – you can visit each directly) and search for your book there.

Even if your book is available at dozens of websites, most customers tend to buy Create-Space paperbacks through Amazon. Some of the sellers listed may never sell a single copy of your book (especially, because a few list outrageous prices). A few of these sellers, such as The Book Depository, do sell some CreateSpace paperbacks. The Book Depository advertises free shipping worldwide and is very popular in many countries.

A couple of major bookstore chains in the United States that may sell your book online through the Expanded Distribution channel include Barnes & Noble and Books-a-Million. Powell's Books, Alibris, and Abe Books are large online booksellers that may also choose to include your book. The Book Depository is a major online retailer that I've already mentioned. Some small businesses and even individuals might list your book for sale on Half.com and eBay (and customers can resell their copies there, too – but in the case of resale, you don't earn any royalty). You will probably also discover other booksellers carrying your book "virtually in stock." Most (if not all) of these booksellers will not carry your book in their warehouses – it's print-on-demand, so they will only order it if and when it happens to sell. Since it can take 2-3 months for an Expanded Distribution sale to show on your royalty reports, it may take several months before your Expanded Distribution sales take off (and, like sales in general, there are no guarantees that it will). If you cancel the Expanded Distribution channel, you run the risk of stopping such sales right when they're starting to pick up, without even realizing it (because the royalties may not show for a couple of months).

None of these booksellers have any obligation to carry your book. CreateSpace lists your book with Ingram's catalog. That's the end of CreateSpace's obligation. Then it's up to bookstores to discover your book and decide whether or not to carry it. There are no guarantees. However, there are many booksellers that want to have the widest selection possible; these are very likely to pick up your book, too – at least, online (probably not on-hand).

Similarly, every bookseller will individually decide what information to display for your book, and what price to charge. Many will only display the thumbnail image and title. Some won't include your description, categories, or keywords. You can try asking CreateSpace politely to have select bookstores (such as Barnes & Noble – although the relations between Amazon and Barnes & Noble may inhibit this possibility) add your description, if possible (it may not be). You might also consider trying to contact the booksellers directly; some may be more receptive than others. If you publish an eBook through Nook Press, your description, keywords, and/or categories may get linked with your paperback edition on Barnes & Noble.

You should visit Barnes & Noble and other online booksellers' websites to search for your book and learn more about their websites and how they work. Find out firsthand what your list price is, whether or not there are periodic discounts, if your description shows up, which categories (if any) your book is listed in, whether or not your book is searchable by any keywords other than words from the title, what the sales rank is (if it's sold), and if there are any reviews. Monitor your sales rank by visiting the sites periodically as this will help you estimate how often your book may be selling there. Note that customer book reviews are most common on Amazon and Goodreads, and are very rare at most other online booksellers.

As we discussed in Sec. 6.2.4, customers won't discover your CreateSpace eStore unless you provide a link to it, and many customers will prefer to buy your book on Amazon instead of CreateSpace. Theoretically, it is possible for customers to find your book on CreateSpace by visiting their homepage, entering a search where it says Search Site, and changing Site to Store in the drop-down menu. In practice, this is very seldom done. CreateSpace also has an affiliate program, but it relates to new authors signing up to publish their books – not commissions on sales.

Search for your book and also search for your name on popular internet search engines such as Google. Note that some places may appear to be giving your book away for free (some will go so far as to quote the number of alleged downloads), but most of these are false appearances. They often don't have your book at all, but have some ulterior motives. I recommend avoiding websites that pretend to be giving your book away for free – if they are dishonest about that, who knows what else may be going on there (and if they are honest about your book being free – when it's not free anywhere else – then they are dishonest in their practice of giving it away, which again is a good reason to avoid that website).

7.2.2 Online eBook Retailers

Your eBook should only be available specifically where you publish it – and if you use an aggregator like Smashwords, at any outlets where sales distribution is enabled (check care-fully, as you may have to disable your eBook's distribution anywhere you don't want to publish – or where you've already published, like KDP or Nook Press – rather than enabling its dis-tribution where you do want to publish). Therefore, you won't have to hunt all over the internet to find your eBook: You should already know exactly where to find it.

Go to Kindle (on Amazon), Nook (at Barnes & Noble), Smashwords, Sony's Reader Store (www.ebookstore.sony.com), the Apple iBooks website (www.apple.com/apps/ibooks), the Kobo bookstore (www.kobobooks.com), and wherever else your eBook is available. Search for your book to see what the listing looks like and which searches pull it up successfully. Check your list price, description, categories, keywords, and free sample carefully. Monitor your sales rank to estimate your sales frequency and see if there are any customer reviews.

Try searching for your eBook with a variety of devices (e.g. Kindle, Nook, Sony Reader, Kobo, iPhone, iPad, etc.) and see what the sample looks like on the device. It would be wise to see what one full-length copy of your eBook looks like on each device (from each eBook store where it is available for that device), since your eBook can easily look great on one device, but have serious formatting issues on another. Ideally, you should test the formatting carefully before publishing, whenever possible. You want to see how your book looks on each device firsthand before your customers do (who will probably complain about any serious formatting issues in a review, if there are any). If you don't have the specific device, you may have a friend or acquaintance that has one that you can borrow (or, more likely, they can do this for you and you can watch).

If you publish an eBook on Nook and have the same title available on Barnes & Noble through CreateSpace's Expanded Distribution, the two editions may get linked together and the description, categories, keywords, and/or author biography may show up for your paper-back edition through this linkage.

Remember that if you enroll in KDP Select, you're not permitted to sell your eBook online through any other retailer until your enrollment period ends. **Enrollment in KDP Select automatically renews every 90 days unless you go to your KDP Bookshelf, check the box next to the book, click the Actions button, choose See KDP Select Details, and uncheck the box for automatic renewal.** If you uncheck this box or even if you unpublish your book from KDP, you're still obligated to publish exclusively through KDP until the enrollment period expires – there is no way to opt out early (except for a very brief grace period of a few days when you first sign up).

You may publish a paperback with CreateSpace or publish other print editions while your eBook is enrolled in the KDP Select program – only the eBook edition of your book is exclusive to KDP. Note that you are not even allowed to give away more than Amazon's free sample on your own website when your book is enrolled in KDP Select.

Some eBooks sell best on Kindle. Some sell very well for the iPhone and iPad – yet, strangely, sometimes more iPad and iPhone users buy the eBook through Kindle than from Apple iBooks. A few eBooks sell very well on Nook. Success with different eReaders can vary widely depending on the genre and even the book. The only sure way to know what works better is to try it. Note that some eBook publishing services have a very long delay in sales reporting, and that some aggregators have a significant delay in distributing the eBook to various eReaders. For this reason, your eBook could be selling well through a variety of outlets and you might not even know it for a couple of months. Just because you don't see sales initially doesn't mean that your eBook isn't (or won't be) selling.

Many authors who aren't satisfied with their eBook sales try switching their options. Some who try KDP Select for its benefits opt out after 90 or 180 days to try Nook, Kobo, Smashwords, and others. On the other hand, authors who first publish with Smashwords, but notice that most of their sales come from Kindle, often decide to try out KDP Select. However, note that there can sometimes be lengthy delays in getting eBooks successfully unpublished from some distribution channels. Amazon sometimes sends emails to authors stating that they are in violation of the KDP Select terms and conditions because their eBooks are still showing as available through one or more other retailers, whereas the authors had unpublished their eBooks from those channels. If this happens to you, first try politely responding to the email (or contact as directed in the email) to explain the situation. Also contact the service where you published the eBook about getting it unpublished.

Yet other authors start with KDP Select, then try to publish elsewhere, and finally return to KDP Select. Some authors claim that they sell mostly through Kindle, while others say that they sell many through Nook, Kobo, and Smashwords. Some claim that KDP Select's free promo days tend to bring them successful results within a few days, others state that it doesn't help them at all. Some authors receive many borrows through KDP Select, but many eBooks very rarely get borrowed (if ever). Again, the only way to know for sure is to try it out for yourself and see firsthand. This is why so many authors switch back-and-forth between these different eBook publishing services.

If you can find authors of eBooks that are very similar to yours – genre, price, length, style, etc. – who have tried both with and without KDP Select, then you may be fortunate enough to save yourself from the trials and tribulations of switching – you can then have some measure of confidence with your initial decision and choose to stick with it, whether it is for better or for worse.

7.2.3 Customer Book Reviews Other than Amazon

The vast majority of customers post their book reviews on Amazon. Very few customers post reviews at Barnes & Noble and other online booksellers' websites. Customers who buy most of their books from Barnes & Noble are far more likely to post reviews there. Barnes & Noble can sell your paperback if you have the Expanded Distribution and if they elect to include your book on their website, and they can sell a Nook edition of your eBook if you publish through Nook Press or an aggregator like Smashwords. Unless you have a strong sales rank at Barnes & Noble for a long period of time, it's unlikely that you'll get more than an occasional review there; you may not receive any. If you're not selling frequently at Barnes & Noble and other online booksellers, don't sweat the reviews – or any lack thereof – on their websites.

Next to Amazon, Goodreads tends to garner a large number of customer reviews. A few customers will post the same review on both Amazon and Goodreads, but many will just take the time to do one or the other. Don't ask a reviewer who posts a good review at Goodreads to also post it at Amazon; it looks tacky and unprofessional – you don't want to appear needy. As mentioned in Sec. 6.2.5, don't comment on any reviews at Goodreads. Don't invade any customer space there – like customer forums discussing books and authors.

Goodreads has a reputation for very strict "review police" and "author behavior police." Many customers at Goodreads absolutely do not like to have their space invaded and feel strongly that authors should not comment on reviews. Defensive comments, appearing needy, taking reviews personally, making requests of reviewers, and especially accusing reviewers of anything – these things can bring responses from the "review police" in swarms, and they may post on Amazon in addition to Goodreads. Many of the Goodreads customers also frequent the Amazon customer forums, KDP community forums, review books on Amazon, and visit several other places online. It's very important to always behave professionally with your author image in mind, remembering that it's at stake anytime you post any information online (even on your own blog). Don't say bad things about reviews or reviewers. Don't get involved in discussions with reviewers. Only *your* reputation is at stake.

Occasional reviews will be bad: It's a fact of life as an author that we must deal with. Customers are entitled to their opinions. Some bad reviews help us grow as writers. Don't react emotionally (you will feel some strong emotions, just don't let those emotions cause action or written words). Don't take it personally – they reviewed the book, not you. Try to wear a thick skin and hope that there are many good reviews to balance occasional bad ones.

There are small customer groups on Goodreads that identify authors and their books who they believe have "misbehaved." Sometimes, you can get on this list just by association – maybe you said something to another author who got on this list, whom you don't even know. Don't try to discover these groups. How you might discover them is when someone sends you a message to let you know that you and/or your book have been mentioned in one of these groups. This message tempts you into making a grave mistake. Don't go there! No customers are going to discover your name or book in that small group. But if you post there, your posts will show up on your author page at Goodreads along with all of the group's responses, which can destroy your credibility and image as an author.

Anything that you post anywhere on Goodreads – and anything that you simply vote on – shows up on your author page at Goodreads. Don't do or vote on anything or rate any books or write any reviews or vote on any reviews that in any way can be construed as being negative by any potential customers.

An interesting feature at Goodreads is that customers can rate books without reviewing books. When customers rate a book, they give it 1 to 5 stars. When customers review a book, they write comments about what they did or didn't like. On Amazon, customers must do both; on Goodreads, customers may rate a book without writing a review. This is kind of neat because some customers don't know what to say or don't want to take the time to write a review, but are willing to rate the book.

Customers can also mark books as to-read on Goodreads, which shows you if there is some future interest in your books. Don't thank customers for marking your book as to-read – again, this looks tacky, unprofessional, and needy.

Another place where you might see reviews of your book is on blogs (see Sec. 8.1.15).

Chapter 8

Marketing Strategies

Chapter Overview

8.1 Low-Cost Marketing Ideas
8.2 Other Marketing Options

This chapter answers questions about the following topics, and more:

- ☑ The importance of marketing, and why every author has to do it.
- ☑ Marketing that every author should be doing prior to publishing.
- ☑ Simple things everyone can easily do to market their books.
- ☑ Free ways to market your book and eBook.
- ☑ The importance of positive feedback.
- ☑ Effectively marketing through discovery instead of self-promotion.
- ☑ Techniques to brand your book's image and your author image.
- ☑ Identifying and reaching your target audience.
- ☑ Friends, family, acquaintances, and word-of-mouth publicity.
- ☑ Preparing a professional press release package.
- ☑ Taking advantage of free media coverage.
- ☑ Book signing, seminars, and other social marketing strategies.
- ☑ Contacting local bookstores that feature local authors.
- ☑ Selling your paperback book directly.
- ☑ Free marketing resources and paid marketing services offered by CreateSpace.[23]

---

[23] Amazon™ and CreateSpace are trademarks and brands of their respective owners. Neither this book, *A Detailed Guide to Self-Publishing with Amazon and Other Online Booksellers*, nor its author, Chris McMullen, are in any way affiliated with any of these companies.

8.1 Low-Cost Marketing Ideas

8.1.1 Why Marketing Is Necessary for All Authors

I t's simply a matter of numbers. With millions of books to choose from and thousands of new books released every day, your book is just another faint star in the sky. Just a small percentage of customers buy their books after searching for keywords online. Most books are bought from customers browsing bestseller lists or specifically for the title or author – as should be expected, since the popular authors and bestsellers account for a huge fraction of book sales. Many customers buy books because of promotional discounts or giveaways. Amazon's Customers Also Bought marketing tool attracts a significant number of customers. Only a few books out of a hundred are purchased through online searches.

These online searches are very significant though because of the very large number of books purchased. But there are also millions of books available, which is why the vast majority of books sell only a few copies per month (or less). Out of millions of books, only the top hundred thousand or so average about a sale per day.

Unfortunately, books just don't sell themselves. Let's consider the life of an unmarketed book. When it's first published, it's at the bottom of the pack both in its category and in keyword searches. Sure, the Last 30 Days filter helps a little, but there are thousands of other books in this category, many of which have developed great sales ranks and have received some good reviews because of effective marketing. Those books are far more likely to be discovered than an unmarketed book. The unmarketed book sells very little, so it's sales rank – once it acquires one – quickly rises up to the millions, which adversely affects its visibility. It hasn't sold enough for the Customers Also Bought lists to help it out.

The successfully marketed book, on the other hand, sells many times when it's released, giving it a healthy sales rank, which aids its visibility and helps create an early Customers Also Bought list. It may have a few early reviews earned through advanced review copies. Not all of these reviews may be good reviews, but it's better than no reviews. The effectively marketed book is selling frequently and generating new reviews through those sales. Buzz has been growing since before the book's launch and word-of-mouth sales are helping its sales along. If it's very successful, it may reach one of the top 100 bestseller lists and receive great exposure.

It's a tale of two stories. If you want your book sales to be successful, you must help promote sales through effective marketing, and the sooner you begin this, the better. Amazon helps authors who help themselves: The more you perfect your book prior to publishing and the greater you stimulate sales through effective marketing, the more Amazon's Customer Also Bought and top 100 bestseller lists may reward your efforts. Amazon gives every book a chance, but the odds are highly uneven: Unmarketed books have very slim chances, while effectively marketed books are the clear favorites.

Even traditionally published authors must market their own books. Publishers mainly help with editing, typesetting, formatting, sending out advance review copies, and including the books in their catalogs, but still expect authors to do much marketing on their own. In fact, publishers expect this – and may contract for it – because they know that they won't sell enough books unless the author is willing to follow through with effective marketing. Many writers are becoming self-publishers not just to avoid the countless rejection letters that are typically involved in the hunt for a traditional publisher, but because they are still going to have to do the marketing themselves anyway. Authors who have highly successful marketing skills are desired by publishers, but these authors can just as well market their own self-published books – and that's what many of them are now doing.

8.1.2 Effective Marketing Isn't an Afterthought

Hopeful authors who just throw their books out there to see what happens are almost always very disappointed: not much happens. After seeing firsthand that books don't sell themselves, they begin to realize that everybody may have been right – indeed, marketing skills might be required to sell books. **By then, it's too late!** They have missed the golden opportunity. Once the sales rank has risen very high, it counts against the book's favor – it becomes more and more challenging to rebound from this history of poor sales.

Starting off with a strong sales rank gives your book its best chance of success. This gives your book greater visibility, improves your prospects for getting early reviews, and helps to quickly generate Customer Also Bought lists. Also, a great start can lead to increased exposure on the top 100 bestseller lists.

Marketing is something that should begin before the book is published – when the book is still being written. There is a great deal that you can do for <u>free</u>:

➢ Utilize the ideas described in Sec. 8.1.7 to generate "buzz" for your upcoming book both in person and through social media.

➢ People like to buy books from authors whom they've personally interacted with – in person or online. Let them discover that you're a writer, rather than advertising this openly. Many people should be aware of your writing before you ever publish.

➢ Let others see your passion for your writing. This increases their interest in your book.

➢ Get feedback on your cover, title, and blurb before you publish. This not only lets you see how people react firsthand, but also helps to create interest in your book.

➢ Think about what is special about your book – such as extra time spent doing research or multiple revisions from a professional editor – and let this slip naturally in conversations once in a while (don't overdo it).

➢ Don't talk about your book every time that you interact with friends and acquaintances or you'll be tuned out. Rather, let them inquire about your book.

- ➢ Use Amazon Advantage to enable preorders of your paperback (see Sec. 7.1.8). This can give your book a headstart in sales rank and Customer Also Bought associations.
- ➢ Send out advance review copies via Goodreads or relevant blogs, for example, to help improve your chances of earning a few early reviews.
- ➢ Perfect your cover before your book is published because it's a valuable marketing tool. It can attract attention and signify the genre with a relevant, striking image. A memorable cover makes it easier to recognize and describe to others.
- ➢ Write a killer blurb and perfect the Look Inside before you publish because these can have a profound influence on sales.
- ➢ Perfect your editing, formatting, and storyline before you publish. If people love your book and the writing, they are far more likely to leave good reviews and recommend your book to others by word-of-mouth.
- ➢ Develop your websites and post relevant content there before you publish your book.
- ➢ Start your blog and gain a small following before you publish. Post content relevant to your book and genre that will help attract customers and also interest fans. You don't want readers who enjoy your book to visit your blog only to find it mostly empty.
- ➢ Setup your social medial (Facebook, Twitter, etc.) with relevant content prior to publishing. Your friends, family, and acquaintances can help you generate early sales.
- ➢ Setup fan, book, author, and/or imprint pages at Facebook. Fans who go to your author pages should find fresh material. Your preexisting fan base may give you some early sales and a few early reviews.
- ➢ Don't tackle more than you can handle. Definitely, create online webpages or sites that require very little maintenance. However, for things that require you to make regular content (blog, Twitter, Facebook, etc.), you need to budget your time wisely because these are commitments that you are making to your readers.
- ➢ Use the same author image and logo everywhere to help with brand recognition.
- ➢ Choose an imprint before you publish and develop a website (free, perhaps) to help lend it some credibility.
- ➢ Setup your AuthorCentral and Goodreads author pages.
- ➢ Develop a marketing plan in three stages – before, during, and after publication.

8.1.3 Marketing Is Different from Advertising and Salesmanship

Many self-published authors often fear marketing because they believe they lack the skills of a salesman and the motivation to sell and advertise. But marketing is different from advertising and salesmanship. In fact, direct advertising – especially, outright self-promotion – and direct persuasion don't tend to generate book sales. Advertising and persuasion may sell cars, but they don't tend to sell books. Marketing is more subtle and can be far more effective.

Effective book marketing has more to do with discovery and branding. If a stranger walks into a room and says, "Hey, I just published a book. You should go check it out," most people will think, "Great. Another salesman telling me what I need to buy." The same is true even in an online forum. If a writer posts, "I just published a book. Here's the link for it," in an online forum, such self-promotion does <u>not</u> tend to sell books. That's because most people don't like self-promotion, and it's not permitted in many online forums where people interact. Marketing isn't about self-promotion.

Discovery tends to be more effective. Consider the following two scenarios. (A) One person walks up to you and says, "I just wrote a book and now I need to find people to read it." (B) Another person comes to sit near you, a conversation begins, and because you enjoy the interaction, you each inquire about what the other does for a living. You discover that you've just met a writer. In which case are you more likely to check out the book? With the vast majority of people, the correct answer is (B).

People like to read books by authors whom they have personally interacted with. People who have read hundreds of books sometimes don't know any of the authors, which makes the occasion special when you can read a book by an author you've actually met. People are more likely to know a few authors in this age of self-publishing, but out of every hundred books read, knowing a few of the authors is still a treat. Don't think self-promotion. Think discovery.

Just as marketing is often confused to mean self-promotion rather than discovery, advertising is often misinterpreted. Many people believe that commercials work like this: A company says, "This is our product and you should buy it because it's the best," and that this works because millions of people are foolish enough to listen to it, march right out to the store, and buy the product. Advertisements actually make very few (if any) sales this way.

The reason that advertising is successful has to do with branding, and not because people are foolish enough to listen to instructions about which product is better or that you should buy a particular product the next time you're at the store. (Okay, maybe they do make a few sales this way, but that's not how *most* of the sales occur.) The main goal of commercials and other advertisements is to get as many people from the target audience as possible to remember and recognize the brand. Companies strive to build brand recognition, not to generate direct sales. Advertisers know that brand recognition results in indirect sales. Such indirect sales are plentiful and long-lasting when the advertising is successful.

I'm not suggesting that you spend money on advertising. You can create a similar effect for <u>free</u>. I want you to understand the true nature of advertising, and to see how this fits in with the marketing suggestions of this chapter. You want to brand your image as an author, using a variety of free techniques, so that readers in your target audience remember and recognize you and your book(s). Paying for advertisements may not be effective for book sales, but there is no reason to pay for it when you can do this for free. Some writers wish that they could "buy" their way out of marketing by just paying for advertisements, but doing the work and marketing with free methods tends to be more effective.

Here is an example of how advertising works, which you may be able to relate to (it doesn't involve books). Imagine that you're in the grocery store buying detergent, and you're looking at two similar products. You've heard of detergent A, but not detergent B. Which one will you buy? Very many people will go with detergent A, simply because they recognize the brand. Most aren't buying it because a commercial said that it was better; most aren't buying it because a commercial told them to run down to the store and buy it; most are simply buying a product that they recognize. A brand name is a brand that customers recognize.

Sure, some people will buy the cheaper product to save money. Others will buy the expensive product hoping to get what they pay for. A rare customer will actually do research to see what others have to say about it. But if they're buying online, many customers will check out customer product reviews. Not everybody makes purchase decisions the same way. Nevertheless, successful branding does influence a very large number of consumers.

The same holds true for books. If you can get members of your target audience to see your cover, read your title, hear your name, and/or view your author picture multiple times, this helps to brand your book and image as an author.

Let's consider a second non-book example of marketing, which involves more than just advertising. Suppose that you decide to buy or sell a home. Which realtor will you choose? Most people will choose a realty company that they've heard of, which relates to company branding, or an agent whom they know, which relates to discovery and/or person branding. If you've ever met a real estate agent socially who made a nice impression during your brief encounter, this may greatly influence your decision. This is the discovery method that we discussed earlier in this section; you discovered that this person sold homes during a conversation. This gives the small hometown realtor a chance against the major brands. Similarly, discovery, branding, and marketing give self-published authors a chance to sell books alongside popular authors and major publishing houses. These are your most valuable tools, and they're free; you just have to learn to use them effectively.

Some people may choose a specific agent whom they haven't even met. Maybe they recognize the name and photo of the realtor from signs, posters, business cards, ads, etc. Authors can similarly brand without personal contact. Readers may recognize your photo, title, or book cover from your website, blog, and other online activities (e.g. maybe clicking on your profile somewhere). The more visible you are – in a positive way – among your target audience (*not* just anybody with eyes), the greater such discovery may impact your sales.

Another way that you might select a specific realty company or a particular agent is by word-of-mouth recommendations. If any friends or family members, for example, personally recommend a realty company or agent they've done business with before, this may have a very significant influence on your decision. The better job they do, the greater the prospects for receiving word-of-mouth recommendations. This can have a very significant impact on book sales, too. The way to achieve this is to have a great story that's perfected as much from the front cover to the back, and then to get a large number of customers to read it.

Discovery, branding, and word-of-mouth are three major methods of marketing books that relate to marketing and advertising techniques that big businesses use. These are the main ideas, but there are several specifics – which we will explore in this chapter. We can also relate many of the specifics to big business marketing.

For example, authors should devise a hook for their books, which works sort of like a catchy slogan. The hook is a very short sentence that's easy to remember, which helps stir interest in your book. It should tell something about your book so that your target audience will recognize the genre. If mystery readers hear a hook for a mystery book, but can't tell that it's a mystery, for example, then the hook won't be as effective. A highly effective hook will also create interest in reading the book.

Another similarity is the use of a product name that's very easy to spell and remember. What brands come to mind? Coke, Sony, Levi's. Similarly, a book title should be short (two to three words), easy to spell and remember, and relate to the genre and content.

8.1.4 Ways that Marketing Can Be Ineffective or Even Backfire

There are several different ways that marketing can be ineffective. This is very important, and not all of it is obvious – otherwise, there wouldn't be nearly as many books suffering from such ineffective marketing. In addition to discussing how marketing can be ineffective – even when the marketing techniques employed are often highly effective – we'll learn how to avoid mistakes that can make normally sound marketing decisions produce poor results.

The last thing you want is to successfully market hundreds of people to your book, but have most of the potential customers decide not to buy your book – or purchase the book only to return it shortly afterward. If you get people interested in checking your book out, you want to close the deal, and then you want them to keep the book once they have it.

What determines whether people will buy your book once they find it?

➤ A lousy cover says, "This author didn't put much effort into the book, and didn't seek feedback from others to learn what suits his/her target audience."

➤ Suppose that the cover looks like a great sci-fi book, but it's really a fantasy. The readers who are attracted to the cover think, "That's not what I was looking for."

➤ If the blurb contains mistakes, this doesn't bode well for the content. The same goes for the Look Inside. Proofreading or formatting mistakes can blow the deal.

➤ Does your blurb create interest in your book without giving too much away? Does the blurb seem like a good fit for your target audience? A great blurb helps to stimulate sales; a lousy blurb may inhibit your marketing efforts.

➤ The Look Inside should look professional and the beginning of the book should create interest in the book. Wise customers try the Look Inside before buying the book. If the sample impresses them, they buy it; if it's just so-so, they're more likely to pass on it.

What determines whether people will keep your book after they purchase it?

➢ They enjoy the first part of the book (more than just the Look Inside). For fiction, the story must engage their interest. For nonfiction, they must appreciate the information and the way that it is presented.

➢ The content is what the reader was expecting. Prospective customers have some idea of what they expect the book to be about based on the title, cover, and blurb. If they begin reading the book and it doesn't seem to agree with these expectations, they are likely to abandon their efforts.

➢ The book is well-edited and well-formatted. When people invest money in a product, they expect to receive something that appears professional. For a book, this means that it should be well-written and visually appealing.

After customers read the entire book, you want them to recommend it. They might recommend it in a customer review, by word-of-mouth to friends, family, or acquaintances, or even online (e.g. at a blog or website). The customer has to feel strongly to recommend a book. Most readers don't recommend a book; only a fraction do. Customers who dislike a book, however, are more likely to post a bad review. Marketing is most successful when most customers enjoy the book and when a significant percentage of the customers recommend it to others, while marketing is ineffective when few customers enjoy the book and a significant percentage dislike it strongly. Following are some factors involved in customer reactions:

➢ Customers who love it or hate it are most likely to leave a review. If they enjoy it or dislike it mildly, or if they feel indifferently about it, they are less likely to review it.

➢ Only customers who love some aspect of the book are likely to recommend it to others. Even then, it must be well-formatted, well-edited, and suitable for the people they recommend it to; they're unlikely to recommend books that seem unprofessional.

➢ For fiction, memorable characters, scenes that evoke strong emotions, and great plots tend to generate more reviews and recommendations. For nonfiction, useful content and clear explanations achieve this. For either, a wonderful way with words can leave a good impression.

➢ There are also genre-specific issues. Readers in each genre have certain expectations and if you violate these unspoken rules, it could have a very negative impact on sales. For example, an action thriller should have a fast pace and a romance should have a happy ending. Protagonists shouldn't have character traits that upset the readers.

➢ Controversial books are more likely to be reviewed. In this case, the reviews are likely to be mixed with both very good and very bad reviews.

Self-publishers tend to make titles that sound good to them, covers that have images that mean something to the author, and other styles that they appreciate. But you're not selling the book to yourself! Take the time to find out how others – especially, strangers in your target audience – will react to your book. Don't just go with a minority of reactions that happen to agree with what you wanted to hear. Listen to things that you hear repeated, even if you disagree with them. The difference between selling just a few books or selling very many books can often be something simple in the title or cover that makes the book less or more appealing to your target audience.

I've seen many authors solicit feedback on their title, cover, and blurb after a few months of slow sales, only to discover that something – an image on the cover that didn't seem to fit, colors that didn't work well together, etc. – was putting people off. It's especially common for the author to be partial to an image that really doesn't belong on the cover – and to be quite stubborn about it. For example, the story might involve a ring, which at some point becomes important in the story, but only the author knows this. Unless the title mentions a ring, this ring just confuses prospective readers. Consistency and unity among the title, cover, and blurb – and signifying the right genre and content – are far more significant than most indie authors tend to realize. Inconsistency there can be a sales deterrent.

There are also some other important ways that marketing can be ineffective. One major problem that can arise is a target audience mismatch. If your marketing efforts are attracting mostly adult romance readers, for example, but your book is actually a teen romance, many of the customers who check out your book may pass on it. The first step in effective marketing is to identify, as precisely as possible, your main target audience. Then you gear your marketing efforts toward that specific audience. The title, cover, blurb, and Look Inside need to send a unified message about the genre and content so that the same audience who comes to check out the book feels that the book is a good fit for them. This is another reason why it's so important to invest the time to get representative people from your target audience to offer you opinions on your title, cover, blurb, first chapter, and even the entire book. Companies use a focus group in their marketing efforts for this very reason.

One of the worst things that can happen is that hundreds of people buy the book, but then find a glaring mistake that you missed. Almost all books have a few minor mistakes. What I'm talking about is a major mistake that would ruin the book (and your image). A misspelled word in the title, grammatical mistake in the title, misspelled author name, major formatting mistake inside the book, or a major problem in the appearance of a key picture, for example, can produce a very negative reaction from customers who order your book. It's critical to catch all major problems before you publish your book. Scrutinize your printed proofs and eBook previews very carefully. There are a few horror stories circulating the internet from authors who delivered hundreds of books with major mistakes that they missed prior to publication. Don't let that happen to you.

If you succeed in generating much buzz for your book, resulting in a large number of preorders or early sales, it becomes even more crucial that the book be free of major issues.

Perhaps the most common marketing mistake – aside from not marketing at all – is to only do what the author feels most comfortable doing or to only do what seems easiest. For example, many authors mainly market through Facebook and Twitter. Social media is great for generating early sales among your friends, family, and acquaintances, and for early sales and reviews among your established fan base for your subsequent books. You can also reach some new readers using hashtags, for example. But social media is very limited in its ability to attract new members of your target audience, so if this is the only thing that you do, your marketing efforts are not likely to yield long-lasting success.

Just browsing through this chapter, you will find a wide variety of ideas that you can use to market your book. If you decide not to utilize all of these ideas, don't simply discard those that fall outside of your comfort zone and don't simply look for those few that seem like they might involve the least amount of work. Instead, try to determine which of these ideas are likely to be most effective in driving your specific target audience to your specific book. Some strategies work better for some kinds of books than for others. You definitely want to apply the techniques that are likely to be most effective for your book. The only reason that you should discard an idea is if you have good reason to believe that it won't be effective for your particular book. Unfortunately, most authors choose based on what's easiest and most comfortable for them. Or maybe I should say "fortunately," since having fewer people do what's most effective leaves the door wide open for those who choose to do it. Get out of your shell and market in ways that you don't prefer – it could make a big difference in sales.

Another common mistake is giving up with marketing efforts prematurely. Marketing involves work. Writing is the kind of work that authors like to do; marketing isn't. So when we begin marketing, we want to see results. It's easy to use the lack of quick results as an excuse to stop doing this work – marketing – that we didn't want to do in the first place.

Unfortunately, marketing doesn't always pay immediate rewards. Branding, for example, can be a long-term process. Branding takes repetition – so first people in your target audience need to see your cover and photo, hear your name, and read your title a few times over a period of months. Then they're not likely to be in the market for their next book in your genre immediately. Branding pays off when they finally get around to looking for a book like yours, which can be several months down the road. It's the same way with advertising on television: We get branded over a period of months, then several months after that when we're making a purchase decision in the store, the branding may finally make a difference.

One of the best marketing tools is often hidden and very slow to develop: this is word-of-mouth sales. First, customers have to find your book. They might not buy it when they first find it. When they finally do buy it, they need to read it. The might not read it as soon as they buy it. When they finally start reading it, they need to finish it. This might take many months. Most readers aren't going to recommend your book to others until they finish reading it themselves. It can take several months before a significant number of people have read your book, at which point – if your book is very good – they may recommend it to others. Don't get discouraged if you don't see early results. Keep marketing actively and your patience may pay off down the road. Continued marketing is essential to long-term success. Don't give up!

Marketing doesn't supply instant satisfaction. You must be very patient. It can take a year before consistent marketing efforts really begin to pay off. If you give up prematurely, you may never fully realize the fruits of your early efforts. Don't give up; keep at it. Focus on your next book and the prospects for the first book helping the second book. Visualizing positive success in the future can help you be patient with your marketing efforts.

The way that you market can also impact its effectiveness. As discussed in Sec. 8.1.3, self-promotion tends to be highly ineffective, whereas branding and discovery tend to be more effective. Similarly, with social media and blogs, posting about yourself and your book tends to be less effective, whereas posting useful content tends to be more effective. No more than 10% of your posts should be geared toward yourself, your own book, or your own websites; in fact, you needn't do this at all since anyone who is interested in learning more about you, your book, or other websites can find such information on your profile or end-of-posts.

A marketing tactic that can backfire is making a book sound far better than it really is. Making a book sound like the best book ever loses customers two ways. First, potential customers often avoid books where the blurb or author brag about how great it is. They're skeptical: If the book is great, this should be easy to see on its own merit, so there shouldn't be any need to boast. Let readers discover how good it is and judge this for themselves. Secondly, customers who do read the book are very likely to be disappointed that the book isn't the best book ever written. Don't create expectations that are impossible to fulfill.

On the other extreme, you can't sell many books if you lack confidence in yourself. If you make statements like, "My book probably isn't very good," you might draw a little sympathy, but most people are going to think, "Well, if you don't believe in your own work, it must not be worth reading." Somewhere there is a fine line: You need to show confidence, but don't sound boastful. Your confidence and passion for your work help to create interest in your work, but any bragging tends to detract from it.

Let me conclude this section with the bad news: Not all book ideas can be good sellers, and not all writing styles make for good reading. Marketing has its inherent limitations. For marketing to be successful, the first step is to develop a book idea that has good potential, perfect the book cover to cover, and have a writing style that will appeal to many readers. If any of this is a significant problem, no amount of marketing can offer you long-term success.

With that said, you must show confidence in your book. Don't worry that it might not pay off. Worry and doubt don't help at all. Instead, worry and doubt affect your attitude and mood, hampering your ability to successfully market your book. You must believe in your book wholeheartedly. If you can't sell your book to yourself, you definitely can't sell it to others. Remember, show confidence, but don't boast.

Let prospective readers see your passion for your book and your passion for writing, and your confidence but not your ego. Your image as an author is very important toward your success. Be knowledgeable, trustworthy, and professional. Behave like someone who may write such a book as yours to establish credibility as a writer.

8.1.5 How to Motivate Yourself to Market Diligently

Most authors easily motivate themselves to write because they either enjoy the topic that they're writing about or the art of writing itself (or both). However, most writers feel that it is quite challenging to motivate themselves to market. I will try to convince you that this is not logical – that authors who are motivated to write should be equally motivated to market their books when they finish writing.

Writers tend to look at marketing as persuasion and salesmanship. They see writing as an art, but book sales as a business. Most authors love the artistic elements that they see in writing, but not the business side of writing – well, selling books and earning royalties they appreciate, but striving to earn this through marketing they don't.

Let's look at the business perspective for a moment. Don't worry, you don't have to become a business person to sell books. I'm not trying to convince you to think like a business person. I'm not suggesting that you gear your writing toward money. It is, however, useful to see how the business-minded person approaches writing because business-minded people are often successful at marketing. Have a little patience and I will try to show you how you may become successful at marketing without thinking like a business person. But – like it or not – we're going to look at the business model first. Then we'll modify it significantly for writing.

Editors and publishers often see the business side of writing more than the artistic side. Those who favor the view that writing is a business tend to be successful marketers. The business-minded writer doesn't want to waste his/her time writing. The first thing he/she does is research: Which books are already on the market, which are selling well, what kinds of book does he/she have the expertise to write, of these is there a need that he/she can fill, what large potential target audience can he/she reach, what kind of writing will appeal to this audience, and what is most likely to sell well?[24] This person is writing to sell and everything revolves around how to sell books beginning with the writing. Since this person is motivated to sell, marketing comes very naturally. The business person uses his/her passion to sell in order to motivate himself/herself to write.

If you're not a business-minded individual, what you have to do is invert this: Use your passion for your writing to motivate yourself to market your books.

It's simple, really. You infused your passion into your book, and now you wish to share it with others. If you're passionate about your writing, then you must develop a passion for sharing it, which means that you must be passionate about marketing it – for that's how it will be successfully shared. If you can't get passionate enough about your very own writing to feel that it's worth sharing with others, why on earth should others want to read your writing? Use this to motivate yourself to market your book. Let your passion for your work show.

---

[24] When an editor looks at a query letter and book proposal, they're thinking about the business side of writing. Editors want to find books that were written to sell because publishers are businesses that sell books. One great thing about self-publishing is that the non-business-minded author can succeed without giving in to this mindset.

Passion is the secret ingredient that can bring writers and readers together. Readers want to read books (in genres that they enjoy reading) which are written with passion by authors who are passionate about their work. Which writers have so much passion for their work? Those authors who actively market their books, whose sense of passion shows – not those who advertise their passion overtly, but those whose passion is implicitly, yet clearly, present.

From the reader's point of view, authors who don't market their books must feel that their books are lacking in some way or must not have passion for their work. Why else would they be so reluctant to share their books with the world, if not for some inherent problem? Therefore, you must first perfect your book in order to convince yourself that it is ready to be shared with the world, and then when you believe in your own book, you must market diligently in order to share your book. You must also be passionate about your work within. First convince yourself that your book is worth sharing. If you cannot do this, then why should anyone else want you to share it with them?

But don't go overboard expressing your passion. Boasting, bragging, and overconfidence tend to turn readers off. They want to discover your passion – not have it thrust upon them. You want your passion for your writing to show without overdoing it. Let others inquire about your work, then show your passion as you discuss it. This way, they are discovering it. Don't tell others what to think – e.g., "This book is the best," "It will make you cry," etc. Bragging like this doesn't allow others to discover it for themselves. Statements of the form, "Oh yeah, when an idea hits, I just can't stop writing," don't tell others what to think, while conveying your sense of passion and dedication.

Also, don't let your passion for your writing let you take criticism or negative reviews personally. When it comes to criticism, you must wear a thick skin and keep your passion in check. They are reviewing your work – which you are very passionate about – but not you personally. While you love your writing, not everybody will. You just have to accept this. Although you have passion for your book, you can't afford to react emotionally or this will quickly ruin your reputation and credibility as a writer. The trick is to use passion to motivate yourself to market and create interest among potential readers, without letting your passion show in boasts, overconfidence, or difficulty receiving criticism.

Why must you market your book? You published your book, so it's available. Isn't this sharing, since others can now read it? Why can't people discover your book this way? If my book is good, won't people realize it and spread the word? Why should you have to sell a great book? Shouldn't great books sell simply because they're great? These are thoughts that most new self-publishers wonder. If you have similar questions, perhaps you can use one or more of the following answers to continually remind yourself why you need to market:

➢ There are millions of books out there, and thousands of new books released every day. How will people find your book if you don't market it?

➢ For the author who wonders why he/she must market his/her book, the reader is wondering why the author doesn't care enough about his/her book to market it.

> ➤ No sales rank or poor sales rank suggests to the reader that the book isn't very good. While you wait for your book to be discovered amongst millions, the low frequency of sales will have a long-lasting effect on your sales rank.
> ➤ Nobody will know if you're book is great until it's discovered. Without marketing, it will be buried in the search results. This means that it may take months or years for the book to get any attention, and by then it will be too late to overcome its slow start.

Some self-published authors may be able to let traditional publishers fuel part of their motivation. Until recently, big publishing houses have been deciding what people can read. Self-publishing provides freedom and opportunity for both authors and readers. Some writers have a stack of rejection letters from publishers that they use for motivation. Others draw motivation from the hope of succeeding without publishing traditionally. Another option is to let the freedom that self-publishing provides fuel part of your motivation.

Self-publishing doesn't tend to reward laziness. Writing successfully is hard work. Success takes a great idea, months of writing, months of editing and formatting, honest feedback, and effective marketing. Even if you publish traditionally, you still need a great idea, months of writing, and effective marketing – and you may have a contract for marketing expectations. Publishers require authors to market their own books, knowing that this hard work is what it takes to be a successful writer. If traditional publishers need their authors to market their work in order for sales to be a success, it's even more important for self-publishers. The more that you realize how important marketing is (without having to learn this the hard way, hopefully), the more diligent you are likely to be in your marketing efforts.

Once you start marketing, you must be patient and constantly remind yourself that continued marketing is essential if you're to sustain long-term success. Resist the urge to give up. Keep marketing. Don't let early results fool you: If sales start with a bang, that doesn't mean that you can slack off; and if sales start out slow, you must keep marketing in order to give your book a chance. Remember, it can take a year for your marketing efforts to fully pay off. Branding takes months. Word-of-mouth referrals can be especially slow in coming. Keep marketing to give your book its best possible chance.

Visualize a positive future for your book sales. Keep up your marketing in an effort to achieve this positive outcome. You must work toward it; sales won't just come to you. Focus on writing your next book. Working diligently on your marketing and writing your next book help to keep your mind off sales and reviews. Sales tend to fluctuate, so anytime they seem to be slipping, it can be agonizing; and reviews are sometimes critical. Instead of focusing on sales and reviews – or worse, responding to reviews – devote your mind to your marketing campaign and to writing your next book.

Think about the prospects for your next book improving sales of your first book. This will give you something to hope for and to work toward. It may help you exercise patience, keep your mind off of numbers and reviews, and help you stay positive. ☺

Another thing you can do to try and stay positive is to keep track of milestones. This can be fun and give you something to look forward to, whether you just notice it and enjoy it for a moment or keep a scrapbook. Here is a sample of some milestones that you can look for:

✓ Your first sale. Heck, you could even buy it yourself and frame it.
✓ When you sell your 10th, 100th, 1000th, etc. book (paperback and eBook, separately).
✓ When you first make $100, $1000, etc. overall (i.e. not just in one month).
✓ The first time that you make $100, $200, $300, etc. in royalties in one month. Fourth quarter sales may help you show improvement; so can releasing your next book.
✓ The first time that you sell 100, 200, 300, etc. books in one month.
✓ Also keep track of annual totals for both royalties and sales; try to improve each year.
✓ When your sales rank first cracks 200,000, 100,000, 50,000, 20,000, 10,000, etc. I have screenshots from a few of my books the first time that they cracked 5,000, and several other authors have done the same (because it doesn't always last long).
✓ Your first good review and your first five-star review.
✓ The first time a fan contacts you to say something nice about your book.
✓ When you sign your first autograph.

The best thing about these milestones is that no matter how good or poor your sales are, there is always something to look forward to – i.e. there is always a way to improve. On the other hand, your happiness can't depend upon reaching the next milestone, otherwise you will never be happy. Use the next milestone to help you revamp your marketing efforts.

8.1.6 Branding Your Author Image

As described in Sec. 8.1.3, branding is largely about recognition. The more you see and hear a brand name – like Heinz, Skechers, and Dell – the more you are likely to recognize it. Branding isn't about getting people to go out and purchase a product immediately. Rather, the idea is that if people recognize the brand from having seen and heard it enough, this may influence their purchase decision when they eventually shop for such a product. It can take months for branding to take effect, and many more months before customers are searching for such a product. This is the case with books. Branding doesn't bring immediate results, yet it can be a very powerful tool: When most customers are buying a product in the store, they very often choose a brand that they've heard before.

Branding a book or author isn't quite the same as branding laundry detergent or soda, but – as we will see – there are many close parallels. One of the main differences is that paid advertising probably won't be as effective for branding books. For one, everybody buys laundry detergent, but not everybody reads books similar to yours (yes, almost everyone does read books – but they read many different kinds of books – whereas any single laundry detergent is suitable for nearly anyone; also, there are millions of books for readers to choose from, but only a dozen or so laundry detergents – a huge difference in buyer-to-product ratio).

The similarities between branding a book or laundry detergent can help us apply common advertising methods to our books. For one, most brand names are very short and easy to spell and remember, like Nike, Timex, and Ford. Why? Because that makes it easy to remember, type in a search engine online, or refer to a friend. Would you like for your book to be easy to remember, type in a search on Amazon, or refer to friends and family? Then you should strive for a short title with three words or less, which is easy to spell and remember. It will be easier to remember if the title fits the genre and relates to the content. This is very common in traditionally published fiction.[25] Another advantage of short titles is that at the bottom of your email, blog posts, and online profiles, you can concisely say, Your Name, Author of X, Y, and Z. With a long title, you can just mention one book this way, instead of two or three.

Your cover plays a similar role in branding – the more people see the same cover, the more likely they are to recognize it. It might seem intuitive that if you had a wacky picture on your cover that would make it easier to recognize, but research suggests otherwise. Also, you don't just want your cover to get noticed by making it look zany – it needs to signify the genre and content, and it must look professional. The covers that work best for branding feature one striking, memorable image, where the title and cover send a consistent, unified message that relates to the genre and content. When the title, picture, genre, and content all easily relate to one another – without having to know anything about the book! – this makes the cover easier to remember. Unity is very important and too often ignored: Authors tend to favor cover images that mean something only to people who have read some of the book, but you're trying to sell the book to people who haven't yet read it. Keep this in mind.

Use the same book and author photos everywhere. Many authors make a temporary cover, feeling that it's better than nothing and that they can upgrade it later. When they change their covers, this hurts their branding efforts. It would be far better to perfect the cover prior to publishing. Similarly, post your same author image on all of your websites to help with branding your author image. There is a time issue – every few years you may need to update your author photo – but it should still be the same at all of your websites.

There is more to branding than just creating recognition. Companies want their brands to symbolize a particular trait – such as quality (like Sony), luxury (like Mercedes), or affordable (like K-Mart). One way that companies try to achieve this is with a catchy slogan. This helps people remember something about the brand. There is a similar tool that authors use with books: the hook. This is a short sentence that helps create interest in the book, and will give potential readers a glimpse of what to expect – something they will associate with the book.

---

[25] Perhaps I should have simply called this book *Self-Publishing with Amazon*. Titles are sometimes longer in nonfiction than in fiction, as a couple of additional words can help to match the content to a specific audience. In fiction, extra words usually hinder rather than help. For this book, the combined title and subtitle are too long. Even if you publish nonfiction, I recommend keeping this combination much shorter than mine.

Use your hook whenever you talk about your book in person. You can also use your hook at the end of a book reading. It's useful online, too – at the bottom of an email, blog post, or other online activity where you write your name and title (under that you can write the hook).

Companies also use a logo to help with branding. If you use your own imprint, you should develop some logo to put on your cover and copyright page, and anything else – such as a website – that is associated with the imprint. All of the books using the same imprint will feature the same logo.

Brand names establish status. You want your book to have status, too. Part of status is actually established with price. An underpriced book loses status – the price makes it seem cheap. Being way overpriced won't work, but a modest price may. The quality has to match. If people thumb through the book and it appears highly professional and if the book is very well-written, this signifies quality. However, a book with poor formatting or spelling and grammar mistakes won't command the higher price of a higher-quality book.

Some status comes by word of mouth. For example, if you list an editor by your name and readers are talking about how well-written your book is, while other authors are asking you if your editor may be interested in helping them – this greatly helps your status. Sir Arthur Conan Doyle had a different type of status with his protagonist, Sherlock Holmes. In fact, his sidekick, Dr. Watson, immensely helped build up Holmes's status as a super sleuth. In this case, the status is two-fold: a very memorable character and clever mysteries.

Another important part of branding is visibility. You need to get your target audience to see your book's title and cover along with your name and author photo in order for branding to take effect. Both discovery and branding require first identifying and then reaching your target audience. We'll discuss this in Sec.'s 8.1.9-10.

Branding the author's image is just as important as branding the book's image. Anything that you post online – including your biography and photo (see Sec. 6.1.3) – must help to reinforce your image as an author. You want to sound confident and knowledgeable, with a personality that relates to your book. All of your behavior must be professional.

Credibility takes much time to establish, but can be lost online in a heartbeat through forum clashes, arguments, rash behavior, controversial remarks, political comments, replies to reviews, etc. Don't risk your credibility by looking unprofessional. As explained in Sec. 7.1.6, perceived bad behavior by authors can lead to No votes and negative reviews, and sometimes a mob mentality develops when an author responds to reviews – especially, when done so emotionally, defensively, or repeatedly.

Maintaining good public relations is an important part of becoming a successful author. A single post anywhere online can destroy your author image. You must always be thinking about how each post may affect your brand as an author.

It's not always easy. Once you have several reviews, you are likely to have at least one critical review. If you attain success, some people will make accusations and try to show that you've done something wrong. You must wear a thick skin, avoid commenting on reviews, avoid complaining about bad reviews anywhere online, never get into an argument online, not behave defensively or react emotionally, and always behave professionally.

Branding occurs in person, online, and also through social media. Consider how you appear in your Facebook and Twitter activities. Posting bad things about negative reviews through social media, for example, hurts your reputation.

In addition to your own image, there is also the image of self-publishing in general to consider; both are important. On the one hand, the self-publishing industry has already been branded with some criticism (which indies have largely brought upon themselves), including:

- ☹ Authors who have abused the system with numerous fake five-star reviews for books that turned out to be not so good, giving malicious reviews to other books, getting into forum arguments, etc. Bad behavior doesn't just hurt your own image: it affects indies at large.
- ☹ Some websites that criticize indie covers.
- ☹ References to self-published books that were poorly written, edited, formatted, or thought out. Even if nobody reads them, the Look Inside of the worst books still affects the image of self-publishing.
- ☹ There is some criticism of free promo and 99-cent books cheapening the market – especially, those books that didn't turn out to be good.
- ☹ Very short books seem to be the new fashion – sometimes, just a chapter that's not even self-contained. Some authors are hoping to create interest by giving a short sample away for free; others are even just looking for feedback before completing their books.[26] Customers like to get their money's worth.

Unfortunately, there are even self-published authors who are contributing toward the negative image of self-publishing by frequently talking about the "slush pile" of poorly written and formatted indie books. The better the image of self-publishing, the more customers will be willing to buy self-published books. Similarly, the better the image of eBooks, Kindle, Amazon, or Smashwords – the more customers will be willing to buy these products.

Consider this: If you invest time and effort marketing your own books, while at the same time you're often disparaging other indie authors, eBooks, or eBook sellers, this is neutralizing your own marketing campaign. The better the image of self-publishing, the better for your own sales. If indie sales or eBook sales decline because this image declines, that hurts sales for all authors – not just those at the bottom. Fewer eReaders = fewer eBooks for everyone.

Everyone can help to improve the image of self-publishing:

- Don't disparage other indie authors or indie works.
- Don't complain about the slush pile, free promo books, or review abuse. Reminding people about these problems is negative advertising.

---

[26] You want your first impression to be a great impression. Don't publish material that's not ready for publishing, especially not just to get feedback. Go to a writer's forum and exchange feedback there.

- Strive to paint a positive picture for indies in your blog, conversations, etc.
- When you hear someone disparage indies, refer to the slush pile, etc., make a quick, positive, tactful, "Actually…" comment. Don't get in a debate, don't sound defensive. Just make one short, swift, positive statement and let it go.
- When someone asks you, "Don't you hate the effect that all of those lousy self-published books have on your image," politely and quickly refute this.
- Do your best to perfect the covers, editing, formatting, and stories of your own books.
- Once you have achieved mild success, occasionally lend a hand to help a newbie start out on the right foot and avoid some common mistakes.
- When your friends and acquaintances self-publish, give them honest feedback and help them improve their covers, blurbs, Look Insides, storylines, and writing.
- Bring attention to great indie covers, great indie books, and indie success stories.
- Recommend quality indie books to others.
- Don't give good reviews to lousy indie books. Do give good reviews to good indie books. Be careful what you say in any bad reviews of lousy indie books.

One thing we have going for us is strength in numbers. There are over a million self-published authors. Add to this number their friends, family, and acquaintances. Almost every-body knows somebody who is a self-published author. Together, we can help overcome this stigma and build a positive image for self-publishing. Discuss advantages of self-publishing, like not having an editor decide what we can read and artistic freedom for the author.

8.1.7 Creating Buzz for Your Book

The importance of marketing before your book is published – or even written – was stressed in Sec. 8.1.2, which listed several marketing techniques that you should be applying prior to publishing your book. Many of these help to generate "buzz" for your upcoming book – i.e. to get people talking (in person and online) about your book. This process should begin a couple of months prior to the release date, and you want to create buzz before, during, and after its release. This helps greatly in stimulating early sales and reviews, and gives your book the best possible start.

It should all begin when you first start writing your book. "What have you been up to?" Questions like this provide you an opportunity for friends, family, and acquaintances to discover that you're working on a book. Weeks later, they may ask, "So how's your book coming along?" This way, they can follow your progress.

The trick is to create interest in your book, but not to give too much away. The more you reveal about your book, the less they need to read to learn about it. Arouse curiosity. Don't answer every question – let them read it and find out. Also, let people ask you questions so that they can discover that you're writing a book, or look for opportunities to bring this up naturally – e.g. if it happens to relate to the conversation. Refrain from advertising out of the blue that you're written a book, as this doesn't tend to generate nearly as much interest as when people discover it.

Feedback is invaluable for two reasons: It provides you with a variety of opinions about things that people do and don't like (so if there is any feature that is widely disliked, you may improve your book's chances of success by correcting this prior to publishing) and helps create some buzz in the process.

As described in Sec.'s 5.1.1-2, you should separately solicit feedback on your title, cover, blurb, Look Inside, and even the book itself. Strangers in your target audience (who aren't yet fans) will most likely give you the most honest, relevant opinions. Friends and family are far more likely to be supportive, even if you feel that they are usually very critical. Don't rely on just friends and family to provide feedback. Besides, the more people who provide feedback, the more buzz you can generate.

Begin with family, friends, and acquaintances. If you happen to have a conversation with someone, you can pull out your title or cover, for example, and request a little feedback. Any busy (yet safe; bring a friend) place where soliciting isn't prohibited can help you solicit feedback from strangers in person. You can also post questions – including a link to your prospective cover – online at discussion forums (best if it includes your target audience), your blog, social media, and your website. (Remember, the fewer posts about you – like 10% or less – the better. Providing valuable content for your target audience helps to attract followers.)

You generally don't want the same person to offer feedback on everything at the same time. Start out with the title. First, show people your title and ask them what they think the book is about – if they can't guess, a better title is desirable. Also ask their opinion of your title, and any suggestions that they may have. Then show your cover. The better your cover is the first time you show it, the greater will be the effect – especially, if there is a striking image. The blurb requires some reading and thought, so opinions won't come in as quick and casual a setting as the title and blurb.

You need a few people who can provide good critiques to carefully comb through your Look Inside. Your goal is to make this immaculate – beautifully formatted, perfectly edited. You need to approximate the Look Inside and get this feedback before publishing. The first couple of paragraphs can be shared more widely. You want to know if the first couple of paragraphs hook the readers into the story.

A bigger challenge is getting some people to read your book – and not all at once, so you can make one set of revisions before seeking further help. Ideally, the first person to help with this would be an experienced editor, whose previous work (one way to verify this is if they are listed as the editor and you – or someone with great grammar skills – checks a sample of it) looks excellent. Most very well-written books have gone through a few separate edits. Don't rely on a single person to do all of the editing. A few close friends can help, too.

The more positive publicity your book gets prior to publishing, the more you may get people talking about your book before, during, and after its release. Do you know people who love to socialize? You want them to know about your book, so that if there is something about your book that they like (just the cover, perhaps; they don't necessarily need to read it), they might be more inclined to say something like, "Did you know that so-'n'-so is writing a book?"

Think about what makes your book special. You would like to find ways that people can discover this – i.e. without your prompting. Multiple edits might make it seem well-written, use of a professional formatting service might make people want to check out what it looks like, a couple of years doing research helps make you seem knowledgeable about the subject, sharing excerpts about a memorable character can get people discussing the characterization, a few people who've read the whole book can advertise if the storyline is excellent, etc. There are many things out of your control, but one thing in your control is what you say when you answer questions about your writing and what parts of your book you reveal to others. For the purpose of branding, if most people are describing just one or two main things that really make your book stand out, this helps with recognition. People have their own opinions and express ideas differently, so it won't just sound like the same thing is being repeated over and over – but, for example, if a prospective reader happens to hear from a few different sources that your book is very well edited, this could make a favorable impression (but then if the facts contradict the gossip, it will backfire).

Any professional services that you use might give you a little publicity. For example, if you hire a professional illustrator or editor, find out if he/she has a website and, if so, if he/she will feature your thumbnail image on his/her website. This person might also mention your book to his/her friends, family, and acquaintances in order to help create some buzz for your book.

Sending out advance review copies can help you create word-of-mouth buzz and earn some early reviews. Goodreads can help with this (Sec. 6.2.5), and so can bloggers who have a following among your target audience (Sec. 8.1.15).

The more early sales that you can stimulate through effective marketing, the more people may be talking about your book shortly after its release. Word-of-mouth publicity is among the best marketing that your book can get. The first step toward this is getting many people to read your book. The next step is for your book to be as good as possible. Some books tend to garner word-of-mouth referrals more than others. Nonfiction that is very clear and helpful or fiction that evokes powerful emotions are more likely to benefit from this. Memorable characters and great storylines can help, too. Poor editing or formatting detract from this – or worse, provide some negative publicity.

Amazon Preorders allow you to generate a sales rank before your book is even published, and can get your book listed in the Coming Soon category. We discussed this in Sec. 7.1.8.

Many of the other marketing ideas described in this chapter – such as writing articles, book signings, and book readings – can help generate buzz before, during, and after the release of your book.

8.1.8 Launching Your Book

The launch of your book should involve more than merely pressing the button to publish your book. The large number of authors who do just that are missing out on many possible benefits. First, you should create buzz for your book, as described in the previous section. For your paperback, arrange for preorders on Amazon (this was discussed in Sec. 7.1.8). Of course, you should be marketing from the get-go (in fact, starting a couple of months in advance). In this section, we'll mention a few specific marketing strategies that you should be using when you release your book, but you should also be applying many of the other techniques from this chapter, too – like how to make a press release kit (described in Sec. 8.1.14).

Arrange a book launch party among friends and family on the release date. I recommend not investing in decorations or a fancy dinner; this is an occasion to start earning royalties, not to be spending money. Maybe someone will be nice and treat you to dinner in celebration of your accomplishment. If not, a low-cost barbeque or pizza party might be in order. If you frequently go out to dinner, you might be able to use a "normal" dinner occasion to celebrate your book launch without incurring any additional monthly expenses.

You might want to have some paperbacks available to sell during your party. Friends and family might wish to get them free, but you need sales. If they buy your book on Amazon, this affects your sales rank. They might appreciate buying copies in person as a compromise, as you can earn more royalties while they can also receive a discount due to the low price of the author cost. Remember, anyone with a financial interest in your book – a family member who lives with you, for example – isn't allowed to review your book.

Two other events you should be arranging around the publication date are book signings and book readings. A signing is when you sit down at a table and autograph paperback copies of your book, such as at a bookstore. At a reading, you read part of your book for 10 to 30 minutes and answer questions. Such events help stir interest in your book, establish your credibility as an author (it looks professional), and can earn early sales. We'll explore this much further in Sec. 8.1.11.

Many authors fail to take advantage of free media (newspaper, radio, and television) opportunities. Local press especially likes to feature local authors, and local papers often have column inches that need to be filled somehow (your story might just be that "somehow"). You should get some local press when your book is released, and may earn better publicity later if your book really takes off. We'll describe how media can help you market your book in Sec. 8.1.14 and the use of videos and writing articles in Sec. 8.1.13.

Decide whether to release your paperback book and eBook at the same time. Traditional publishers often release different editions in stages, often by price. Usually they begin with a more expensive hardcover edition, then come out with less expensive paperback and eBook editions. If the paperback is more expensive, but you draw a greater royalty from your eBook, then this strategy doesn't really make sense for you.

8.1.9 Identifying Your Target Audience

All of your marketing efforts will be wasted if they are not directed at and geared toward your target audience. You must first take the time to identify and truly understand the target audience for your book. Then spend time thinking about and researching precisely where you can find your target audience. If you have visibility with an audience that's not a good match for your book, you won't be attracting much interest in your book.

Your audience is <u>not</u> anyone with a pair of eyes. Sure, anyone who can read could read your book, but almost all readers buy books in just their favorite genres. Very, very few book sales come from readers who don't ordinarily buy in your book's genre – except for those people who buy your book primarily because they already knew you or met you and became interested enough to buy your work. Marketing toward a very specific audience that's a great match for your book is far more effective than marketing across the board.

If you want a wider market, write books in very popular genres like romance or suspense. There is a trade-off, though – there is a great deal of competition in the most popular genres. Meeting a need in a niche market may have a smaller audience, but you're more likely for a good book to attract a high percentage of a niche audience.

Note that combining genres that are too different may hurt more than it helps. Intuitively, some authors expect a mystery/romance to attract more readers than either a mystery or romance novel because it could be of interest to every mystery and romance reader. But it may not work out that way. Most mystery readers are looking for a good mystery; if it has some romantic elements, that's fine, but if the blurb says it's a romantic mystery, it may sound like too much of a romance. Similarly, romance readers are looking for a good romance novel; some mystery in it is okay, but if it seems more like a mystery that has some romance, they may prefer another book. You really need to choose one or the other and gear your book that way. The problem is that the romantic mystery isn't attracting – as intended – all of the readers from both genres; instead, it's only attracting the few readers who read both mystery and romance frequently. The difficulty lies in writing a blurb that is attractive in both genres.

Similarly, authors want to list their books in as many categories as possible, thinking that this widens the book's visibility. However, some readers will actually check out the categories to see what kind of book they are getting. If they see two significantly different categories listed, like mystery and romance, they might think, "Oh, that's not what I was looking for."

To make matters worse, if you run the idea of combining genres by friends, they will often support your intuition. They will probably even give you an example, such as, "I buy both sci-fi and fantasy, so I think a crossover is a great idea." Gearing your book toward a specific genre is best for marketing your book.

In the other extreme, the toughest books to market are books that blend three or more categories and books that don't quite fit into any category. A few books have a blurb that states that they are part romance, mystery, horror, and fantasy, for example. Such books are very difficult to sell. Your best chance of having stellar sales is to write a book geared for a popular genre, which adheres to the unspoken rules of that genre (i.e. read the bestsellers in that genre to learn what is allowed, not allowed, and generally expected).

On the other hand, if you write a mystery book where the majority of the book involves bowling, for example, then it is a good idea to target both mystery readers and bowlers. Here, we're not combining two separate genres. In this case, we're instead identifying both a genre and a common interest among the target audience.

You want to identify your target audience not only by genre, but also be age group, gender, occupation, hobbies, interests, and any other category that may be relevant. It's to your advantage to pinpoint this precisely. The more precisely your marketing efforts match the perfect audience for your book, the greater will be the yield. It's a common mistake to try to find every possible audience member. For example, if you think, "Oh yeah, fantasy readers might be into computer programming, too," and start reaching out to computer programmers to brand your fantasy book, you're wasting your time unless your book features this skill, too.

Identifying the specific audience for the book is what publishers do, and it's what the editor expects to find in your book proposal when you try to get traditionally published. If there is a mismatch between the book you propose and your target audience, the editor will likely think that your marketing efforts won't be successful and reject your proposal. For self-publishers, it's equally important: If you don't market your book to the right audience, it really hurts your prospects for good sales.

Note that romance, for example, isn't a precise genre: You must distinguish between teen romance, adult romance, and erotica. Even within adult romance, there is contemporary, historical, gothic, and more. First, pinpoint the target genre.

Next, do some research to try to learn more about your target audience. You can try searching online for help or conducting surveys, for example. When you meet and interact with fans, you can get some idea directly (without making them feel that you're collecting and analyzing statistics). Are they mostly male or female? What age group is predominant? What main interests and hobbies are they most likely to have? How about their careers? Will they have anything in common among their educational backgrounds?

The more you know about your target audience, the easier it will be to find them. In the next section, we will discuss how to reach your target audience, assuming that you have already correctly identified who they are.

8.1.10 Reaching Your Target Audience

Now that you've identified your target audience, the next step is to find them. For example, if you write a book to help troubled teens, you need to start thinking about where to find troubled teens and their parents. In this case, doing volunteer work in your community to help troubled teenagers or to help their parents deal with them will let you personally interact with members of your target audience – and there may be indirect benefits, such as authority figures getting to know and trust you, who may recommend your book once they discover it, if they believe that it would be helpful. There are discussion forums online for parents to share experience and advice with one another. If you're an active and helpful member there, you improve your presence – and if the website allows you to fill out an online profile, you may be discovered or branded. You could post articles on a blog to help troubled teens and their parents, try to publish articles in magazines (in print and online), and ask bloggers on this topic if they would consider reading an advanced review copy and, if they like your book, consider posting a review on their blog.

As another example, suppose that you wrote a book that closely relates to golf – it could be a nonfiction book about golf, or a fictional work that is set on the golf course. In this case, you should be visiting golf courses and golf shops with several books in your trunk. Sell them at a healthy discount that's a good compromise for both you and the seller. Have a press release package, business cards, and a sample book handy. Start locally where people know you and work your way up. Keep some copies handy when you visit the driving range or play a round of golf. Contact golf magazines, starting with smaller publications, to see if they have an interest in showcasing your book or writing an article about you. Look for online golf websites, too. If you write a golf article, you may be able to get it published in print or online, indicating that you're the author of Your Book at the bottom. Figure out where golfers hang out online: You may be able to write an online golf article or interact with golfers at a discussion forum.

Unfortunately, I can't work out every possible example. Let me do one more, and hope that these examples will help to inspire ideas for your unique book. Suppose that you wrote a science fiction book. If so, then you should already be a member of one or more sci-fi clubs and organizations. Many of these allow you to meet and interact with others online, where they may be able to learn more about you from your user profile. They also have parties and get-togethers (you could throw one yourself, but if you have a good social presence, you will receive invitations), where everybody gets to dress up. You can meet several people at sci-fi conventions. Try to find a science fiction book club (being a member would help). A blog is a little trickier because it's difficult to attract many new readers with short fiction pieces – it's a big commitment to read blog fiction when you're not already familiar with the author, and it's hard to know what to expect until you start reading. Instead, it may be more effective to post nonfiction articles that are relevant for a sci-fi audience.

Once you've established who your target audience is, it's just a matter of resourcefulness, willpower, and motivation to find them. You can do it! You're not under pressure to find every avenue today; other ideas may pop into your mind from time to time. Keep pondering this and good ideas will come.

The most effective way to market your book to your target audience is to meet and interact with them in person. This is more personable than online interactions, and benefits from the fact that the reader can say that he/she actually met the author of a book that he/she has read. The next time they see you, they can even get your autograph. A significant number of self-published books are actually sold to customers who have personally interacted with the author. It's important to let them discover that you've written a book, rather than advertising this information – i.e. let them ask, or at most work this into the conversation at a relevant moment.

Of course, there is a limit to how many people from your target audience you can meet in person, so you must also use social media and/or online tools. These may not provide as large a percent yield, but this is compensated by the much greater number of people whom can potentially be reached this way. You can use branding and discovery effectively with social media, online forums, your blog, your websites, writing and posting articles online, and other online resources – provided that you're interacting with or presenting information to your target audience (not just to people in general).

Most places (including Amazon's customer discussion forums) don't allow self-promotion, which means that you're not allowed to say, "I'm the author of This Book." That's okay because self-promotion isn't effective anyway. Instead, many forums do allow you to include your name, occupation, and sometimes a link in your profile. When you interact with members of your target audience, people whom you interest may click on your user profile to learn more about you. It's not reasonable to expect to generate many sales in the near-future this way. This is just one step in your overall discovery and branding scheme, which helps people recognize you when they finally (which may be months from now) go to buy their next book.

One of the more effective marketing resources available to you online is the opportunity to write and post an article with content geared toward your target audience in a modestly high-traffic area on the internet. There are very many online magazines and other websites that feature articles – so many that you can find several where useful content is in demand. This will be described in more detail in Sec. 8.1.13.

You can also make a video and post it online, or publish a poem or short story in a magazine, journal, or high-traffic website. We'll also discuss this in Sec. 8.1.13.

Social media can be useful at a few different stages. When you publish your first book, Facebook and Twitter help you reach out to family, friends, and acquaintances for useful feedback, to help generate buzz, and to stimulate early sales. As you gain new readers, they help you establish a fan base. When you publish subsequent books, social media can help you utilize your fan base to get early sales and reviews. Attracting new readers from your target audience requires posting valuable content that will be useful to your target audience. At least 90% of your posts must include valuable content for this to be effective; only 10% can be links to your own websites or posts about you and your book (except, perhaps, for a separate Facebook fan page, which will consist almost exclusively of already established fans). At Twitter, research relevant hashtags at www.hashtags.org to understand them prior to using them with your posts. We discussed the use of Facebook and Twitter in Sec. 6.2.6.

Socializing in person is generally better than the distant, impersonal interactions with social media. Interacting face-to-face provides the personal touch. When people meet the author in person, they feel like they have really met the person; interacting with the author online doesn't produce the same feeling, and definitely not nearly to the same degree. Face-to-face socializing with the right audience is more likely to impact sales. Get out of the house and interact with your audience in person. It's only because there is a limit to how many people you can interact with in person that social media is effective – although it is less likely to stimulate a sale with a single person, social media can easily reach much larger numbers.

Ordinary media is often more effective than social media. Too many authors aren't taking advantage of newspapers, radio, and television opportunities. Local papers usually like to cover local authors and normally have free column inches to fill. Free media coverage is the subject of Sec. 8.1.14.

Ideally, you should have your blog up-and-running prior to publishing. This helps you establish a small following prior to your book's release, and ensures that there is some content available when your first fans check out your blog. As with everything you do online, post valuable content to get people interested in checking out your profile. This is true whether you blog, use social media, or just post online in a forum. Posting about yourself or your book won't attract people unless you're a celebrity, but content will slowly develop a small following. A highly successful blog may also lead to other possibilities, such as advertisers that pay you. We discussed blogging in Sec. 6.2.2. Remember to feed your blog and Twitter posts into your Author Page at Amazon (see Sec. 6.1.6).

An author website – i.e. more than just a blog – can also include valuable content to attract prospective readers from your target audience. If you add a mailing list for fans to sign up at your author website, be sure to send valuable content – don't just plug your books. Sec. 6.2.3 described how to go about creating a website for you as an author.

Whenever you post a link to any of your books at Amazon, be sure to use the short link, as explained in Sec. 7.1.1, or an affiliate link, as described in Sec. 7.1.8.

Think of where to meet people from your target audience in person. Find a book club for your genre. Knowing what interests are common among your target audience will help you immensely, which is why it's so important to first identify and try to learn more about the people who are the best fit for your book. This is a little easier with nonfiction, and with fiction that features a main topic or hobby. For example, a book may be geared toward raising kids with disabilities, involve a great deal of basketball, or have much to do with aviation. You just need to find where you can meet people with similar interests. Since you wrote about this topic, hopefully you will naturally fit in there; you don't want to seem out of place, like you're only there as an author hoping to sell books.

Get involved in community service that relates to interests that are common among your target audience. You can arrange workshops, guest lectures, and other presentations. You may be able to setup book readings at libraries, schools, bookstores, churches, theaters, big brother or sister organizations, civic centers, etc. Don't sign up for readings everywhere – focus your energy on your target audience. You can also do book signings at libraries and bookstores. We'll discuss readings, signings, presentations, and workshops in Sec. 8.1.11. Organize other types of events (or get involved in events organized by others) that let you meet potential readers.

The more you socialize, the more your work may be discovered in person, which can significantly impact sales. Anyone you interact with could buy your book – maybe not right away, but sometime down the line. They might also recommend your book to someone else even if they don't buy it themselves. For example, if you interact with someone who doesn't read mystery, they probably know a friend who does. Socializing with people in your target audience is most effective, but all interactions are useful. I can't emphasize enough the importance of letting them discover your work, rather than you advertising your book.

When you meet people, charm them. Make a good impression. Think of your image as an author. Brand yourself as professional, knowledgeable as a writer in your genre, passionate about your work, engaging in conversation (people may expect your book to be as exciting or boring as your conversations – true or not, this impression is likely), and credible as the author of the type of book that you've written.

People who enjoy interacting with you and happen to discover that you're an author are not only more likely to buy and read your book, they're also more likely to spread the word about your book among friends and family (provided that they like your book). Many authors tend to be highly introverted, and so would rather sit comfortably at their computers and type than socialize. As I mentioned earlier, some of the most effective marketing strategies involve doing things that lie outside of your comfort zone. Get out of the house and meet new people – it will be a healthy change for authors who tend to prefer being unsocial.

It's not just people from your target audience whom you want to interact with. You also need to attend events where you can meet other authors, editors, literary agents, publishers, bloggers, advertisers, and publicists. Build useful contacts. In life, who you know is sometimes more valuable than what you know. Like it or not, you can benefit from this principle if you simply accept it. It's the underlying principle of marketing – people need to learn about you and your book before they will buy it. It's "who you know" first (i.e. your marketing campaign is designed to get more people to know you as an author through branding and discovery) and then "what you know" later (once they read your book, they get this from the content). Similarly, if you want to find a good editor who is willing to work with you, get good press from a high-traffic blogger, or get traditionally published, you must first market yourself in these circles so that they can learn "who you are" before you can sell them "what you know." Even careers tend to follow this principle.

People often wear many hats or change hats. Most authors are also bloggers, and many authors who have a humble blog now will have a high-traffic blog in the future. Some authors who write very well and gain some experience helping others revise their work will become freelance editors someday. A few people who enjoy major success marketing their own books may transform into publicists to help aspiring authors succeed. As you begin to wear more hats or as you change hats in your own career path, the various contacts that you build in the world of writing may come in handy in ways that you would never have imagined.

What is unique about you – the author? Do you have any marketing advantages? For example, if you happen to be a triplet, this improves your prospects for getting great press coverage. If you have expertise – such as an advanced degree – it should help you publish a nonfiction article in a magazine with high circulation. If you have marketing contacts – e.g. in the media, or a publicist – they may be able to help you promote your book. Everybody has something special going in his/her favor. Think about what it is and how to use it to your advantage. You have interests and experience that relate to your book: This not only helps you connect with readers who have similar interests and experience, but can also help you get exposure in these areas, too. People you already know in this area may be able to help you promote your book. If you feel that nothing is special about you and that you don't know anybody that can help, then you need to spend more time pondering this or ask others for ideas. For example, if you write a suspense novel that features chess, you must know some chess players or instructors, be in a chess club, or play online. Start with these contacts.

Your successes and accomplishments can sometimes help you work your way up the ladder. For example, climbing up the bestseller list, improving your sales rank, and earning reviews may show that your work is serious enough for higher-traffic websites to consider working with you. Publishing articles on smaller venues and achieving mild success with it may open doors with larger venues. You can't leap from local to national exposure in a single bound, but you can slowly work your way up the ladder.

There are sometimes opportunities to plug your book or eBook. Discovery and branding tend to be most effective, while self-promotion tends to be ineffective. In between, someone may plug your book for you or prompt you with a question. During a radio, television, or blog interview, for example, the host is likely to plug your book or directly ask you about your book. A plug can greatly increase your exposure in a high-traffic zone. There are sometimes creative ways to plug your book. For example, I was watching a baseball game once when one of the announcers mentioned the name of a book that a fan had sent him in the mail. The fan had written a baseball book that consisted of pictures of memorabilia. The television station even took a moment to show excerpts from the book. That was a great plug, as there were over a million viewers in the author's target audience.

Plugs, YouTube videos, and publicity stunts can help you get a little exposure among a very wide audience. However, you must strive for positive publicity. Remember, your author image is at stake. Negative publicity of any kind – including publicity stunts – can ruin a writing career. Don't do anything that may give you a bad name.

Use your hook – a short sentence that helps to create interest in your book. This comes in handy during conversations, interviews, and all of your personal interactions.

Are there any popular books that are very similar to yours? If so, drawing a comparison can help you describe what your book is about. For example, when someone asks you what to expect from your book, you might say something like, "It's a cross between *The Lord of the Rings* and *Harry Potter*" (and for a case like this, it arouses curiosity – they will want to know how that's possible). You can also write statements of the sort, "If you enjoyed *Twilight*, you may also like *My Book Title*."

But you must be careful. Saying, "If you like Book A, you'll love Book B," is dangerous. First, it sounds boastful. If Book A is a bestseller and Book B is self-published, saying that Book B is better creates unrealistic expectations. People are more likely to check out your book if you say that they may like Book B, and less likely to do so if you say that they will like or will love Book B. Those who do buy Book B expecting it to be better than Book A are likely to leave a negative review if Book B doesn't live up to these lofty expectations. Even worse is saying, "*My Book* is better than *This Book*." Be confident and passionate about your writing, but don't be overconfident or boastful. Bragging deters sales, while passion encourages them.

Always carry business cards in your wallet or purse; you can't have too many, but you can have too few. Your cards should include your cover photo, book's title, author name, and mention your website(s). If you wish to sell some books through your CreateSpace eStore (see Sec. 6.2.4), consider including a discount code on your business card. There are other press release materials that may come in handy, too, in addition to business cards (see Sec. 8.1.14). You should always have books on hand – i.e. in the trunk of your car (nicely stacked in a box where the covers won't get wrinkled or start to curl).

If you can get inexpensive bookmarks printed that look nice and feature your book, these will probably be more effective than business cards. What do you do with a business card that you find in your pocket when you get home? Many people toss it in the garbage or a pile of other business cards. What would you do with a nice bookmark that includes information about a book, but doesn't look like an advertisement? Many readers will actually use these, especially if they enjoyed personally interacting with the author. Guess what? They will be reminded of your book every time they read.

We'll discuss promotional contests and giveaways in much more detail in Sec. 8.1.17, including discounts and freebies.

8.1.11 Book Signings, Readings, and Presentations

A book signing is an event – often hosted by a library or bookstore – where the author sits down at a table and fans wait in a line to get their copies of the book signed. A reading is an event – which could be at a theatre, school, or church, for example – where the author stands before a podium and reads a portion of the book for 10 to 30 minutes, followed by a question and answer session. Very often, an author will sign books at the conclusion of a reading.

Bookstores have an incentive to work with authors in arranging book signings: Customers may purchase the author's book while in the store – and may even buy other books and products (like bookmarks or coffee). Local bookstores – especially, smaller specialty shops and antique stores that sell books – are most likely to be receptive. With this and many other marketing strategies, starting small and working your way up is a good idea. For one, this gives you some experience and confidence – plus, you can honestly say that you've done this before – prior to approaching the bigger bookstores.

Why won't all bookstores be receptive? Unfortunately, whenever a bookstore may have a bad experience with a book signing, this ruins the chances for other authors to do this. Make your book signing professional and successful, leaving a good impression with the bookstore managers and owners, and you're more likely to get additional opportunities in the future (not just with the same bookstore – news tends to spread).

But don't be discouraged – some bookstores, libraries, and other places will be receptive to book signings. It's a valuable opportunity to meet people from your target audience who you know in advance have some interest in your book. Many authors don't think to try this or don't realize how effective it can be when done right. Book signings and readings lend you credibility as a professional author.

With bookstores, you'll need to make arrangements in advance regarding the sale of your book. They might expect you to sell copies to them at a discount, which they can then sell to customers, with the option of returning unsold copies to you for a refund; or they might allow you to sell them on consignment while you're there – i.e. they will take a commission for each sale. We'll discuss all of the ways that you might sell books to bookstores in Sec. 8.1.16, but the best option usually is for you to buy the books directly from CreateSpace at your author cost and then sell them to bookstores in person at a significant discount.

For libraries and other places that won't sell your book, you will probably bring your own stack of books to set on the table where you do the signing and sell them yourself (since author copies are quite cheap, you can offer a discount from the list price and still make more than your Amazon royalty).

Always clarify the arrangements in advance – especially, the exact arrangements for how to sell your book at the signing. Bring a few nice pens. Even though you're the one who should be using the pen, nice pens have a tendency to disappear, so you want backups. Also, use a pen that looks very nice, yet which you can afford to replace if you must. Dress appropriately – you should look credible as the author of the type of book that you wrote.

Be polite, personal, and charming, while also appearing professional and confident (but not boastful or overconfident). Get their name and remember it, but clarify the spelling. Write with care and absolutely avoid any need to cross anything out (that's very tacky). Mistakes happen though. How do you cover up non-erasable ink? With a sticker or adhesive label that will look very nice inside the book. A sheet of these may come in handy. Come prepared to answer questions about you or your book. Don't give away too much information about the story. Make eye contact with each reader and strive not to blush (this makes you appear amateurish). Engage in a brief conversation individualized to each reader – this makes everyone feel special and worthy of your attention. If someone is dragging things on too long and holding up the line, make eye contact with the next person briefly and gently wave him/her forward. Develop an autograph that differs from your bank signature.

Help populate your book signings, readings, and other events. It's totally embarrassing for both you and the host if you sit at a table for half an hour and scarcely anybody shows up. You have to promote your event. At least get friends, family, and acquaintances to populate some of your events (maybe try to spread them around so that they don't all show up to the same event, leaving others empty – while still getting enough to attend each event that in the worst-case scenario, it's not too vacant).

Have a friend take pictures of you signing books. You can post one of these on your Author Page at Amazon, your blog, or your author website. It will help to establish your credibility as a professional author. If the photo features you and just one other individual, ask for that person's permission to post it on your author pages. If it features you signing a book with many others in the background, since they came to a public event, as long as they aren't doing something embarrassing in the background, posting the picture shouldn't be a problem. Of course, if you want legal advice, you should consult an attorney; beyond legalities, you also don't want to offend or embarrass any of your fans.

Let your fans know about your signings and readings through your fan page, author website, blog, social media, Goodreads, and your Author Page at Amazon (you can post information about events and tours there). Remember, you need a regular dose of relevant content on your blog and social media sites so that when you have an event to announce, the posts about you and your other websites don't amount to more than 10% of the overall posts.

There are many places where you can give readings of your book, such as theaters, schools, churches, civic centers, big brother and sister organizations, etc. Theaters and other businesses that often market events may help you promote your reading – they might even have contacts in the press to place a note in the local paper.

When you call or visit in person (don't email or text – it's far too impersonal) to make arrangements, sound (and appear, if in person) professional. Avoid saying, "I don't know." Prepare for questions and think of details that you should ask about. If they've done readings before, inquire about prospective attendance counts and expectations for what percentage of the audience may purchase books. Make arrangements for selling your books – e.g. all on your own, will they take a commission, or do they want to sell them? Some theaters have a gift shop and may even want to keep some extras for a few days because people who couldn't attend sometimes call afterward to inquire about the event. Ask if they will help promote your book and how – e.g. with press coverage or sending emails to their fan base.

Be sure to place an order for author copies well in advance. In fact, just having several extra copies lying around the house and in the trunk of your car can come in handy. It's quite embarrassing to not have a book when you need it. If you can get a good estimate for the prospective attendance count, this will help you bring the right number of books. Some authors sell copies to 70% of the audience at a book reading. A few authors like to bring enough books for 100% just in case. If you bring too many copies, you will be able to use the unsold copies in other ways. Business cards and press release material can come in handy for the unlikely case that you run out of books (well, it should be unlikely if you're well-prepared).

You might not sell 70%. Prepare for the possibility of only selling books to a small fraction of your audience, but don't be discouraged if that happens. Everyone who shows up is interested in your book – otherwise, they wouldn't be there. Some might not buy your book for months. Having attended your reading, they now know about your book, which is one step in branding your book and image. So even if sales are dismal at your reading, you should be encouraged by the prospects for future sales. You've planted the seed.

However, if sales at a reading aren't too good, you should also request some feedback a couple of days later from a few individuals. They might have suggestions for something that you could have done better. Don't ask for criticism at the reading, but politely accept any suggestions that may be offered at this time. Don't ruin your image by getting into a debate at a signing or reading, and don't make any disparaging remarks about anybody or anything.

Many readings last 10 to 30 minutes and allow for about 15 minutes of questions and answers. Contact your host regarding expectations for the duration of your reading. Keep in mind that we tend to speak twice as fast when we're on stage as we do when rehearsing at home. Err on the side of your reading being a little short rather than too long.

Choose suitable material. Rehearse to see if you have too much or too little material for your allotted time. Reading the first couple of chapters is typical, but if it contains material that may not be suitable for the audience, you can read something else. Select material that is likely to be engaging and get people interested in reading your book, without giving too much of your story away. The end of your reading should leave them hanging in suspense so that they feel like they have to read more. At the end of your reading, use your hook – that short sentence that you use to generate interest in your book.

Show up early and test the microphone out before your reading begins. Introduce yourself to the people in charge and shake hands with them when you show up. Also, shake hands with and introduce yourself to people as they enter instead of waiting alone by yourself.

If you may be using technology – such as a PowerPoint presentation – inquire in advance about exactly which hardware and software they have and visit the venue a few days in advance to check that everything will work. Test it out again a half hour or more prior to the reading – occasionally, there are room or equipment changes and the same equipment does not always work the second time. If there is a helper on-hand on your first visit, the same helper may not be there on the day of the reading. You must have a back-up plan in case there are any technological problems. Things don't always go as planned, and the last thing you want to do is cancel your reading for lack of preparation on your part.

Use the restroom shortly before the reading begins. Have a bottle of water with you near the podium or desk where you will read.

Don't read your work in a monotone. Show your passion and make it sound interesting. Vary your tempo and pitch to match the story, and stress select words for emphasis. Pause between paragraphs. Slow yourself down if you have a tendency to speak too quickly on stage. Pronounce your words clearly. Your audience will forgive occasional stutters and other speech issues if your passion shows through and the material engages their interest.

When audience members ask questions, repeat them for everybody to hear. Don't show any frustration or anger regardless of the nature of any questions. Be polite, courteous, and professional at all times – your reputation and future success is at stake. Prepare in advance for obvious questions:

❖ What is the significance of your book's title?
❖ Where did you get the inspiration for your characters?
❖ What challenges did you encounter in writing and publishing your book?
❖ Where did you learn how to write?
❖ Have friends and family members who have read your book ask you their own questions a few days before the reading so that you can practice answering them.

It would be wise to attend book signings and readings of other authors to learn more about them before arranging your own. You may find video footage posted online (e.g. try YouTube). Study them and decide what you believe they did well and poorly. Did the reading bore you or entertain you? Would you have bought the book when it was over?

Arranging and preparing for workshops, lectures, and presentations are very similar to handling book readings. You may be able to give workshops or lectures to provide valuable training or knowledge that relates to a nonfiction book, for example. Once you become a successful self-publisher, you can even get involved in workshops to help share your skills and experience with new authors.

8.1.12 Word-of-mouth Publicity

Word-of-mouth referrals can be the best publicity for your book, and it's also the hardest to come by because you can't get it directly. To some extent, friends, family, and acquaintances who like your book may be able to help spread the word locally. But for word-of-mouth sales to be highly successful, you need complete strangers who have never met you simply to enjoy your book so much that they mention it to their friends.

The best thing you can do toward this end is to have your book be the best it can be. People are less likely to refer a book that has editing mistakes, formatting problems, or a lousy cover – even if they loved the story – because it reflects poorly on them if they recommend a book that looks unprofessional. In fiction, a great storyline, memorable characters, or a book that evokes strong emotions tends to gain more referrals. In nonfiction, a very informative book with clear explanations achieves this. There are also some genres and specific kinds of books that tend to garner more word-of-mouth sales than others. The more initial sales you get through effective pre-marketing, the more people there will be who have read your book; and the more readers you have, the more potential there is for referrals. If you write a series, many readers may wait until it's complete before recommending it to others.

Branding (see Sec. 8.1.6) plays an important role in word-of-mouth sales. An easy-to-remember title that relates to the content and genre helps – if a customer can't remember the name of your book several months after reading it, they won't be able to recommend it.

Gifting your book to others may or may not pay off. It depends on your audience and the likelihood of your book being recommended. For example, if you write a book geared toward teenage girls in a genre that is very popular among them and if they love your book (that's a big IF), just imagine the incredible publicity that your book could receive if many of them get their hands on your book and start texting about it and posting comments about it with Facebook and Twitter. In this case, giving copies of your book to teenagers you know could very well pay off. Gifting books is an investment, and like all investments, it carries a risk. There are no guarantees that people will like or recommend your book. The more social your target audience is, the more likely they are to spread the word if they enjoy your book.

8.1.13 The Power of Articles and Videos

There are numerous online websites with thousands to millions of daily visitors that need content that will continue to attract their readership. The most popular sites have a high demand from authors who are trying to publish their articles with them, but the very large number of websites out there means that there are also many sites with modest traffic that have a need for valuable content. Some magazines and newspapers also have significant circulation numbers. While it's a challenge to get articles accepted in the most popular magazines, it's easier to get an article accepted by a more modest magazine – and, again, there are so many magazines out there that this increases your chances of a quality article being accepted somewhere. Just imagine having an article published someplace where a thousand or more viewers will read it every day for a month or so, with your name followed by *The Title of Your Book* appearing at the bottom.

You really have nothing to lose. In the absolute worst-case scenario where nobody wants your article, you can always post it on your blog. So no matter what, it will get used.

Start out by writing some articles for your blog. This is something you should be doing once per week anyway. You gain some experience when you post articles on your blog and see firsthand which types of articles tend to generate more interest. This experience can be useful when you prepare a query letter to send with your request for publication. Start out with a modest website. Success that you achieve there may help you breakthrough with higher-traffic sites. Focus only on websites that are great matches for the interests of your target audience. Check out each website and read several articles before submitting your query letter (which describes your proposal) to see how relevant it is for your work and to get an idea of what kinds of articles they publish. Read the submission guidelines.

Try small print magazines and newspapers, too. If you have an advanced degree that's relevant for your book, this can help you to break in with scholarly magazines in your field. Journals are more appropriate technical publications; if your work is more popular and less technical, then you should be looking for magazines that will be of popular interest with your target audience. Either way, well-researched and thought-out articles have an advantage.

Poetry and short fiction can also be published in relevant magazines – in print and online. A short story in a high-traffic area among your audience can gain you some nice exposure.

Maintain a professional image in your interactions with prospective publishers. See the following section regarding how to prepare a press release kit.

Another way to gain exposure is to make a video with content that relates to your book and will likely interest your target audience, and post this video online in a place that will be highly visible and attract your target audience. The most obvious place to upload a video is YouTube. Be sure to link to this video from your author websites and social media.

Relevance is key. It doesn't do you much good to make a cute video about cats purely for the sake of attracting attention and then mention that you're an author of a book that doesn't relate to cats in any way whatsoever. You want to attract your target audience, so you should make content relevant for them. Also, don't try to make a video that will go viral with negative attention. You want positive publicity in order to build credibility as an author.

Nonfiction writers can make a video lecture or demonstration that provides useful skills, knowledge, or training that is relevant to your book and target audience. The video may attract new readers, and you can also provide a link to it in your book – this way, it also serves as supplemental content for your current readership.

Some authors make a video introduction – or trailer, like a movie preview – for their books. These can be posted on YouTube or your AuthorCentral page, for example. A video to go along with a free short story is another way to garner interest in your writing. You can find a few sample video trailers that authors have made for their books by searching YouTube or the CreateSpace community forums.

8.1.14 Free Media Coverage

Local newspapers, magazines, radio stations, and television networks have many readers in your area, without much competition. In contrast, the online sites with the highest traffic have much more competition – both in terms of competing sites and with the number of other writers trying to get their work published there, too. Local also seems more personal.

Another advantage of local press coverage of your book and/or you as an author is that it helps you build credibility. You can post a link to it from your author websites, for example, and include information about it on your Author Pages at Amazon and Goodreads. Most other authors aren't doing this (but they should be!), which makes it look more professional for you when you get featured in a newspaper, in a magazine, or on a radio or television show.

In the previous section, we discussed how to publish an article that you write. In this section, we're talking about an article that a journalist writes about you and/or your book(s). This is great exposure for you, and can be far more effective than a blog (but you should mention it and post a link to it on your blog and social media sites – remembering to post at least nine times with useful content for every post about you, your book, and your websites).

If you already have contacts in the media, use them. If not, you should be establishing these as you gain media attention for your work. Contact local newspapers and local radio and television stations. For radio and television, make sure that your target audience fits in with their image. It would be kind of funny for you to be interviewed by a radio station, for example, where neither you nor your book relate to the listeners in some way. Local and regional public broadcast stations that often feature talk shows and interviews are a good place to start for radio and television appearances. You have a better chance to gain national exposure if you're a celebrity, if your book becomes a bestseller, or if the topic of your book is a perfect fit for the radio station or television network. For example, if your book relates to tennis, see if you can get any press with a tennis or sports channel. Some smaller cable or satellite stations may be more receptive. If they can just briefly post a note about you and your book somewhere on their website, that in itself will be a great step in the right direction.

Newspapers often have column inches that they need to fill. Radio stations and television networks occasionally have minutes to fill; some shows are looking for ways to use all of their airtime. Contact local newspapers, radio stations, and television networks (and specific shows, separately) regarding your book. Tell them that you're looking for local press to write an article or do an interview about you as a local author and your book. Many small-time authors have gotten featured this way. The first step is to ask (while appearing professional).

Even newscasts online can give you unique publicity as a writer. Some high-profile bloggers interview authors periodically. Your interview will be most effective when their audience coincides with your target audience. See Sec. 8.1.13 regarding videos.

What is unique about you that might help you gain more press coverage? You can gain some press coverage even if nothing seems to stand out. But if there is something about you that's newsworthy – like overcoming long odds – use it to your advantage. Many people have a marketing advantage and don't even realize it. For example, universities have internal marketing departments that not only recruit new students, but assist faculty with press coverage. Even if an instructor writes a nontechnical book (instead of a journal article or a textbook), it still benefits the university to help the instructor receive press coverage for the book – as the increased popularity of what the instructors are accomplishing helps attract new students. Even students and alumni who publish books can receive help from the university in getting local media coverage. Former students can get featured in an alumni magazine.

A press release package can help you appear more professional in your interactions with the press, making arrangements with book signings and readings, bookstore dealings, etc. Your press release package may include one or more of the following (the combination that you use should depends on the circumstances):

❖ A well-written announcement for the launch of your book, featuring your cover photo. (You can make similar announcements for awards and other achievements.)

❖ An informational sheet about your book, including the description, cover, price, and any quotes that you have permission to use.

❖ Your author biography with your photo. Customize your biography for the occasion and the market of whomever you're submitting your press release package to.

❖ A professional-looking book review request form (for an editorial review).

❖ Your business card for your work as a writer, or relevant expertise for nonfiction.

❖ A bookmark. What reader wouldn't mind enjoying the benefit of a visually appealing bookmark that doesn't look like an advertisement? If it features your cover, title, and name, this is a product that's likely to get used while helping you with branding.

❖ A copy of your book. If you may use this on a wide scale, you could consider making a separate edition (with no sales channels enabled) that says Advance Review Copy on it in large letters, noting that it's not available for resale in smaller print. (Instructors can make a similar evaluation copy when they publish textbooks.)

❖ If you want bookstores and other retailers to stock your book, they may want to see sheets that outline your marketing plan and provide sales figures, copies of reviews, and other data that can convince them that your book may be worth stocking.

❖ Post a digital copy of your press release material on your author website (but don't post personal info) and link to it (or email it as an attachment) in your online dealings. On your website, this material may help lend you credibility as an author.

Just like sending cover letters and resumes to a company when you apply for a job, your press release package should look highly professional in appearance. You want it to look impressive at first glance. It should also be completely free of mistakes if you wish to make a good impression of your ability to write well. All of your material should look uniform, with similar imagery. Your front cover may appear on most of it, and so might your logo. Use the same page border for each full-sheet document.

Following is the link to a local paper that included an article about myself and my books: http://www.natchitochestimes.com/view/full_story_2/19369910/article-Northwestern-State-faculty-member-writes-book-on-basic-astronomy?instance=nsu_news.

8.1.15 How to Get Book Reviews

Let's begin by discussing some <u>wrong</u> ways to go about getting reviews. Some of these violate Amazon's review policy and may cause the review to be blocked or removed (and can also lead to account suspensions or worse). Most are unscrupulous, and provide a negative image for the author as well as self-publishing. All make the author look unprofessional and needy.

➤ Don't review your own book. Don't create fake accounts or use other accounts to review your own book. This is against Amazon's customer review policy. It is also frowned upon as highly unscrupulous and will permanently tarnish your reputation as an author. Amazon has found and removed thousands of such reviews, outsmarting the authors who thought that they were outsmarting Amazon's system.

➤ Don't allow anyone who may have a financial interest in your book – spouse, parents, children, household family members, editor, illustrator, coauthor, publisher, etc. – to review your book. This is against Amazon's customer review policy.

➤ Don't allow genuine customers that you've sold books to in person to post reviews from any computer or IP address that you've ever used. It will be blocked or removed. If multiple customers post reviews from the same IP address – even if you've never used it – the same result is likely.

➤ Don't buy reviews or offer to pay for reviews. This is against Amazon's customer review policy. Believe it or not, there are ways to track this and Amazon and others are trying to prevent such abuse – which means that people may be investigating this and setting "traps" for authors. There are stories circulating of authors who have respond-ed to advertisements from customers willing to sell good reviews, claiming that the customer actually left a negative one-star review instead.

➤ Don't offer anything other than an advance review copy (i.e. one free book to read) in exchange for a review. Don't approach just *anyone* with this offer; see the list for the right way to seek reviews to find ways to use advance review copies appropriately.

➤ Don't beg for reviews. Don't go to online forums and ask for people to review your book. Don't go to online forums and ask people how to get reviews. All of this makes you look needy, branding you as unprofessional.

➤ Don't exchange reviews with fellow authors. Don't offer to review other authors' books if they will review yours. Amazon is likely to remove one or both reviews if they see (and they have a computer program that searches for review abuse, so this is likely at some point) that two authors have reviewed each other's books. (Critiquing each other's books and exchanging these critiques personally is fine. Posting them on Amazon is a problem.) Now if you review a book and that author discovers your book and decides to review yours, you did nothing wrong; but it won't look good if others see that there is a mutual review, and Amazon may remove the reviews at some point. Amazon won't know that it was an accident, and may treat it like it was intentional.

➢ Anyone who has written a book that is similar to yours is not permitted to review your book on Amazon.

➢ Similarly, don't use any of these strategies to get Amazon or Facebook Likes, Google Plus One's, etc.

Following are some legitimate methods of getting customers to review your book on Amazon, Goodreads, blogs, media, etc.:

➢ Effectively market your books to stimulate sales. Nothing is better than the reviews that customers who discover your book leave at Amazon and Goodreads. They look more genuine than any reviews that you request, and it's most useful for prospective customers to see what other customers have to say. Unfortunately, only a small percentage of customers post reviews, which is why it takes active marketing to get more sales to improve your chances of getting customer reviews.

➢ Traditional publishers encourage early reviews by sending out advance review copies. Goodreads has an author tool to help with this (see Sec. 6.2.5); some recipients will rate and/or review your book on Goodreads, and a few on Amazon, also – but some won't review your book. Keep in mind that any customers who don't buy your book from Amazon won't have Amazon Verified Purchase showing on their reviews; it may look suspicious if you have many reviews with unverified purchases, even though the customers have read (and sometimes purchased, just not from Amazon) your book.

➢ Find bloggers on your topic (e.g. health food) who review books in your genre. First, Like their blog posts and Follow their blogs to learn more about them. Then, when you feel that they are a good fit and you've been a follower for a while, politely ask if they would mind reading an advance review copy. If they enjoy your book, they may post a review on their blog. They may or may not post a review on Amazon, and Amazon, at their discretion, may decide not to post bloggers' reviews that aren't Amazon Verified Purchases (just speculating). If your eBook happens to be free – through KDP Select, for example – during that time (if not, you can gift it), they can "buy" it that way. Bloggers with a large following are likely to receive numerous requests, so they are less likely to review your book – and if they do, there may be a lengthy delay (plus the time it takes to read a book). Bloggers with a smaller following may be more receptive. Amanda Hocking, for example, credits bloggers for helping her get noticed.

➢ Try to get newspapers, magazines, and online websites that do book reviews to review your book. This will show in print or online – not as a customer review on Amazon – but you can get legitimate editorial reviews to appear on your book's Amazon detail page through AuthorCentral. Your press release kit (described in the previous section), including the book review request form, can come in handy for this. It's best to call – as it's more personal – but prepare a professional, well-written (proofread carefully) letter for a book review request when you can't make the request by phone.

➢ Some professional review services, like Kirkus reviews, provide a neutral editorial review for a fee. This isn't considered buying a review when it's a well-known company that provides a neutral review – i.e. there is no guarantee that it will be good. Amazon will definitely support Kirkus reviews because this is a marketing service that you can purchase from CreateSpace for your paperback book. This will show as a Kirkus review on your book's Amazon detail page. You must have a lot of faith in your book to do this because the review won't necessarily be glowing or even good. It's also a significant investment. On the other hand, it helps to provide customers with a neutral review.

➢ You may be able to get permission to use some legitimate review quotes (not from Amazon customer reviews) in the editorial reviews section on your book's Amazon detail page, in the Look Inside, and on the back cover – depending on the restrictions of where the review appears. You're not allowed to quote Amazon customer reviews anywhere, but you can provide a link to them from your websites.

➢ If a fan contacts you and tells you that he/she read the book, you could try to tactfully and carefully encourage him/her to leave you a customer review on Amazon. Many authors refrain from doing this because they don't want to appear tacky or needy. Rather, they will simply strive to provide a personal yet professional-looking response, and hope that their professionalism and personal interaction (which was invited, if the customer contacts you by email, for example) helps to implicitly encourage a review.

See Sec. 7.1.6 for more information about customer reviews on Amazon. Note that it's possible to send .mobi and .epub files of your eBook or PDF's, which is cheaper than sending paperback copies. However, some reviewers may only accept print editions for review. If your eBook happens to be free through KDP Select, the review will show as an Amazon Verified Purchase (but the reviewer has the option not to reveal this).

8.1.16 Bookstores, Libraries, and Direct Sales

Recall that we discussed what more you might do – i.e. in addition to selecting CreateSpace's Expanded Distribution option – in order to improve your chances of getting your book in libraries and bookstores in Sec. 4.1.7. I will try to avoid repeating too many details from that section and focus primarily on the pertinent marketing aspects.

It's extremely unlikely for brick and mortar bookstores to pick up your title to stock in their stores simply by finding it in Ingram's database. You must approach bookstores to make this happen. Small, locally-owned bookstores, antique stores that sell new and used books, and other kinds of retailers that sell books are more likely to be receptive. Major bookstore chains like Barnes & Noble will be much more reluctant. A few companies actually have title request forms that specifically prohibit CreateSpace books. Remember to start small.

Look for local bookstores that feature local authors on their shelves. That's a great place to start. If they won't carry your book, they might give you helpful suggestions about who might and how to go about this. Since you write books, you probably read books, so they should realize that you're a potential customer, too. Providing you with good service is in their best interest (but, of course, we don't always get good service everywhere we go, do we?).

Bring your press release kit (see Sec. 8.1.14). Some bookstores will be quite interested in your marketing plan (written professionally and included with your press release kit), copies of reviews, and your sales figures. They want evidence that you're actively and effectively promoting your book. Dress up like a business person; bring a briefcase and wear dress shoes. Make sure you speak to someone who has the authority to decide on this before you begin your spiel. You may need an appointment. However, if you call to schedule an appointment, you could get turned down on the phone; if you show up, at least you made it in the door (though you can still be refused, just prolonging it). Have a business card in your pocket – you might leave it for the manager, for example, if nobody present can help you.

If you have multiple listings, you may want to create a professional-looking catalog of your books and include that with your press release kit. Include contact info and your website in your catalog. You might include your CreateSpace eStore number and discount code, too.

There are a couple of more professional things that you could potentially do if stocking your book in a retail bookstore chain is a major goal. Check out Sec. 8.2.3 for more details.

Bookstores can purchase your book a few different ways. If your book has the Expanded Distribution option, just knowing that your book is listed with Ingram is enough for them to stock it. However, this probably won't appeal to them because the discount is very low and the books are nonreturnable. It's the same way if you refer them to CreateSpace Direct (see Sec. 4.1.7). At first glance, these two options seem professional, but the cons outweigh the pros. A third option is to use your CreateSpace eStore. You can create a discount code to entice them into using this option. But the drawbacks include having to sign up for an account with CreateSpace, and the shipping charges may be prohibitive unless they buy many books or you offer a hefty discount. You may have to settle for consignment, but try to avoid it.

The best option is generally to buy author copies yourself, which are relatively cheap for you, and sell them directly. This way, you can offer a significant discount from your list price while still earning a healthy royalty. You can accept cash in person, money order by mail and ship the books, or sell them from your website or by email using PayPal, for example. Keep in mind that you can order books from CreateSpace at your author price and ship them directly to businesses or customers (the packing slip doesn't reveal the price).

If you succeed in getting your books stocked in any bookstores, reward them by helping to drive traffic their way. You want to sell books there or you won't have the same success with getting your book stocked the next time you publish a book.

Another option is to search for wholesale distributors and contact them about the prospects for including your title. Major wholesalers may want exclusivity agreements that restrict where you can sell your book. You may be able to find small wholesalers online willing to work with you. Some authors have been known to contact new and used bookstores who sell on Half.com and eBay, for example, to see if they have any interest in selling their books. If so, they will probably need a hefty discount to offset all of their costs and fees.

Include information on your website regarding how potential booksellers can contact you. If nothing else, this makes your website look more credible when customers and fans check it out, and when prospective bookstores verify your information.

Always have books in the trunk of your car when approaching businesses about stocking your book. It would be awfully embarrassing for someone to say, "Sure, we'll take 10," pull out some cash, and watch your jaw drop as you wonder how you're going to get the books. Be prepared (and be prepared for the same line to be a joke, too – assume it's not a joke unless and until proven otherwise, and behave professionally).

There are other places where you can sell books, too, besides bookstores. For example, teachers can post books and other teaching materials for sale at Teachers Pay Teachers, while golf books may be able to get stocked at golf stores and pro shops.

When you approach libraries, much of the same applies, except they will want to know that your book is available through Baker & Taylor. That's the most professional way for them to order your book, although a small, local library might be willing to purchase through other means. You should have a few copies in your briefcase just in case, at least to let them look it over. Some libraries want to see neutral reviews – especially, editorial reviews. It doesn't have to be at the level of the *New York Times*; a book review printed in a local paper or from a legitimate online book review website would be better than nothing.

There are a variety of ways for you to sell your books directly to customers. Pricewise, the best deal for everyone is for you to buy the book at your author price. This way, you can provide a significant discount while still making a substantial royalty. You don't have to accept cash, checks, or take payments directly through PayPal (although this is a good option for selling books directly from your website): You can order books from CreateSpace and ship them directly to customers (the packing slip shows CreateSpace as the billing address, and there is no receipt with pricing – send a copy to someone you know to check it out).

You can also provide a link to your eStore and optionally provide a discount code (see Sec. 6.2.4). However, this requires customers to sign up for a CreateSpace account, and they will have to pay shipping, which will offset any discount.

There are many advantages for both you and your customers to encourage sales directly from Amazon. For customers, they tend to trust Amazon and their guarantee, may qualify for Free Super Saver Shipping (and two-day shipping if they have Amazon Prime), might find your book on sale, and can check out customer reviews. It's beneficial for you because when customers buy from Amazon, this improves your sales rank and if they leave a review, it will show as an Amazon Verified Purchase. You can also earn a commission on sales that you refer to Amazon from your website using your affiliate link (see Sec. 7.1.8).

For a few rare books that tend to sell much better in person than they do through Amazon, it may be better to try to sell books directly. This is sometimes the case, for example, for businessmen who tour the country giving presentations and sell many books in person when it's over.

If you have expertise, going on tours to give lectures, presentations, and workshops in major metropolitan areas is a good way to sell your books – and possibly get paid for your presentation, too. Stack up books on a table at such events so that people can thumb through them and offer to sell them in person.

The main challenge of marketing books to the United Kingdom and other countries is overcoming the shipping charges. If you enable the Amazon UK and Europe channels, customers can buy your books with low-cost (or free, if their purchase qualifies) shipping from European Amazon websites, in which case CreateSpace has them printed in the United Kingdom or Europe. Unfortunately, at this time CreateSpace doesn't print in Europe for eStore orders or author copies – in these cases, they print the books in the United States and charge a significant shipping fee to send them internationally. You might be able to cut down on the shipping charges by ordering author copies to be sent to you first and then shipping them internationally yourself. However, you should first visit your local post office with some of your books and try to get precise shipping estimates for your precise needs (the prices may depend on the packaging materials, too). Selling them directly this way requires the international customer or merchant to pay you directly (through PayPal, for example).

8.1.17 Free Book Promotions, Discounts, Price-matching, Giveaways, and Other Promotions

Many authors try to generate interest in their books using free book promotions, creating discounts through price-matching, and promoting giveaways and other contests. Note that freebies and discounts are sometimes unsuccessful. Like all investments, giving your book away for free is a risk that may or may not pay off. When it doesn't, there are dozens or hundreds of customers who now have your book for free, who might have purchased it sometime in the future if not for the free giveaway.

The most common way that authors make their books free for a limited period of time is through enrollment in KDP Select. Bear in mind that you can only make your eBook free for 5 out of every 90 days with the KDP Select program. Enrollment in KDP Select has a few other benefits – like paying royalties on borrows – but doesn't permit you to publish an eBook edition with Nook, Kobo, Apple, Smashwords, or anywhere else during the enrollment period (paperback is not restricted). Some authors take advantage of the benefits of KDP Select for the first 90 days, and then if they aren't happy with it, try publishing with other eBook sellers. Other authors sell a significant number of eBooks through Apple, Sony, and Kobo, for example, and don't want to lose those sales by agreeing to KDP Select's terms and conditions.

A significantly growing number of authors feel that the free promo days are becoming less effective than they had been when the program was first introduced. Many are preferring the new Kindle Countdown Deal (see Sec. 4.2.7). Here are some things to consider carefully:

- ❖ The free promo days tend to be most effective when the first eBook in a series is made free, or when an author has multiple eBooks that are very similar. See Sec. 8.1.18.
- ❖ Many customers hoard the free eBooks, but never get around to reading them. If you succeed in giving away 1,000 books, only a fraction of those will get read.
- ❖ Of those customers who will read the eBooks, some won't begin reading them for a few months, and then it may take them a month or more to read it.
- ❖ Authors do receive increased exposure from those customers who do read the eBook. The more people who read the eBook, the greater the chances for word-of-mouth sales and customer reviews.
- ❖ On the other hand, you may be losing sales by not having your eBook available on Sony, Apple, Kobo, Smashwords, etc. If so, the customers you are losing this way may be in your genre, whereas many of the free promo readers may be outside your genre.
- ❖ Customers who believe that they get what they pay for often undervalue free eBooks.
- ❖ Indeed, an increasing number of customers are avoiding free eBooks because of one or more poorly written or poorly formatted free eBooks that they have downloaded.
- ❖ Free eBooks attract readers from outside of the genre, who often don't have realistic expectations. This is occasionally revealed through low-star reviews.
- ❖ Customers who buy the eBook are more likely to read the description and Look Inside to see what they are getting. Those who get free eBooks usually don't take the time to do this, yet may be unhappy with what they get and might state this in a review.
- ❖ Unfortunately, there are a few readers (and worse, authors and publishers) who loathe the free promo days and maliciously leave bad reviews to eBooks that were free. Note that these show as Amazon Verified Purchases. This is quite rare, but does happen.
- ❖ With recent changes in Amazon Advantage (Sec. 7.1.8), many websites have stopped advertising free eBooks through affiliate links, which appears to have significantly diminished the number of eBooks that are given away for free during the promo.
- ❖ However, there are some dedicated blogs and websites that still promote free Kindle eBooks (they just don't use the affiliate links). Research the blogs and websites that do this (use Google, for example) and contact them to let them know when your eBook will be free. Politely ask if they could include your eBook, too.

I still have most of my eBooks enrolled in KDP Select. I used the free promo days more frequently until 2013, at which point I have started using them only occasionally and for just a few of my eBooks. I have some sets of arithmetic flashcards, for which the free promo days have a similar effect as series (see my first point above). There are other benefits besides free promo days and the Countdown Deal.

Some eBooks sell a significant number of copies through Apple, Sony, or Kobo. If you have such an eBook, you may benefit greatly from selling it through as many sales channels as possible. The problem is that you don't know until you try. Another problem is that once you try, you may experience some delays and hassles trying to return to KDP Select: When you publish with an aggregator like Smashwords, it may take a month or so to completely remove your eBooks from all of the catalogs where your eBook was published. KDP will email you if your eBook is available in another catalog while enrolled in KDP Select. If this happens to you, send them a polite explanation that your eBook has been unpublished. I did this once, and they replied to confirm that it wasn't actually available for purchase where they had found it. I had to go through this again a few weeks later for the same eBook, but that was the end of it.

Another way to offer your book for free or at a discounted price is by price-matching. Of course, you can create your own "discount" at any time by simply adjusting the list price (but at Kindle, you can't set the list price lower than 99 cents – and if your converted .mobi file is larger than 3 MB or 10 MB, the limits are $1.99 and $2.99, respectively). However, this doesn't look like a discount – it just lowers the list price. If you have a paperback and Kindle edition linked together, the eBook will appear as a discount off of your paperback price.

Amazon may choose to price-match an eBook if they discover a lower price elsewhere. There is no guarantee that Amazon will do this, and it may take months before they do. It's solely at Amazon's discretion. However, customers may report a lower price, which may or may not influence whether Amazon will match the price.

Some authors have succeeded in getting their eBooks price-matched by setting a lower price elsewhere. Note that if you publish with Nook, you're not permitted to set the list price lower than the Nook list price. Authors who want to make their eBooks permanently free (as opposed to the five free promo days that come with KDP Select) price their eBooks free at Kobo or someplace that allows free eBook pricing, and hope that Amazon price-matches it. Amazon may be more likely to price-match a retailer like Kobo than Smashwords, but again it's solely at their discretion. You <u>don't</u> earn royalties for eBooks that are given away for free.

If you succeed in getting a free price-match from Amazon, it may take several weeks to undo this if you later change your mind. Simply raising your list price at the original eBook publisher (e.g. Kobo) by itself won't work: Amazon will still be giving your eBook away for free (or whatever the discounted price was). You must contact KDP and specifically request the ability to regain control of your price; you will need to agree to stop discounting the price of your eBook elsewhere. Note that it may take 4-6 weeks for all of the prices to raise if you used an aggregator like Smashwords, and that Amazon may continue to price-match until the price is successfully raised in all published catalogs that they can find online.

There are other kinds of promotions and giveaways that you can use besides freebies and discounts that may attract interest in your books. Some of these may even be more effective than making your book free. For one, if you want to put your book on "sale" temporarily, you can do this. Price-matching may result in delays of weeks or more, as noted previously. The alternative is to simply change your list price for a day or so and announce this change on your blog, through social media, by email, etc. Just like any other retailer that has a sale, you simply announce that your eBook is on sale for today only, this week only, or whatever the period may be. Remember, no more than 10% of your posts should be about your books.

Note that eBook price changes made through KDP may show up in 12 hours or so (in the United States), while paperback price changes made through CreateSpace may take longer – especially, through the Expanded Distribution channels. (A Countdown Deal doesn't require republishing.) Short-term price changes are best made on your eBook and not your paperback. Remember, Nook doesn't allow you to price your eBook lower anywhere else.

It's very important to realize that price doesn't sell books. Marketing is what it takes to sell books. A discount can bring success when you use it as a marketing tool – i.e. you promote the discount. Just playing with the price by itself probably won't help. Even "free" is just a price unless you actively promote your eBook.

You can also announce free giveaways and contests. Facebook, for example, has a special page just for this (see Sec. 6.2.6). Announce and promote your giveaways and contests on your blog, through social media, at your website, etc. This helps you create market buzz for your book. The prizes can include bookmarks, signed paperbacks, t-shirts, etc.

Bookmarks make for great gifts. You can print a large number for a low cost. They should look professional (people are very picky even about free merchandise – but mainly you want the bookmark to be used, so the nicer it looks, the better), feature imagery from your front cover, and include the title and author. Don't make it look like an advertisement.

There may be legal restrictions on how often your book can be on sale in a given time period. There may also be rules and regulations concerning prizes and giveaways (e.g. to ensure fairness). If you have legal questions, consult an attorney.

Authors of textbooks have an issue with students reselling their used textbooks at a deep discount. If you publish a textbook where this may be a problem, you can deal with this the way that the big publishers do: They make revisions every year or two to create a new edition. Some old exercises that instructors didn't like disappear, being replaced by new exercises, with the order of the exercises changing. For courses where exercises are assigned from the textbook, this compels students to buy new editions. On the other hand, this upsets many people who feel that it's unscrupulous. If you simply make changes for the sake of forcing students to buy a new edition, the complaints may be justified. However, if the revisions are what you would honestly do anyway to improve your textbook, that's a different story.

8.1.18 Marketing Series and Similar Books

Some highly successful indie authors have derived much of their success by publishing series of books and strategically pricing them. If you have a series – or, to a much lesser degree, a set of similar books – then you have a significant advantage at your disposal. Provided that the first book in the series is very good and hooks the reader, then your focus should be on how to get as many people as possible to read the first book. The other books in the series will virtually sell themselves if, in fact, readers enjoy the first book enough to want to finish the series. Authors who have a series for which they believe that the first book will hook the reader often strive use price-matching to make the first eBook free or price it at 99 cents.

However, price doesn't sell books, and free and even 99-cent eBooks suffer from some of the problems listed in the previous section regarding free promo days. For this strategy to be successful, you must do more than just make the first book cheap:

❖ Have a great cover on the first book to attract attention. All of the covers in the series should match to help with branding.

❖ Write a super blurb for the first book that encourages potential readers to Look Inside. Have a great start to the first book that compels readers to try it out.

❖ Perfect the first book. It has to be very compelling to get readers to buy the next volume or purchase the omnibus, leave reviews, and refer the series to friends.

❖ Perfect the series so that subsequent books also get good reviews.

❖ Actively promote any free or discounted books or editions on your blog, through social media, on your website, etc. (but no more than 10% of your posts can do this – at least 90% must provide useful content that attracts your target audience).

❖ Give away as many copies of your first eBook as you can to your target audience. Offer to gift the first volume to anyone you know in your target audience. Buy paperback copies of your first volume and give those away, too; even sign them.

❖ Place a sample of the next volume at the end of the previous volume (but not longer than Amazon's Look Inside). But beware of having too much front and back matter to the point that customers feel that they haven't received much content for the money.

❖ Price an omnibus edition (i.e. a special edition that includes the entire set) such that readers have an incentive to buy it. For example, if you have 4 books in your series, the first is 99 cents, and the other three are $2.99, pricing your omnibus at $6.99 is like getting the fourth volume for free. Some buyers will try the first volume for 99 cents and then buy the omnibus (which includes book one) if they are hooked. Referred customers may go straight to the omnibus.

❖ Occasionally discount the omnibus – e.g. regular $5.99, now just $1.99 or 99 cents. Promote the daylights out of this sale. Do this just rarely and it will be more effective, and you will also sell many books at the regular price. When the sale comes too frequently, word spreads. Then customers will wait for the next sale (as your sales rank plummets), and the expected sale price will cheapen your book in some minds.

If you just have a single eBook by itself, a 99-cent list price may not be the best price (unless it's very short) because it suggests that the eBook is cheap and it only provides a 30-

cent royalty. However, when you have a series of eBooks, pricing them all at 99 cents makes them impulse buys, and when the omnibus is cheaper yet, that's a good deal, too. But don't forget the fundamental rule that price doesn't sell books for you. You must promote your books in order for them to sell. Discounts and sales can help with your promotion and make the promotion of a series more effective, but they don't promote the books for you.

If you write multiple books that are similar, this strategy may also help you sell these books, although it probably won't be as effective – unlike a series, customers don't have to purchase the other books to discover how the story ends. Also, there is no "first" book in this case. If you give one eBook away for free one day, and give another for free another day, then eventually customers can collect all of your eBooks without spending a dime. Instead, if you always give the same eBook away for free, it helps to sell your other, similar eBooks.

Recently, many authors have been trying to take advantage of the business strategy for marketing series using a free short story. It doesn't have the same effect. For one, a series usually has roughly equal-length volumes, so the first volume is representative of what to expect; a short story is simply different, not representative. If the "short story" is really the first chapter, this tends to frustrate customers – who are then unlikely to buy your other books, but are more likely to leave bad reviews. Even if it's free, many customers expect to get more than a short story when they download an eBook (even if the word count is clearly stated in the description). I'm not saying that a short story can't be used effectively – just that there are some possible pitfalls. It's definitely not an easy way out for writers who are hoping to avoid the need for marketing their own books. The short story idea is most likely to work well if you market your short story and other books effectively and if you are able to succeed in generating many early sales and reviews for the short story.

8.1.19 Book Contests and Awards for Authors

Note that there are two distinct kinds of contests: There are contests where customers can win a prize (mentioned in Sec. 8.1.17) and contests that authors can enter (which we will discuss in this section).

I highly recommend entering your book in several different contests (but first read each contest description to make sure that your book is eligible and is also a good fit). There are hundreds of contests for authors to enter their books into, such as the annual Amazon Breakthrough Novel Award, which you can enter through CreateSpace.

Entering these contests helps give you some free exposure and may also improve your writing skills – including the art of writing an effective blurb, since some contests make their first cuts solely based on the blurb. You don't have to win the contest to gain exposure: Just getting your name on the list of quarterfinalists would give you nice visibility, for example (which you could link to from your websites).

Thousands of authors enter any given contest, so you can't be disappointed if you don't win. There are thousands of excellent writers, so winning the grand prize is sort of like winning a lottery. However, if you enter several contests, there are reasonable prospects for great writers to make it to the later rounds in an at least one contest. Many contests reveal the winning titles and blurbs, which may help you generate good ideas for how to improve next year if you don't have any success your first time. You can also check out the winners; reading their books and comparing with your own may help you grow as a writer.

If you make it to the later rounds, some contests have authors critique one another's work. It's very beneficial all around for top writers to get together and exchange criticism this way. There are many benefits to entering contests and striving to do your best, then entering again the next year with an improved book – even if you never win. If you do win, several contests have amazing rewards – such as publishing contracts with an attractive advance.

There are many contests and awards out there, such as awards for the best indie cover. Use your favorite search engine to find websites and blogs with contests and awards for authors. Check out the contest to make sure it's legitimate before submitting your manuscript to them (because, unfortunately, there are some people who try to take advantage).

8.1.20 Follow-up Work: Thank You's and Fan Mail

Take time to respond to your fan mail. When readers contact you via email, on your fan page at Facebook, through Twitter, by posting on your website, via a private message at Goodreads, or on your blog, for example, take a moment to respond. Don't reply immediately – as that makes you look needy – but do respond in a timely manner. Think about what your fan wrote and also consider your response carefully before you reply. If you respond right away, you're much more apt to let your emotions get into the message or make a blunder.

Remember that your author image is at stake. Anything you write may be copied and pasted elsewhere and used against you (even out of context) – even if you wrote it in a private email (whether or not this is legal is a separate matter – even if it's illegal, it may not be worth the hassle to take action, and it's certainly negative publicity to take any action against a reader for just about any reason). Be courteous. Don't be disparaging or defensive.

Write a professional, yet personal response. Keep it concise. The less you write, the less the chance of making a mistake. Be careful to address him/her by name and to spell his/her name right (copy/paste of the name may help). Just accept any criticism (don't be defensive).

But don't respond to reviews – not even to thank customers. If you write a thank you note to good reviews, it makes it look like the reviewers are your friends (i.e. as if the author had fake reviews planted, which discourages sales). If you respond to negative reviews, it looks like you're needy and can't handle criticism. If customers want to interact with you, they will contact you by email or some other way. We discussed reviews in Sec. 7.1.6.

Check your email periodically (including any special email accounts for fan mail), and also your fan page at Facebook, customer discussions or feedback at your website, posts at your fan club, and anywhere else readers may go to contact you. They're not likely to leave a good review or refer your book to friends if you leave them hanging for several days.

8.1.21 The Team Marketing Concept

Companies often use the concept of teamwork in their marketing efforts. A few authors also apply this to self-publishing. If you know fellow self-published authors, you might consider collaborating together in some way. But don't apply any unethical or unscrupulous team marketing ideas (like reviewing each other's books), as this can ruin your reputation as an author (or cause account suspensions or worse).

The general business notion is that team marketing trumps an individual's marketing efforts. There are a couple of ways that authors can use the team marketing spirit (ethically). One way is combine skill sets. For example, one author may be highly regarded for editing, another for cover design, another for website development, another who has achieved much marketing success, etc. This way, one author has the primary editing responsibilities, another designs the covers, another gets the website up-and-running and maintains it, another does much of the marketing work, and so on. It's not easy to meet and recruit a good combination of authors willing to do this, and it can be a challenge to iron out the details and establish enough trust in teammates (and that the distribution of work is fair) to pull this off – and then there is the problem of an author who wants to opt out. However, a successful publishing team such as this has much more potential than one self-publisher trying to do all of these tasks by him- or herself.

It almost sounds like a small publishing company, which it sort of is. They can put the same imprint on all of the books and develop a website specifically for the publisher. If one person has the finances to invest in a company and hire others on contracts, then there is even greater resemblance to a small publisher.

8.1.22 So Much to Do, So Little Time: Choose Wisely

If you're feeling overwhelmed with the many different things that you could be doing to market your book, just focus on doing one thing at a time and eventually you'll have many things working for you. You can do it all the same way that you run a marathon – one step at a time will get you to the finish line. Try to get several marketing ideas up-and-running prior to publishing your book. Don't start out with the things that are easiest to do or which you feel most comfortable doing. Instead, base your marketing priorities on what's most likely to be effective and relevant for your unique book (what's most effective for others may not be for you). When you're unable to do everything, you must choose wisely. Specifically, consider which ideas are most likely to reach the most new members from your target audience.

I myself haven't applied *every* idea from this book, but I have utilized the vast majority of it. There are many things that I've been doing for years, while others I've only implemented recently. Next on my to-market list is more use of social media. You'll have to make similar decisions about which tools you believe suit your specific needs the most and use those first.

Another thing I don't do is send out advance review copies. Most of my books are math workbooks. Many similar titles earn reviews at a very slow rate, including a few relatively popular series. I thought that it may seem strange if I sent out several advance review copies and earned a modest number of reviews this way right off the bat. Customers may wonder how this relatively unknown, new author (not anymore, but when I started) might suddenly have more reviews than other series with somewhat more well-known names. I also have the benefit of having a Ph.D. in physics and being a university professor; I sell many books just from my expertise, and so the reviews aren't as critical for my math and science books.

To be clear, I absolutely treasure every single review that I receive; I'll never reach the point where a good review fails to make me smile and lift my spirits for the next few days. But I don't use advance review copies or other methods to attempt to garner more reviews.

Most books need the benefits of advance review copies. Most fiction, for example, needs several early reviews to help customers decide whether or not the book is for them, and are critical toward success for new authors. The same is true for many areas of nonfiction. You shouldn't avoid sending out advance review copies simply because I mentioned that I don't use them. In fact, I have a couple of fictional works that I may be publishing in the future, such as *Romancing the Novel* (an extended analogy about dating a book), for which I may be using the Goodreads author tool to send out advanced review copies.

8.1.23 Providing Related Services

Many authors who self-publish excel at one or more of the tasks, such as proofreading, cover design, illustrations, formatting, cleaning HTML, marketing, etc. Especially, once you have several years of experience and have perfected an art, others may be interested in your services. There aren't enough very good proofreaders to go around, so if you happen to excel at this, people may be interested in your service even if you don't yet have much experience. Formatting, on the other hand, is a precise art with many technical issues that the majority of indie authors never even realize they are doing wrong. The formatting of print books, in particular, really requires extensive experience working with graphics and printing before you can compete with the many small publishers out there who do exceptional jobs. A different art is involved in the formatting of eBooks, which also entails much experience to perfect.

If you excel at one or more of these skills in order to provide valuable help to others, you may be able to offer these services freelance. You can mention them on your websites, but you really must market these services much the same way that you would market your books. A benefit of this – aside from supplementing your royalty income – is that your efforts to market your publishing services help a little to market your books, too. You get more traffic coming to your websites this way. When you satisfy customers with a publishing service, it helps your branding – i.e. creating a positive image for yourself and a reputation to associate with your name. They might check out your books, and may refer your services and/or books to their friends.

Realize that it works both ways. Your reputation is adversely affected every time you have a dissatisfied customer. There are also many other experts out there competing with you to offer these services. They might feel that you're stepping on their "turf" when you first come on the scene. You want to uphold your image as a credible author by behaving professionally at all times. As with book promotion, discovery and branding are much more effective than self-promotion. At some discussion forums (where permitted), editors or illustrators, for example, indicate at the bottom of their posts that they provide such services (and may provide a short link to their websites) – or they will make this clear on their online profiles.

If you decide to offer any publishing services now or in the future, you'll need to draw up a contract. It's common to request a partial payment (such as half) upfront and the remainder once the customer is happy and accepts the service. Allow yourself a reasonable time period to complete the work, and expect numerous requests and suggestions for changes. Customers like to see signs of progress, and want to be involved in the ideas. Remember that it's their work, not yours. The quality of the final product does reflect well or poorly on you, but their books are their babies and not yours. Request to mention your name on the copyright page and the service you provided (for example, "Cover design by Your Name") – you can include this in the terms of the contract. Don't let the author write your name on the front cover – it's very tacky, and there is a trend that the larger the name, the worse the quality of the service – unless you are the editor (then there is a special field to declare you as the editor) or illustrator (not a cover designer). Professional cover designers have their declarations on the back cover in fine print by the price or UPC bar code; amateurs have their declarations in a large font on the front cover. The contract should specify, among other things, when the project will be completed, how much will be paid when, who owns the copyright for the work, and that you have the right to mention the work on your website (if you're a cover designer, you also want the right to display the artwork and front cover on your website and any promotional materials that you use to market your services).

Simple proofreading is something that you can get involved in with little experience, provided that you're good at it. Offer to edit a sample chapter (limit the word count) free or at a low cost. After designing a few awesome covers, you can get into cover design easily by making your samples available and doing some effective marketing.

8.1.24 Other Marketing Resources

One of the best ways to learn about marketing is to read about the success stories from self-published authors. They obviously did something right, and many describe their rise to the top in articles or blogs on the internet. Their results show that self-publishers can succeed. When you read their stories, it may help provide you some needed inspiration, motivation, and/or confidence that you can do it, too. Study the sales tactics that they reveal to try to learn their secrets. Follow their blogs and social media posts to learn what they do. But beware, now that they're celebrities, they can afford to blog much more about themselves and their own books and websites – and even advertise – whereas you must restrict such activity to 10%.

There are a few things in common with many of the indie success stories:

➢ They usually have a pile of rejection letters from traditional publishers that helped to fuel their motivation.
➢ These authors often researched and studied business plans. The most popular authors often approach both the writing and publishing from a business perspective.
➢ They wrote books in very popular categories and wrote them in a way that would likely appeal to a very large target audience. They didn't break the "rules" of the genre.
➢ Their books generally have great covers and short, easy-to-remember titles.

CreateSpace actually has some great <u>free</u> marketing resources on their website, which I highly recommend checking out. It's amazing how many self-published authors are unaware of this, and these resources are better than you might expect – especially, for being free. At the top of their website, click Free Publishing Resources, then select one of the three options under Marketing Your Work. For example, under Marketing Central, you can find some genre-specific marketing plans and a guide to targeting your audience. Also in Marketing Central, look for a link to a featured resource on social media. Some of the authors who write these articles for CreateSpace also have helpful blogs and websites.

CreateSpace also has paid marketing services – see Sec. 8.2.1.

8.2 Other Marketing Options

8.2.1 Paid Marketing Services

aid advertising for books might not pay off; you might not even recover the money that you invest in it. Unfortunately, paying for advertisements does not provide an easy way out of the necessity of marketing. One problem with advertisements is that books are genre-specific and so have a much narrower audience than other inexpensive products, like bath soap. For an advertisement to be effective, it must be geared specifically toward your target audience. Since few authors advertise their books – compared to cereal and many other products – it may seem out of place if you do this. Also, as noted before, books tend to sell better through discovery and branding, not through self-promotion. Any branding that you might achieve through advertising may be little better than what you can achieve for free with an effective and diligent marketing campaign. Since branding can take months of dedicated marketing, advertising to help brand your book is likely not to pay off for a very long time. Finally, advertising can be expensive, so you must sell a large volume of books just to recover your investment. Therefore, I don't recommend paying for advertisements. There are many free marketing tools that you can use, which can be highly effective for a very good book and don't involve risk.

You can find many individuals and companies willing to offer you paid marketing services. Marketing yourself is much more personal, and personally interacting with people sells books better than any service that you might buy to market for you. A marketing service that you use in conjunction with all of the free tools that you should be using is likely to be more effective than any service that you try to use in order to get out of doing the work yourself.

CreateSpace offers a few paid marketing services, and you can find other individuals and businesses that provide similar services. One thing to consider carefully is whether the service might boost your sales enough to make the investment worthwhile. You can easily calculate how many books you must sell in order for the royalties to add up to the cost of the service (just divide the service fee by your royalty). If you have money to invest in your book, buying a great cover and very good editing or formatting may provide the best yield.

To check out CreateSpace's paid marketing services, go to their homepage, click Books at the top of the page, and select Marketing. Their writing services may come in handy. They can help you write a compelling description or press release, which many authors struggle with. Note that their bookmarks just have a small front cover image, and are mostly text – so they look like advertisements. A beautiful bookmark filled with imagery or designs that match your front cover, which just has the title and author, may be more effective by receiving more use and not looking like a sales pitch – but this isn't an option with CreateSpace. Nice bookmarks can be effective as free gifts, since they are cheap and likely to be used. Their business cards look very nice, but the price is a bit steep. They also offer unbiased reviews – which could be good or bad – for which the cost of the investment is significant. We discussed CreateSpace's free services in Sec. 8.1.24.

8.2.2 Audio Books and Other Formats

Consider making an audio book edition of your book, or other media, such as a video DVD. The KDP newsletter advertises the Audiobook Creation Exchange (ACX), which is an Amazon platform. From the KDP help pages, click Announcements near the top of the list at the left, then click on a recent newsletter from the KDP Newsletter Archive to find a link to ACX. (Once you are signed up with KDP, you should also receive these newsletters monthly by email.) There are many truckers, for example, who listen to audio books during their long drives. If audio books may be a good match for your target audience, it may be worth doing. Search for books in your genre and see if there are any audio books available with a good sales rank.

If you or someone you know has any potential for being an indie filmmaker, CreateSpace offers DVD on Demand and Amazon Instant Video options for publishing movies.

8.2.3 Other Publishing Options

Once you've published a couple of paperbacks with an imprint, you might be eligible to publish with Lightning Source (LSI) – a major print-on-demand company that many small publishers use. This may be appropriate if your self-publishing efforts are growing toward becoming a small publisher. CreateSpace provides an unbeatable value. Lightning Source offers hardcover print-on-demand books and more options than CreateSpace does, and is highly regarded for their full-color books (if you choose the better of the available formats). It's possible that publishing with Lightning Source might look more professional in the eyes of bookstores that you might want to work with, but it's still a print-on-demand service – so it won't open all of the doors for you. At least, one or more major retail chains that specifically state that they don't work with CreateSpace published books don't (yet) also list Lightning Source as a deal-breaker (to be fair, most don't specifically state anything about CreateSpace, and some CreateSpace authors have gotten their books stocked in various bookstores).

Another option very similar to, but not as affordable as, CreateSpace is Lulu, which does have more printing options.

8.2.4 Publicists, Agents, and Traditional Publishing

A good old-fashioned publicist for authors who feels that the author's work is highly marketable can really help with branding, marketing, and especially helpful connections. Such publicists may charge a very hefty fee. Someone advertising him- or herself as a publicist charging a much more affordable fee probably isn't providing nearly the same degree or quality of services and probably doesn't have the same experience and contacts.

Authors who are able to gain the interest of a reputable publicist have a significant advantage in the publishing world. At the early stages, such a publicist can provide direction in the writing itself from a business and marketing perspective, recommend excellent editors, and connect authors with relevant literary agents. When these authors submit their query letters and book proposals and prospective publishers see that these authors have been working with publicists for several months, this looks very favorable as a book that is likely to be written following a good business model and very successfully marketed. This is what traditional publishers want – authors whose books are easy to market and who are likely to be successful marketers. They don't want authors who lack marketing experience or authors who make empty promises. Previously published authors who have successfully marketed their books have an edge. New authors are more likely to get a foot in the door by having a publicist.

The same business models and publicity plans that traditional publishers seek can also work for self-publishers. Whether you want to self-publish or get traditionally published, studying business models, marketing strategies, and the techniques that publicists use can help you achieve high levels of success.

Did you know that Amazon has some publishing companies? Check out Amazon Encore and Kindle Singles, for example. Like traditional publishing, Amazon's publishing companies are highly selective. There are very many submissions, and most are rejected. You can find Amazon's imprints at http://www.amazon.com/gp/feature.html?docId=1000664761. To learn more about Kindle Singles, visit Amazon's homepage, click Kindle and then Kindle Books, and choose Kindle Singles from the list at the left.

RESOURCES

Here you will find a collection of handy resources, all of which are conveniently and freely available on the web. My intention was <u>not</u> to compile a comprehensive list of every possible resource, as I didn't think it would be as useful if you had to sort through a long list to discover a few helpful resources. Instead, I limited this collection to resources which I believed would be very handy to most readers. Also, by limiting the list to popular resources, this list is much less likely to become quickly outdated. You can easily find more resources – as most of the following websites provide several links to yet other resources.

Let's begin with a few major online booksellers of physical books – namely, paperback and hardcover – books:

www.amazon.com
www.barnesandnoble.com
www.booksamillion.com

Following are the websites for some major online bookstores that sell eBooks (these are the bookstores where the eBooks are sold – <u>not</u> the same as where you publish the eBook):

www.amazon.com/kindlestore
www.barnesandnoble.com/nook
www.ebookstore.sony.com (now closed; use Kobo books)
www.kobobooks.com
www.apple.com/apps/ibooks
www.smashwords.com

If instead you want a few major websites for where you can publish your eBook, look here:

kdp.amazon.com
www.nookpress.com
www.kobobooks.com/kobowritinglife
www.smashwords.com

Here is CreateSpace's website, where you can publish a paperback book:

www.createspace.com

If you need help formatting or publishing your eBook, try searching these help pages:

kdp.amazon.com/self-publishing/help

For Smashwords, click the link at the top of their homepage. For Nook, login to Nook Press and click Support. For Kobo, login to Kobo Writing Life and click Learning Center.

Another way to get help is to use the community help forums. You can also meet fellow self-published authors and share ideas. CreateSpace even allows you to post a preview of a portion of your book and solicit opinions and advice. Who knows, some people you meet here may even buy your book. ☺ But don't explicitly promote your work here. Your best chance of selling books this way is when someone gets interested in your work and clicks on your profile – every post you write is a sample of your writing style, personality, and character. Here are the links to community help forums for Kindle, and Nook Press. At CreateSpace, click Community. For Smashwords, look for "Socialbuzz" on their homepage.

https://kdp.amazon.com/community/index.jspa

http://bookclubs.barnesandnoble.com/t5/NOOK-Press-Help-Board/bd-p/NOOKpress

Following are a few publishing or marketing guides that are both free and very useful. All of these are available for free from Amazon (if you don't have a Kindle, you can download the free Kindle for PC software). The Kindle guide is also available in PDF format from the KDP self-publishing help pages (see the previous page). The second Kindle guide below is also available in a few other languages, and there is also an English guide for Mac users. The Smashwords guides are also available directly from their website in a variety of formats.

Publish on Amazon Kindle with Kindle Direct Publishing

Building Your Book for Kindle by Kindle Direct Publishing

Smashwords Style Guide by Mark Coker

Smashwords Book Marketing Guide by Mark Coker

Secrets to Ebook Publishing Success by Mark Coker

If you want to visit Amazon's websites, look here:

www.amazon.com (United States)

www.amazon.co.uk (United Kingdom)

www.amazon.ca (Canada)

www.amazon.es (Spain)

www.amazon.fr (France)

www.amazon.de (Germany)

www.amazon.it (Italy)

www.amazon.cn (China)

www.amazon.co.jp (Japan)

Following are some major social media websites:

www.facebook.com

www.facebook.com/publishedauthors

www.twitter.com

www.myspace.com

Looking for applications that can help you format your Kindle eBook? Click the Tools and Resources link on the left-hand side of the KDP self-publishing help page (see the bottom of the first page of this Resources list) under Preparing Your Book.

Every author should have an Author Page at Amazon's AuthorCentral (as described in detail in Chapter 6). The US Amazon Central website is listed below. For other Amazon websites, visit that country's Amazon page, search for a book that has an Author Page, click on that author's Author Page, and find the link for AuthorCentral (it will sure be handy if you speak the native language, or if you can find a friend or acquaintance who does). Some countries, like Canada, may not have an AuthorCentral feature.

https://authorcentral.amazon.com

Here are a couple of websites where you can posts blogs:

www.twitter.com

www.wordpress.com

www.blogger.com

You can purchase ISBN's directly from Bowker at:

www.myidentifiers.com

The homepage for the Library of Congress is listed below, along with a website that provides more information about LCCN assignment.

www.loc.gov/index.html

www.booksandtales.com/pod/aloc.php

Learn more about copyright at:

www.copyright.gov

Adobe provides a free reader for viewing PDF files and also sells professional PDF conversion software (but, remember, you can convert to PDF for free using Microsoft Word). Another useful PDF converter is Nuance's PDF Converter Professional.

www.adobe.com

www.nuance.com

Want to learn more about the use of color (which may be relevant when you design your cover, for example)? One place to look is HGTV. Click the Color Guide link at the top of HGTV's homepage:

www.hgtv.com

Chris McMullen created a free marketing opportunity for authors. Participate in a Black Friday type of sales event just for books, but on a Tuesday in December. Check out Read Tuesday:

http://readtuesday.com

THE AUTHOR

Chris McMullen has written and self-published over a dozen paperback books with CreateSpace and over a dozen eBooks. He enjoys writing books, drawing illustrations on the computer, editing manuscripts, and especially the feeling of having produced a professional-looking self-published book from cover-to-cover.

Chris McMullen holds a Ph.D. in physics from Oklahoma State University, and presently teaches physics at Northwestern State University of Louisiana. Having published a half-dozen papers on the collider phenomenology of large, extra, superstring-inspired extra dimensions, he first wrote a two-volume book on the geometry and physics of the fourth dimension geared toward a general audience, entitled *The Visual Guide to Extra Dimensions*. When he learned about self-publishing on Amazon through CreateSpace, he wrote a variety of golf and chess log books, and published these to gain some experience as a self-publisher before self-publishing his work on the fourth dimension.

Since then, Chris McMullen has self-published numerous math workbooks, a couple of books on self-publishing, and several word scramble puzzle books. The math workbooks were written in response to his observation, as a teacher, that many students need to develop greater fluency in fundamental techniques in mathematics. He began writing word scramble books along with his coauthor, Carolyn Kivett, when he realized that it was possible to make over a thousand words using only the elements on the periodic table. Chris McMullen and Carolyn Kivett first published a variety of chemical word scrambles using elements from the periodic table, and have since published several 'ordinary' word scrambles using the English alphabet instead of chemical symbols.

Check out the blog with free self-publishing resources:
http://chrismcmullen.wordpress.com
The author website: https://chrismcmullen.com
Email: chrism@chrismcmullen.com
Facebook author page:
https://www.facebook.com/pages/Chris-Mcmullen/390266614410127
Twitter: @ChrisDMcMullen

Free marketing opportunity created by Chris McMullen:
http://readtuesday.com

CATALOG

Self-Publishing

How to Self-Publish a Book on Amazon.com
A Detailed Guide to Self-Publishing with Amazon and Other Online Booksellers, Vol. 1
A Detailed Guide to Self-Publishing with Amazon and Other Online Booksellers, Vol. 2
Formatting Pages for Publishing on Amazon with CreateSpace

The Fourth Dimension

The Visual Guide to Extra Dimensions, Vol. 1
The Visual Guide to Extra Dimensions, Vol. 2
Full Color Illustrations of the Fourth Dimension, Vol. 1
Full Color Illustrations of the Fourth Dimension, Vol. 2

Science Books

Understand Basic Chemistry Concepts
Understand Basic Chemistry Concepts (Large Size & Large Print Edition)
An Introduction to Basic Astronomy Concepts (with Space Photos)
An Introduction to Basic Astronomy Concepts (Black-and-white Edition)
Basic Astronomy Concepts Everyone Should Know (with Space Photos)
The Observational Astronomy Skywatcher Notebook
An Advanced Introduction to Calculus-Based Physics (Mechanics)
A Guide to Thermal Physics
Creative Physics Problems, Vol. 1
Creative Physics Problems, Vol. 2
Creative Physics Problems for Physics with Calculus, Vol. 1
Creative Physics Problems for Physics with Calculus, Vol. 2
A Research-Oriented Laboratory Manual for First-Year Physics
Laboratory Notebook for Physics Experiments

Improve Your Math Fluency Series

Addition Facts Practice Book
Subtraction Facts Practice Book
Multiplication Facts Practice Book
Division Facts Practice Book
10,000 Addition Problems Practice Workbook
10,000 Subtraction Problems Practice Workbook
7,000 Multiplication Problems Practice Workbook
4,500 Multiplication Problems with Answers Practice Workbook
Master Long Division Practice Workbook
Addition and Subtraction Applied to Clocks
Practice Adding, Subtracting, Multiplying, and Dividing Fractions Workbook
Practice Adding, Subtracting, Multiplying, and Dividing Mixed Fractions Workbook
Practice Arithmetic with Decimals Workbook
Practice Addition, Subtraction, Multiplication, and Division with Negative Numbers Workbook
Fractions, Decimals, & Percents Math Workbook (Includes Repeating Decimals)
Algebra Essentials Practice Workbook with Answers
Trigonometry Essentials Practice Workbook with Answers

Radial Math Workbooks

Radial Arithmetic Facts Math Workbook (Adding and Subtracting 1-12)
Radial Arithmetic Facts Math Workbook (Multiplying and Dividing 1-12)
Radial Math Arithmetic Workbook (Addition and Subtraction)
Radial Math Arithmetic Workbook (Multiplication and Division)
Radial Math Long Division with Remainders Workbook
Radial Fractions Math Workbook (Addition and Subtraction)
Radial Fractions Math Workbook (Multiplication and Division)

Pyramid Math Workbooks

Pyramid Arithmetic Addition and Subtraction Math Workbook
Pyramid Arithmetic Multiplication Math Workbook
Pyramid Arithmetic Long Division (without Remainders) Math Workbook
Pyramid Arithmetic Long Division Math Workbook
Pyramid Fractions – Fraction Addition and Subtraction Workbook
Pyramid Fractions – Fraction Multiplication and Division Workbook
Pyramid Fractions, Decimals, & Percents – Fraction Basics Math Workbook

Word Scramble Puzzle Books (Coauthored)

Christmas Word Scrambles
Fun Word Scrambles for Kids
Football Word Scrambles
Golf Word Scrambles
Teen Word Scrambles for Girls
Song & Artist Music Word Scrambles
Negative/Positive Antonym Word Scrambles Book
Positive Word Scrambles (A Fun Way to Think Happy Words)
Positive Word Scrambles (Fun Positive Visualization)
English-French Word Scrambles (Level 1 Basic)
English-Spanish Word Scrambles (Level 1 Basic)
Igpay Atinlay Ordway Amblesscray
Word Scrambles that Make You Think
VErBAl ReAcTiONS – Word Scrambles with a Chemical Flavor (Easy)
VErBAl ReAcTiONS – Word Scrambles with a Chemical Flavor (Medium)
VErBAl ReAcTiONS – Word Scrambles with a Chemical Flavor (Hard)
Chemical Word Scrambles Anyone Can Do (Easy)
Chemical Word Scrambles Anyone Can Do (Medium)
Chemical Word Scrambles Anyone Can Do (Hard)
Travel-Size Chemical Word Scrambles (Easy to Medium)

Chess Books

The Chess Match Log Book
Make a Personalized Book of 500 Chess Positions

Golf Books

The Golf Stats Log Book
The Golf Stats Scorecard Book
The End-Of-Round Golf Diary
The Practice Session Golf Diary
A Scorecard Sketchbook for 50 Rounds of Golf

Self-Publishing eBooks

How to Self-Publish a Book on Amazon.com
A Detailed Guide to Self-Publishing with Amazon and Other Online Booksellers, Vol. 1
A Detailed Guide to Self-Publishing with Amazon and Other Online Booksellers, Vol. 2
Formatting Pages for Publishing on Amazon with CreateSpace

Math eBooks

Digital Addition Flash Cards in Color (Ordered and Shuffled 1-9)
Digital Subtraction Flash Cards in Color (1-9 Shuffled Twice)
Digital Multiplication Flash Cards in Color (Ordered and Shuffled 1-9)
Digital Division Flash Cards in Color (1-9 Shuffled Twice)
Far Out Addition Flash Cards 1-12 (Decorated with Shuttle, Astronaut, and Satellite Photos)
Far Out Multiplication Flash Cards 1-12 (Decorated with Solar System Photos)
Counting Numbers 1-20 Astronomy (with NASA Space Photos)
Trigonometry Flash Cards: Memorize Values of Trig Functions

Science eBooks

Understand Basic Chemistry Concepts
Understand Basic Chemistry Concepts (in Color)
An Introduction to Basic Astronomy Concepts (with Space Photos)
Basic Astronomy Concepts Everyone Should Know (With Space Photos)

Word Scramble eBooks (Coauthored)

Teen Word Scrambles for Girls
Word Scrambles that Make You Think

The Visual Guide to Extra Dimensions takes you on a journey into the fourth dimension. It begins with some fascinating features of the second dimension: Intuitively, it might seem like the second dimension should be easier to understand than the third dimension, but it turns out that the second dimension has some surprising features. Most of the book is dedicated toward understanding the fourth dimension – the geometry and physics of a fourth dimension, not spirituality or religion. There are some novel figures of a variety of 4D objects – not just the standard tesseracts and hyperspheres, but other geometric objects like the hecatonicosachoron and spherinder. The book helps you visualize what it would be like to walk on a 4D staircase, for example.

UNdErSTaNd BaSiC Chemistry CoNCePtS focuses on fundamental chemistry concepts, such as understanding the periodic table of the elements and how chemical bonds are formed. No prior knowledge of chemistry is assumed. The mathematical component involves only basic arithmetic. The content is much more conceptual than mathematical. It is geared toward helping anyone – student or not – to understand the main ideas of chemistry. Both students and non-students may find it helpful to be able to focus on understanding the main concepts without the constant emphasis on computations that is generally found in chemistry lectures and textbooks.

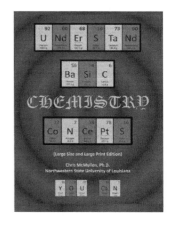

This *Christmas Word Scrambles* book consists of words or phrases that relate to Christmas where the letters have been scrambled. Solve each puzzle by rearranging the letters to form the word or phrase. For example, rearranging the letters T R O F Y S, we can form the word F R O S T Y. Each puzzle consists of a group of related words or phrases, such as common Christmas cookie shapes or images from a Nativity scene. Knowing that the words in each puzzle are related may help you unscramble any words or phrases that you don't see right away. A hints section at the back of the book provides the first letter of each answer, which is handy if you just need a little help; a separate section provides the answers so that you can check your solutions.

CHECK IT OUT

Here are a few cool books that were published with CreateSpace and/or KDP:[27]

- ❖ *CIN: "Lynn, Lynn, the City of Sin,"* by Christina Leigh Pritchard. The title is catchy, the cover is striking and features lightning (which is a big part of the story), and the story is a highly engaging read geared toward the teen audience.
- ❖ *Ghostly Cries from Dixie* by Pat Fitzhugh. This is an entertaining yet well-researched guide to haunted houses across America. It's also well-written.
- ❖ *Thoroughly Modern Monsters* by Jennifer Rainey. The concept is neat: These short stories creatively explore the integration of monsters into human society.
- ❖ *My Stupid Girl* by Aurora Smith. This book tells an interesting tale of a Goth teenager who meets a beautiful Christian girl after saving her from drowning in a pond.
- ❖ *SEO Black Book* by R.L. Adams. As a self-publisher, it's worth checking out both the cover and description for this book. (But I can't tell you if the content is sound because I'm not an expert on search engine optimization and haven't tried these ideas myself.)
- ❖ *Grace Lost* by M. Lauryl Lewis. This series features some cool zombie covers. Let me warn you that it's really intended for an adult audience because it does include that three-letter word.
- ❖ *Through These Eyes* by Michael Risley and Tom Bradford. I recommend that you take a look at this cover – it's a simple design, yet quite effective. Don't copy the same idea; rather, I hope that this cover will help to inspire a simple, effective design of your own. If you enjoy legal thrillers, you might like the content, too.
- ❖ *My First Kakuro Book: 200 Puzzles* by DJAPE. These math puzzles start out small and grow so that you can learn the technique (without step-by-step instructions – as I implied, this type of puzzle is for people who like to figure things out by themselves).
- ❖ *Wacky Sentences Handwriting Workbook (Reproducible)* by Julie Harper. If you have children in elementary school and would like a fun way for them to practice their cursive writing skills, this is a neat workbook.
- ❖ Find more: Search for CreateSpace Independent Publishing Platform on Amazon.

---

[27] I know Julie Harper personally. I discovered a few of these other authors at online forums and enjoyed their books. The remaining authors I have never interacted with; I simply found these books on Amazon. The authors did not pay to have their books included here, and they did not contact me to advertise for them. When this book was published, they had no idea that I would be including their books on such a list.

INDEX

B

D

F

G

H

I

J

K

L

N

O

P

S

T

U

V

W

Y

Z

Made in the USA
San Bernardino, CA
24 August 2014